THE AUTOBIOGRAPHY

Victor Ceserani

CATERING FOR LIFE

Edward Arnold

A division of Hodder & Stoughton

LONDON   NEW YORK   MELBOURNE   AUCKLAND

© 1989 Victor Ceserani

First published in Great Britain 1989

British Library Cataloguing in Publication Data

Ceserani, Victor
  Catering for life.
  1. Cooking. Biographies
  I. Title
  641.5′092′4

  ISBN 0–340–49456–5

Typeset in 10/11 pt California Medium by Colset Private Limited,
Singapore
Printed and bound in Great Britain for Edward Arnold, the
educational, academic and medical publishing division of Hodder
and Stoughton Limited, 41 Bedford Square, London WC1B 3DQ
by Biddles Ltd, Guildford and King's Lynn

To my wife Letty as a token of grateful thanks
for the unfailing love, encouragement and support she has
given me over the past fifty-two years.

To Dave

I hope you enjoy this book as much
as I did.

Now you start on this new chapter
of your career, never loose the
joy + pride in teaching + passing
on your skills to students
about our wonderful industry
Best Wishes
Jane.

April 2022

Victor Ceserani is co-author with Ronald Kinton of:

Practical Cookery, Sixth Edition
Questions on Practical Cookery (to accompany *Practical Cookery*, Sixth Edition)
The Theory of Catering, Sixth Edition
Questions on Theory of Catering, Second Edition (to accompany *The Theory of Catering*, Sixth Edition)
Cookery: an Introduction

co-author with Ronald Kinton and David Foskett of:

Contemporary Cookery

and editor of the British edition of:

Understanding Cooking (US edition by Donald Lundberg and Lendal Kotschevar)

Contents

'For half a century, Victor Ceserani has been the Messiah of good cookery in this country both as a fine practitioner of his art and as a gifted teacher. His name is synonymous with culinary excellence.'

Lord Forte

'I wish I had had the benefit of Victor's devoted teaching. His influence radiates long after his retirement, and so our industry continues to enjoy his wise judgement.'

Gerald Milsom
Le Talbooth Restaurant,
Dedham, Essex

'I believe that the catering profession owes a great deal to Victor Ceserani — I know that I do.'

Richard Shepherd
Langan's Brasserie,
London

'There are few people who have made a more profound contribution to hotel and catering education than Victor Ceserani. If we had not had the good fortune to have such as he, we would have had to invent him.'

Armand Borisewitz
Head of School of Hotel and Institutional
    Administration,
Robert Gordon's Institute of Technology,
Aberdeen

'One of Victor's great achievements was the encouragement he gave to the younger members of his staff. By this means a far-reaching network of ex-Ealing College staff in senior jobs in hotel and catering departments was built up.'

Dr Geoffrey Cowell
Assistant Principal,
Blackpool and The Fylde College

'His skill, knowledge and judgement have led to his permanent role as the industry's walking reference book. His warmth, sense of fair play and willingness to listen are legendary.'

Bev Puxley
Head of Department of Hotel and Catering
    Studies,
Westminster College

Foreword

The news that Victor Ceserani was to embark on writing his autobiography brought me enormous happiness. To be then asked to write a Foreword to it was indeed an honour.

Reading this account of his life from childhood to the beginning of his professional career at the Ritz, one feels Victor's presence as in conversation. The anecdotes of the incidents in his day-to-day professional and social life are alive and rich with sincerity. In this book we meet a man who has dedicated his life to his profession but at the same time held onto the umbilical cord of his family and friends.

Victor has been able to adapt himself and cope with many different situations. Professionally speaking he has always been able to give the best to his superiors and to work on a sharing basis with his peers. While in a position of charge he has had a fraternal attitude to those working under him. At no time has he raised his voice or lost his temper. The man is in charge and in control. Victor holds the rare balance of being a gifted craftsman with an academic mind. The well-deserved multitude of awards bestowed on him have not changed his humility.

To have judged with Victor has always been a great pleasure. Anyone who has judged with or has been judged by Victor has learnt something. His criticisms have always been positive, objective and helpful to those to whom they are addressed.

No doubt this autobiography will be an inspiration for the younger generation and an example for any leader in our profession in the catering world. I wish him great success with this work. I hope to have the pleasure of his company for years in the many manifestations of our profession to which he brings so much. The catering industry, like all others, only moves forward with leaders like Victor.

Michel Roux
Meilleur Ouvrier de France
Chef/Patron
Waterside Inn, Bray

Acknowledgements

I wish to record thanks to my publisher and friend, Bryan Bennett, who first suggested that I put pen to paper for this book, and to Lee Brown, publisher, for confirming the suggestion.

Sincerest thanks also go to a former Ealing College colleague and good friend, Betty Evans, who so kindly typed all my scribble.

I would also like to express particular appreciation and thanks to my friend Miles Quest, Managing Director, Wordsmith and Company, Albemarle Street, London, for all his helpful suggestions and comments on the text.

CHAPTER 1

1919–1934

Chelsea

Pop emigrated from Italy before the First World War. He stood four feet ten inches in height and was too short for the army. The son of a poor peasant farm worker who lived in Chignola Camatta, near Pavia, he had little schooling and was almost illiterate. His pleasing smile and personality earned him the affectionate nick-name of 'Bobby', and, as such, he was known to many of his fellow workers and regular customers in the Ritz Restaurant, Piccadilly, London, where he worked as a commis waiter.

My mother fled under the fire of German guns from her home town of Charleroi in Belgium, as a refugee during the First World War, and found employment in London in private service.

Mum and Pop met towards the end of 1918, neither understanding very much about each other's language, but as the oldest international language prevailed, yours truly was born on 23 October 1919 at Raphael Street, Knightsbridge, just off the Old Brompton Road not far from Harrods, which gave me the questionable distinction of a birth certificate in the district of Mayfair.

Shortly afterwards we moved to a flat in Chelsea where I lived for the next twenty years. At the age of three-and-a-half, schooldays began: the Oratory Infants, then the Elementary, Secondary and Central Schools in due course. The Oratory Elementary School in Cale Street faced onto a local amenity and landmark known irreverently as the 'tin church' – a round, metal, half-open urinal for men. In such a vulnerable position it was woe betide any occupant blissfully relieving himself when school turned out at dinner-time or four o'clock, particularly when snow was on the ground. The exhilarating pleasure of happy relief could speedily be counteracted by a neck full of slush!

During the summer months, Jack Rea, the local Italian ice-cream vendor, would park his barrow outside the school. Jack's most popular item with the boys was 'halfpenny lemon on paper'. This consisted of a blob of lemon water-ice on a four-inch square of paper (taken from the wafer and cornet boxes), with a thin slice of lemon popped on top. During tedious lessons in the hot summer months, mouths would start to water and minds would easily stray from the class-room to Jack's succulent, refreshing treat awaiting at four o'clock. When the bell went the haste from the class-room on the second floor down the stairs would be most unseemly and the cries would ring out, 'Halfpenny lemon on paper, please, Jack.'

As the Church school of the Brompton Oratory, discipline was firm, regular religious education was compulsory, and on more than one occasion I received six strokes of a whistling, pliable cane, which caused the cheeks within my trousers to blush furiously. On the last occasion, at the age of fifteen, two bigger boys had bullied me into lending them my maths homework, even though I earnestly assured them it was wrong. When three identical incorrect sets of work were marked by our maths master he demanded an explanation. Since we kept silent, we were dispatched to the headmaster's study where he repeated the demand for an explanation. Once again silence prevailed and, without further ado, we bent over in turn, received our thrashing, our names were entered in the punishment book and we were summarily dismissed.

Looking back over my life I cannot recall any instances when the disciplines of school, Church and the Army, and the occasional punishments they imposed, did me any harm. If anything, the reverse is true, as I have often had occasion to be grateful for the instillation of discipline into my character.

Schooldays, on the whole, are a pleasant memory. Although Pop did not earn a great deal of money, my mother supplemented this with part-time domestic service and, as I was the only child, I was well-cared for by loving parents. Pop used to bring home all his champagne corks from the Ritz where he now worked as a wine butler, and twice a year I would help him to sort them. In this way I acquired an early knowledge of names like Mumm, Charles Heidsieck, Piper Heidsieck, Bollinger and Perrier Jouet, for to me, this was a game. As I grew older I realised that the various firms paid a small bonus of a few pence for these corks, and on the occasions when Pop took his corks to cash them in I would receive a few extra coppers pocket money. Pop's station in the restaurant was the royal corner, and I would hear him talking of serving, and the likes and dislikes, of personalities such as Edward Prince of Wales, Nubar Gulbenkian, the Aga Khan, Grand Duke Dimitri of Russia and many others. He would bring home menus and tell us what the customers ate. At the tender age of seven the thought of being able to eat in a restaurant of this calibre was akin to entering Paradise.

At home we could not afford a radio but possessed an old second-hand gramophone with a dozen records. Pop's favourite was 'O Sole Mio' sung by Enrico Caruso, which had a weekly rendering. Pop would accompany Caruso (a most unlikely duo) in a flat, out-of-tune voice, the first strains of which would waken the cat and send it slinking from the room as though in pain.

My daily pocket money was a halfpenny, with a full penny on Saturdays. Most days pocket money was spent in the Little Gem, a sweet shop in Cale Street, on the way home from school. For a farthing one could buy a good selection of sweets, or a 'Vantas' (an aerated fruit drink).

Pop, in common with most hotel restaurant brigades, worked long hours, seven days a week with two half-days off which started at 3 p.m. We lived in a simple first-floor flat at No. 20 Radnor Street with two rooms and a kitchenette, sharing with the family in the downstairs flat an outside toilet, and a scullery with a coal-fired boiler and a large mangle. As there was no bathroom we would go weekly to the Chelsea public baths at the side of the town hall. There, for the charge of a few pence, one would be issued with a towel, the composition of which, to my skin, felt as if it included a goodly percentage of coarse sand. You were then taken to a cubicle containing a bath into which, from taps outside the bathroom controlled by an attendant, were deluged measures of hot and cold water. On testing the water, if more hot or cold was required then a sophisticated communication system went into action. One hollered, 'More hot (or cold) in number five, Jack!' If the voice of a chum was recognised then ribald remarks and anatomical suggestions would be made that usually defied the laws of nature and human capability.

Pop's weekly wage depended considerably on tips, which were pooled into the 'tronc' and distributed weekly by the restaurant manager. Each share was known as a 'potage'. The number of potages given weekly varied according to the level of employee, with the manager receiving the major share, followed by first head waiter, second head waiter, first wine butler, head waiters, wine butlers, 'chefs de rang' and 'commis'. During the London season – Easter to July – one, two or three potages could be received, whereas in January and February when business was at its quietest, maybe only half a potage (less than £1) would be collected.

Occasionally, on a Sunday afternoon in summer, if we had special visitors, I would be sent to J. Lyons tea-shop at South Kensington, about fifteen minutes' walk away, to buy six chocolate éclairs for tea. The éclairs were chocolate coated, unfilled and filled to order by a cream injection machine. If you can, imagine a young boy watching this happening, seeing the delicious cream oozing out into the featherlight fondant cases, the éclairs being carefully placed into a light cardboard box and tied with string, the boy then walking carefully home wondering with greedy anticipation what would be his share of the box! This represented a treat that I would drool about for days afterwards.

Similarly, when a little older, I would sometimes accompany my parents on a shopping expedition to Berwick market and Old Compton Street. For an occasional treat I would be taken into a Swiss pastry shop in Old Compton Street and given an individual, pink ribbon encircled, charlotte russe, which, on my first acquaintance, represented the most delicious thing I had ever tasted. The enjoyment was so intense that I used to discipline myself to eat it in the smallest morsels in order to extend the pleasure for as long as possible. It is probably partly due to boyhood memory that, to this day, a charlotte russe is still one of my favourite sweets.

Living less than five minutes' walk from the Royal Hospital, we boys played football (with coats piled up for goal posts), or cricket, (with the stumps chalked on to a suitable tree), most days after school and at weekends in the grounds, and struck up friendships with some of the Chelsea Pensioners.

Three vivid memories of the Royal Hospital remain clear in my mind. The first is the annual preparation for the world-famous Chelsea Flower Show when, approximately three to four weeks before, hordes of workmen would descend on the grounds, and our favourite playing areas were gradually eroded. It was fascinating watching the ground preparation and gradual raising of the huge marquee, the large cranes building the rockeries on the Embankment side, and the installation of waterfalls and fountains; we would get as close as we dared before the workmen set us on our way. We would be allowed in to play until three days before the show opened, and were then barred until the day following its closure.

On show days, crowds milled up and down all the neighbourhood streets. On the last day, as the show was closing, the majority of plants were sold off and eagerly snapped up by willing buyers after a bargain, although many of the plants looked extremely wilted and unhappy.

The second memory is of two large mulberry trees behind a high brick wall in a private part of the gardens. Once, daringly, four of us organised a scrumping session. Two kept 'cavey', while the other two – one of whom was yours truly – clambered over the wall and collected a handsome haul of very ripe berries. On our way back over the wall our look-outs started waving and whispering 'Keeper!' but, too late. We were caught, well and truly told off, and barred for a week from entering the grounds. On returning home I received another 'wigging' for having my clothes stained with mulberry juice, which only goes to show that crime does not pay!

The third memory is of walking with my parents along the minute allotments that some pensioners cultivated in a special part of the gardens, set aside in a private section called the Ranelagh. Although very small, each plot was meticulously tended and the produce sold off to provide a little extra spending money. We would often buy salad and vegetable items, and got to know some of the pensioners very well during the course of these shopping expeditions.

Our street games were either 'flick-it', which consisted of setting an equal number of cigarette cards up against a brick wall, kneeling some three feet away and endeavouring to knock them down by flicking other cards against them. Whoever succeeded gathered in all the cards. We all avidly collected cigarette cards, especially those of sportsmen, ships and trains, and swopping them to make up complete sets went on continuously. Hopscotch patterns of several kinds adorned many areas of pavement around our homes. Winding and spinning our peg tops, we would play 'chip-'em' up and down the street. This consisted of spinning the top onto the ground, manipulating it into the palm of the hand, and then dropping it down onto a bottle crown-top, attempting to 'chip it' in the required direction. 'Five-stones', marbles and conkers were other games which we played and enjoyed at very little expense. Once a year, during the summer holidays, 'Marbletown' was set up in the grounds of Sutton Flats in Cale Street. This consisted of a myriad of home-made games, side-shows, and every possible activity that young minds could conceive of with the sole currency in all cases being marbles. It was even whispered that in one dark corner of the block one precocious young lady would let you put a hand inside her knickers for five marbles, but I never had the opportunity to test the truth of this.

On Pop's two half-days each week he finished after lunch which meant that he arrived home just before I returned from school. Once a week, if the day was fine, we would walk to Battersea Park and go rowing on the lake. Afterwards we strolled back to the Six Bells in the King's Road. (The pub was bought by Bob Payton in the 1980s and converted into an American-style eating house.)

In the twenties and thirties the Six Bells was a popular, fashionable pub, and through a covered alley by its side you reached the garden at the back. This was of sufficient size to house the green of the Chelsea Bowling Club, and also had space for a fountain surrounded by a cluster of tables and chairs. Pop would have a pint or two and I had a glass of lemonade and a packet of crisps. (There was only one flavour, plain with a twirled piece of blue paper containing salt.) On the opposite side of the pub to the alley was a large room containing two full-sized billiard tables. I spent my time between watching the bowlers (who fascinated Pop), the billiards (and occasionally snooker) players, and feeding the goldfish in the fountain.

These afternoon excursions gave me a great deal of pleasure, and I must confess to more than a pang of sadness when I saw how the Six Bells went down and down from the once attractive pub of pre-war days. A variety of themes considered suitable for the swinging sixties set who flocked to the King's Road was tried out, but in the end it came on the market and was snapped up.

The main carrier of parcels was a firm called Carter Paterson whose fleet of horse-drawn carts was stabled in a large complex, opposite the Pheasantry Club, in the King's Road. From the beginning of December, parcels and crates were left at our flat almost daily. These were Christmas gifts of goodwill to Pop from the wine merchants, and usually consisted of one to four bottles. By Christmas, our sideboard was packed solid with bottles of wine and spirits of all kinds. My mother also subscribed a few coppers weekly to a Christmas club. The money and dividend was issued just prior to the holiday and ensured that there was sufficient extra to buy the trimmings for a bumper Christmas. In the New Year, as there were always plenty of bottles left, the wine butlers from many of London's hotels and restaurants would visit each other in turn during the afternoon break, spending the time in animated discussion about the rights and wrongs of life in general. I always got excited when it was Pop's turn, for as his colleagues left in a convivial mood around five o'clock, young Victor would accumulate the equivalent of a month's pocket money!

In the secondary school we had an Army Cadet Force which was run on military lines. We younger boys had dummy wooden rifles, and once a week a drill sergeant from one of the Guards regiments stationed at Chelsea Barracks, resplendent in an impeccable uniform, red sash, boots with toe caps gleaming like mirrors, a moustache with waxed ends and a swagger stick, would come to put us through the paces at Army drill. This, to us, was playing a game of real soldiers, and arms drill taught by such a martinet and stickler for perfection was something I never forgot (as, indeed, my platoon sergeant noticed when I joined the Army in 1940). In the mid 1930s, however, the peace movement and support for disarmament were gathering momentum, and school military cadet forces were frowned upon. Overnight our beloved cadet force was disbanded and replaced by a Scout troop, which many of us thought, unkindly, was a sissy outfit by comparison, and very few cadets bothered to join.

When I was old enough to see over the banking at Stamford Bridge, I started to support Chelsea Football Club, and remained a loyal supporter for many years. At one memorable match against Arsenal, the English League record attendance of over 82 000 was established. Accompanied by several of my pals, I went early, in order to be able to stand right at the front on the half-way line facing the grandstand. Because of the crowds the police allowed small boys onto the greyhound track which surrounded the pitch. During the match, a full-blooded London derby, the ball came towards us and I caught it and kicked it back into the arms of the legendary Alex James. What a moment of glory that was! At one time, Vic Woodley, the first-team goalkeeper, was an English international player and the reserve-team goalie, Johnnie Jackson, played for Scotland. My maths master in the Central School was J. C. Burns, an amateur who played for Brentford (then in Division I) and who was selected for the full England team on more than one occasion. He never spoke of football at school and we never saw him kick a football with any of the school teams. My sporting heroes were Vic Woodley and Leslie Ames-Kent, an England wicket-keeper batsman. My film star soft spot was for Jessie Matthews, and I kept a cigarette-card picture of her showing a suspicion of a *décolletée* neckline in my breast pocket for several years.

CHAPTER 2
1934–1937

The Ritz Hotel

Shortly after my fifteenth birthday I began to lose interest in school, where the bias of subjects was strongly geared to the world of business and finance. Maths, algebra and geometry were reaching levels beyond my comprehension. Shorthand, typewriting and bookkeeping were introduced – all subjects which failed to stir enough interest in me to activate the necessary motivation. My work began to suffer, and I told my parents that I wanted to leave and become a chef. They were completely supportive; Pop spoke to Monsieur Arsène Avignon, head chef at the Ritz, who offered to take me on as an apprentice. Alternatively, I could have applied to the only hotel school in Britain, Westminster Technical School, for a place on the chef's course. Westminster sounded as though it might have 'schooling' in the curriculum and so I elected to sign on as an apprentice (one of four) for the wage of seven shillings and sixpence a week, supplying my own uniform and knives. We worked a six-day week and split duty, nine-thirty to two-thirty, five to nine-thirty. The bus fare from the King's Road to Green Park was two pence – this meant eight pence a day, which took four shillings out of my wages. At the end of one year I received a five-shilling rise, and at the end of my apprenticeship I earned seventeen shillings and sixpence. I also set about acquiring a push-bike in order that I could cycle to work and save money. My pipe-dream was for a Claud Butler, but as the cheapest models cost twenty pounds I had to settle for something much humbler. My mother and Pop had encouraged me to save by giving me a Post Office book with five shillings in it as a Christmas gift when I was quite young. I used to deposit sixpences and shillings and, over the years, it was surprising how the amount grew. I was able to spend five pounds on a bike.

The first time I entered the Ritz kitchens the luncheon service was getting under way, and I thought that I had entered a mad house. Orders and counter orders across the kitchen, to the larder, to the pastry and across the the hot-service plate were shouted out in the loudest possible voice in French. I began to have second thoughts about my choice of career, but was pleased to learn that we four apprentices were to start work in the pastry, which was twenty yards or so away from the main kitchen.

My first day's work in the pastry, on 5 November 1934, consisted of cutting up fresh fruit for fruit salad and cutting, boiling and peeling chestnuts which were to be made up into one of the most popular sweets, mont blanc. The peeled chestnuts were finely chopped, passed through a fine sieve and worked into a paste with the addition of fresh unsalted butter and icing sugar. This chestnut purée was then forced through a gadget like a mincer onto rounds of meringue, piped generously with whipped cream, and dusted with icing sugar to resemble the snow on the mountain. I was shown how to make short pastry, puff pastry, sweet pastry and choux pastry, and was allowed to give a hand in finishing off afternoon tea pastries which were made very small and neat. Eclairs, for example, were two inches in length, and fruit tartlets an inch-and-a-half in diameter. The pastry chef was Fritz Hofer, a genial Swiss, whom I came to regard as a second father. The first commis was Bill Sandys, who had trained at Frascati's, a famous restaurant in Oxford Street. The second commis was John Anselmi, who had also trained at Frascati's, and the third commis was Charlie Kralik, a Czech, who swayed gently from side to side when he spoke, and also ended many of his words with a distinctive hiss. Mario, an elderly Italian, was our kitchen porter.

Poppa Fritz was a man of moods. At his best he was cheerful, humming snatches of songs, and possessed the right amount of patience needed to handle we four apprentices. Occasionally, he would sink into fits of depression and if these got too bad, Bill and John would take him on one side and quietly advise him to seek solace with one of the ladies of the streets. I wasn't supposed to hear this, but sharp young ears pick up much of what they are not supposed to hear. The morning after these very occasional visits, Poppa Fritz would come to work happy, cheerful and singing like bird.

Poppa Fritz was a craftsman of the old school who never wasted or threw away a scrap of food whether it be liquid or solid. All surplus fruit juice he would keep in 7 lb stone jam jars, ferment with the addition of yeast, strain, and use as his special tipple. I was once given a small glass as a special treat for a job well done, and privately thought that it was ghastly.

Bill Sandys' extra job was to make all the ice-creams. These were made of the finest ingredients and included many specialities in different shapes – hearts and bombes, for example – flavoured with liqueurs and fruits. Our vanilla ice-cream consisted solely of fresh, full-cream milk, double cream, egg yolks, sugar and real vanilla. He also made all the *petits fours*, the tasty little mouthwatering sweetmeats served with coffee after dinner.

John Anselmi was the pulled-sugar man and, in addition to his routine work, he would spend two to three hours daily boiling sugar and glucose to a high temperature. In order to test the temperature, he would have a bowl of ice water as near as possible to the sugar, dip his forefinger and thumb into the ice water, and as quick as a flash back into the boiling sugar, the temperature of which would be about 150°C, and back into the ice water. By rolling the small amount of sugar gathered between his fingers he could tell when the correct degree was reached. The sugar was then poured onto a marble slab, allowed to cool slightly, then worked with a palette knife and scraper from the outside to the centre. Colouring was added, and working continued until it was touchable by the fingers – his, not mine! At this stage it was ready for pulling, and as John was one of the finest sugar craftsmen in the country, he would weave baskets in between frames of copper rods set in wooden bases (all of which were removed when the sugar cooled and set). He fashioned pompon dahlias like Wootton Cupid or Dr Grainger; flower stems were made from wire covered with green-coloured sugar, and individual leaves were carefully shaped between the fingers and fused onto the stems. The baskets were filled with flowers, a tall loop handle attached, and then by fusing two, three or four colours together while warm, he would pull out lengths of thin sugar resembling ribbon. This would be festooned across the basket handle and neatened off by attaching a life-like sugar bow. Sugar baskets were made in various sizes and were used as a centre piece for serving petits fours.

Everything was made fresh, including the paste for raviolis, which we made up with the filling supplied from the larder consisting of well-flavoured braised beef, cooked calves' brains and spinach. Cannelloni squares, 'bouchées', vol-au-vents, tartlets, 'barquettes' and cheese straws would be prepared and cooked for use when required in the kitchen. Short-pastry tartlet cases would be used as a base for some of the poached or soft-boiled egg dishes, like eggs mornay, and the bouchées were filled by the fish cook with a sea-food mixture in lobster sauce, topped with a slice of truffle. Vol-au-vents were filled by the sauce cook with chicken and mushroom pieces in a rich cream sauce, or calves sweetbreads. Cheese straws were served as an accompaniment to turtle soup. Barquettes were filled with devilled shrimps, prawns or soft roes, and served as a savoury. Steak pies sent from the larder using raw meat were covered in short pastry, and chicken pies (a Sunday lunch special) were prepared from raw chicken – each piece was wrapped in thin streaky bacon; sliced mushrooms, finely chopped onion, herbs and chicken stock were added; and the whole lot was covered with puff pastry. Chicken pies were always prepared in blue willow-pattern pie dishes kept expressly for this purpose, and were in various sizes for one, two, four or six portions. Sufficient quantities were baked to ensure a supply for the cold buffet during the week.

I thoroughly enjoyed the work and environment, and took to it like a duck to water. As my confidence increased, so my native cockney humour and cheekiness came bubbling out until, one day, having gone a little too far, I was firmly grabbed by Bill, John and Charlie, the lower part of my clothes was pulled down, and I had the embarrassing experience of being anointed in the nether regions with 2 lb of strawberry jam, and was treated to a few well-chosen words on my behaviour. (I thought that they could have chosen a jam without pips, but did not dare say so!) A pastry-cook's initiation, no doubt, for which, as Gilbert and Sullivan put it, 'the punishment fits the crime'.

In our afternoon breaks I, along with my fellow apprentices, Pierre, Gerard and John, started to explore Soho and, inevitably, we were curious as to the reason why so many ladies paraded up and down certain streets. Gerard, who knew his way around, took upon himself the role of guide, and we learned from him some of the reasons for and economics of the ladies of the streets. Gerard informed us that the Lisle Street ladies were the cheapest and would charge ten shillings. All the streets off Old Compton Street and Gerrard Street had a regular complement of promenaders who would charge fifteen shillings to a pound according to services rendered. In Shepherd Market the price doubled, and in and off Bond Street anything up to five pounds was the rate. In view of our seven shillings and sixpence a week we speedily realised that this was a mystery of life well out of our reach. However, this didn't stop us gawking until one day, when we stopped to stare at a new member of the sisterhood, she, on observing us, let flow in a high shrieking voice such a torrent of abuse and bad language that we were sent scurrying off highly embarrassed and lost in admiration at her use of vocabulary.

At the beginning of December it was time to start the Christmas puddings, and the various ingredients were prepared during the slacker evening periods over two or three days. Then on the big day for the mixing we all moved into the bakery, which was twenty yards along the passage and was occupied by a large German who baked all the bread rolls for the hotel twice a day. When he went off duty at four o'clock the whole pastry staff moved in with all the dry ingredients for the puddings. These were tipped into the baker's wooden trough which was about twelve feet long, and with our sleeves rolled up as high as possible, we started to mix. Mario was dispatched to the bar and returned with a trolley bearing bottles of stout, brown ale, whisky, rum and brandy. Poppa Fritz started to open the bottles and pour the contents into the mixture and, initially, all the contents went in. Then he started to take an occasional swig and pass bottles to Bill, John and Charlie for a swig, before emptying the remainder into the pudding mixture. As the swigs increased in size, so the merriment started up, and when I rashly made some remark out of place, my head was ducked into the mixture without ceremony.

As was the custom in many kitchens in those days, all chefs received a daily drinks allowance; apprentices received two small bottles of lemonade, commis two small bottles of light ale, and 'chefs de partie' one bottle of red wine. The kitchen was organised on the 'partie' system as created by Escoffier, and was broken down into sections, or parties, according to the sections of the menu. Obviously, this system varied from kitchen to kitchen according to the volume of business and the number of chefs employed. Away from the main kitchen, in addition to the pastry and bakery, was the 'glacier' where Bill Sandys worked with one of the apprentices, making the ice-cream specialities and *petits fours*. The larder, which adjoined the pastry, was sub-divided into two parts with a chef de partie in each. In one worked a butcher, a fishmonger and a poulterer, and in the other, all the cold dishes were prepared; hors-d'oeuvres, buffets, canapés, terrines, pâtés, dressed crabs, lobsters, crawfish, oysters and sandwiches for afternoon teas.

Monsieur Avignon had his office next to the glacier, facing the main kitchens, and on the other side of this was the fruit and salad room with a row of glass-fronted refrigerators lined along one wall. Then came the silver room where all the cutlery and silver dishes were washed and polished, and, finally, the china and glass wash up. This took you to the end of the kitchen with stairs leading up to the restaurant and stairs leading down to the grill room. On more than one occasion I saw Monsieur Avignon chasing a waiter who had spoken out of turn out of the kitchen and half-way up or down the stairs. Once this happened to the restaurant manager, who came down displaying a pompous attitude about a certain customer's order, but he speedily retreated at the sight of chef, with eyes flashing, cursing in French and brandishing a large knife!

The main kitchen consisted of four, long, coal-fired, solid-top ranges, set back-to-back in two lines to give eight sizeable working areas. One of these was for the soup partie, one for the fish, two for the sauce, two for the vegetables and, along with a double charcoal-fired grill, two for the roast. In one corner of the main kitchen was the 'plonge', or pot wash, where the vast collection of tin-lined copper pots and pans were washed, dried and polished with a mixture of fine sand, flour and vinegar. In the basement was a large ice-making plant and cool store, and the main kitchen store was near the back door facing the pastry, with a huge wooden table outside. This was for the suppliers to unpack and display their produce ready for Monsieur Avignon's inspection, which was a cast-iron prerequisite before any delivery notes were signed. Woe betide any supplier who dared send commodities that did not match up to the chef's specification! They would be ordered off without ceremony and he would be on the telephone to the unwise tradesman, letting him know in no uncertain terms that if this was the best that he could supply, his order to serve the hotel would be cancelled forthwith. Twice a week, from the markets of Paris, would arrive a large consignment of vegetables of minute size and superb quality, including Brussels sprouts and French beans. Since the vegetables were so small they were time-consuming to prepare, but they cooked in no time at all, remaining appetisingly green, crisp and fresh.

Details of the 1935 Hotel, Restaurant and Catering Exhibition (the first to be held at Olympia) were circulated and Martin, a management trainee who was doing his kitchen 'stage', and myself were talked into entering. My class was that for apprentice pastry-cooks, for which had to be prepared a decorated gâteau, six afternoon pastries and a cold sweet. Coached by Bill and John, I prepared a splendid butter-cream gâteau delicately decorated with a piped bunch of lily of the valley, six of our best and most inviting looking pastries, and for the sweet, a charlotte renaissance, which is a charlotte mould, the sides of which are lined with rectangles of Genoese sponge glazed with white and pink fondant. The mould is then filled with a vanilla-flavoured bavarois (an egg custard enriched with whipped cream, lightly set with gelatine) combined with raw, peeled and sliced apricots, peaches, diced pineapple and wild strawberries, all previously marinated in kirsch. When set and turned out, a slice of pineapple decorated with candied fruit is placed on top. For Martin's class it was necessary to present a cold meat dish and a sweet, and he prepared a dish of lamb cutlets in aspic and a charlotte russe, and he made two charlottes in case of accident.

On the morning of the exhibition we left the hotel by taxi at eight o'clock and were in the kitchen bright and early to complete our entries. I dressed my gâteau on a lace doily on a large, oval, silver dish which gleamed to perfection, then dressed three of each of my pastries around the gâteau which made an impressive display and, gazing at it with pride, I couldn't think how the judge could award me other than the first prize. With half an hour to go I carefully and successfully turned out my charlotte onto a round, silver flat dish and went back to the fridge to get the previously prepared slice of pineapple. As I lifted the pineapple onto the charlotte, to my horror, the charlotte started to sag and it gradually flattened out leaving a mess of liquid on and around the sponge fingers. I almost burst into tears! What I had done was that while preparing the slice of pineapple for the top (I had been given a whole fruit so that I could take out the best slice), two or three tablespoons of pineapple juice had accumulated in a bowl and, in my ignorance, I thought that it would be a good idea to add this to the bavarois mixture. What I didn't know then is that an enzyme in raw pineapple juice counteracts the setting properties of gelatine. Anyway, I borrowed Martin's spare charlotte russe, put my slice of pineapple on top and finally, disappointed but relieved, emerged with second prize.

I so enjoyed my time in the pastry and took to the work that I declared I wanted to become a fully-fledged pastry-cook. Poppa Fritz wisely took me on one side and said that, although he would be delighted to keep me on and that I had the makings of a good pastry-cook, nevertheless, I should go around the kitchen and complete an all-round apprenticeship. If I did this there would be more opportunity open to me in later life. These were true words for which I have often had cause to be grateful.

So, into the kitchen I went, first with Mr Williams, the 'potager' (soup cook), where I learned how to cut vegetables with precision and eventually speed as, side-by-side with him, I cut piles of 'julienne' (fine strips), 'brunoise' ($\frac{1}{8}$ or $\frac{1}{16}$ inch dice) and 'paysanne' (triangles, squares, circles or edged rounds cut flat to a ¼ of an inch) for use in various soups. The importance of care and use of stocks and the making of crystal clear consommé overhung all our soup preparation. Each day the baker would make us French sticks known as 'flutes' one inch in diameter, which we cut into a variety of shapes of croûtons to accompany the various soups. Soupe à l'oignon was made fresh to order at fifteen minutes' notice. Wafer-thin sliced onions were browned in butter in a thick-bottomed pan, lightly dusted with flour, cooked for a further two to three minutes and then moistened with chicken and beef consommé and simmered until tender. The soup was then poured into an earthenware bowl, covered liberally with toasted slices of flute, sprinkled generously with grated parmesan cheese, browned under the grill and served.

'Petites marmites' in special earthenware or porcelain crocks in sizes of one to four portions were simmered gently on the side of the stove. Starting with a good consommé, cubes of blanched beef were added, then at a later stage blanched trimmed winglets of chicken followed by turned carrots, turnips and neatly cut pieces of celery, leek and cabbage, the end result being a double strength consommé. Consommé was made fresh daily as were all our soups. Potage Germiny, made to order, consisted of a third of a pint of consommé thickened with the addition of two egg yolks, mixed with three tablespoons of cream, and cooked gently on the side of the stove stirring continuously until the mixture lightly coated the back of a wooden spoon. The mixture was then strained into a soup tureen in which had been placed a few leaves of sorrel that had been cut into fine julienne and gently sweated in a little butter. Delicious! Many of our soups were thickened with finely ground rice, barley or potato flour known as 'crème de riz', 'crème d'orge' and 'fécule de pommes de terre'. Where appropriate, as in the case of cream soups, as portions were ordered they were ladled into a small pan, reheated and finished by stirring in a little cream and butter before serving.

Every day Monsieur Avignon would come to our corner to taste all the soups and I had to have teaspoons, a small basin of hot water and a clean cloth ready for him. He was thorough and severely critical of any shortcoming, but always in a constructive way. That is the way to achieve perfection and how I developed my love of good soups which still exists today. Whenever I eat in a restaurant where I know the chef to be a good cook I frequently start a meal with soup. This is certainly the case at Langan's Brasserie, in Stratton Street, just behind Green Park station, where Richard Shepherd is responsible for running one of London's most successful restaurants, and at the Heathrow Penta, where Head Chef Michael Sullivan and his team provide consistently good food.

So, on to the fish cook ('poissonier'), François Terraillon, a hard taskmaster who, being well respected by Monsieur Avignon, was obviously a good fish cook. His first commis was Syd Howe who later became Head Chef of the Palmerston, a renowned restaurant in the City of London. I soon got into François's bad books for, on my second day, I was given the job of making a sabayon out of thirty-six egg yolks and a quarter of a pint of water, as the base for hollandaise sauce, by whisking them continuously on the very edge of the stove. The stove was red-hot, my eyes were becoming drawn, my whisking arm started to flag and, before I realised it – scrambled eggs – which meant that the sorry mess had to be thrown away. Every name imaginable in bad English and good French (none of which I remember from school vocabulary) was hurled at me. Without having time to think, I was sent off to the store for more eggs and then, under François's stern eye, I restarted, my whisking arm nearly dropping off, but this time I was successful. It was a lesson I never forgot.

A mouthwatering selection of fish dishes were prepared at the Ritz; hot lobster – Mornay, Thermidor, Newburg, Cardinal, américaine; hot oysters – vin blanc, florentine, au champagne; sole, whole or in fillets – vin blanc, Véronique, bonne-femme, coquelin, meunière and many more. Here was learned the foundation of good fish sauces; fish stock, for which we used only sole and turbot bones, was lightly sweated with a little sliced onion in butter, then moistened with white wine and water. Thyme, bay-leaf and lemon juice were added and the mixture was simmered for twenty minutes only and strained. The stock would then be steadily simmered in a clean pan until it reduced to a gelatinous consistency known as fish glaze. This we kept in jars in the refrigerator.

Whenever a fish sauce was required, whether for an à la carte order of one or two portions, or a large quantity for a luncheon dish or a big party, the principle was the same. After the fish was poached, the cooking liquor was drained off into a clean pan through a fine mesh strainer and reduced to a glaze. This would then be removed from the stove, a sufficient quantity of best quality, softened, fresh butter would gradually be stirred in and it would finally be finished with a generous quantity of three-quarter whipped cream. The seasoning was carefully checked, and if the fish flavour was insufficient, a teaspoon or so of the stored fish glaze added. Finally, the sauce was strained through a large sheet of strong linen cloth, a chef at either end folding the cloth over to enclose the sauce completely and then, by twisting tightly in reverse directions and pulling, forcing the sauce through the cloth thus straining it perfectly. This was also the way we strained hollandaise sauce.

As these cloths aged and weakened with continual wear and washing, there was the danger of them splitting and bursting open during the turning process, jetting the hot sauce all over the place (rather like the top of an emulsifier shooting off when at full speed with a batch of hot soup).

Turbot, halibut, skate, salmon, trout and scallops were regularly prepared, and mussels by the gallon were cooked marinière in the classic style with chopped shallots, white wine and chopped parsley; the cooking liquor was drained off, allowed to stand for any grit or sediment to sink, then carefully strained through fine muslin and lightly thickened with beurre manié (equal quantities of butter and flour kneaded together). This still remains one of my favourite dishes today and I wish that restaurants would not spoil the natural flavour of the sauce by lacing it with cream, which is correct if serving moules à la crème, but unacceptable in a moules marinière. Haddock à la Ritz consisted of 1 lb finnan haddocks, placed in special, individual, oval, tin-lined copper pans and gently poached in a light cream. Four slices of skinned tomato were added, covered with cream, browned under the salamander (over-fired grill) and served in the cooking dish.

Cadgery de saumon (salmon kedgeree) was a popular dish which we served accompanied by a medium strength, slightly sweet curry sauce. When coulibiac (salmon pie) was required, the raw ingredients of salmon, vesiga (spinal marrow of sturgeon), duxelle (a chopped shallot and mushroom preparation), rice cooked in consommé and chopped hard-boiled eggs, were sent to the pastry where they were encased in layers in a brioche dough (rich yeast pastry with eggs and butter). The dough was allowed to rise, brushed with melted butter, a slit made in the top for steam to escape, baked, thickly sliced and served hot with melted-butter sauce. All grilled fish were cooked by the 'grillardin' (grill cook) who also doubled as first commis on the roast partie.

What finer culinary delight than good fresh fish cooked with care and understanding? I am an admirer of the many talented chefs who practise with great skill and innovation today, but sometimes feel a little sad that so few of the outstanding classic fish dishes find their way onto good menus.

By this time I was cycling regularly to work, thus saving four shillings a week which went a long way in those days. As a result of careful saving I was able to afford a week's holiday with my pal Freddie Bridger (a fellow cyclist who lived in Putney), and we booked in at a newly opened holiday camp at Skegness. As active, healthy teenagers we were able to indulge ourselves to the full, and enjoyed a splendid week of almost non-stop activities of all kinds. By the time we returned we both felt in need of recuperation, but our recovery rate was rapid, and we heard that a new school of ballroom dancing was opening above the Pheasantry Club in the King's Road, Chelsea. As on our holiday we had sampled ballroom dancing for the first time, 'dancing' as much on our partners' feet as on our own, we decided to investigate. The school was run by Victor Delaney and his wife, Margery, and classes were held from eight to eleven nightly. The entrance fee was modest, non-alcoholic light refreshments were available and music was supplied on gramophone by strict tempo records, mainly of Victor Sylvester, with a smattering of other bands including Fats Waller. An evening consisted of general dancing in the middle of which Victor and Margery would give a demonstration followed by an explanation of basic and elementary steps. Glaring faults were corrected as one engaged in general dancing. I quickly spied an attractive, lively young girl and, having enjoyed two or three dances with her, asked if I could see her home. 'I'm sorry', she replied, 'but Benny has already asked me and I have agreed.' Benny was a local lad who had also gone to the Oratory School. As I was only able to attend a full class on my one day off a week, I wondered whether this lass, to whom I had taken a considerable liking, would be there next time.

The following week I arrived early in plenty of time for the first dance, was delighted to see my prospective partner on the far side of the room, and manoeuvred into position for a quick dash to make sure that I was the first to invite her to dance. My tactics succeeded; half way through the dance I informed her in masterly fashion, '*I* am taking you home tonight,' she agreed, and that was how in 1936 I met Letty, the girl who was to become my wife in 1942. When I escorted her home I couldn't believe my luck, as she only lived 200 yards on one side of the

King's Road in Cale Street, and we were then in a first-floor flat at No. 9 Tedworth Gardens, about 200 yards the other side of the King's Road.

By this time my weekly wage had increased to twelve shillings and sixpence, and as my confidence increased, so did my enjoyment of work even though I was now, during service time, in the centre of the 'madhouse' that had so startled me on my first day in the kitchen. Working over red-hot stoves we perspired profusely, but the busier we were (within reason), the more we gloried in it. Looking back, I suppose it was the challenge we enjoyed taking on and successfully completing.

The 'saucier' (sauce cook), Paul Lajoie, had Camille Lamouille as his first, Cecil Bill as second, and Bruce Garrard as third commis. This was a busy, important partie which prepared all the meat, poultry and game dishes with the exception of roasts and grills, and almost all the hot sauces required by the whole kitchen: boeuf braisé à la mode, navarin of lamb printanier, fricassée of veal à l'ancienne, tripes à la mode de Caen, goulash à l'hongroise, currie d'agneau, cervelle au beurre noir, tête de veau vinaigrette, ris de veau braisé, langue d'agneau poulette, queue de boeuf en hochepot, rognons sautés Turbigo and truffles au champagne. For this last, fresh peeled truffles were placed in an ovenproof cocotte, a glass of champagne was added, the lid was sealed with a strip of pastry and the whole lot was baked. The seal was broken in front of the customer thus stimulating the palate with a heavenly fragrance. There were so many more interesting and varied dishes. A different chicken sauté dish appeared on the menu each day (there are a selection of 100 in the classical repertoire) and sometimes there would be a superb Irish stew, which was accompanied by pickled red cabbage. Steak and kidney

In the salad room, Ritz Hotel kitchen, 1936
From the left: Syd Howe, Bruce Garrard, Robert Benveignin, Victor Ceserani, Freddie Bridger

pies and puddings were often served (sometimes snipe or oysters were put into the puddings) and choucroûte garni, pot-roasts of pheasant, duck, partridge, plover and salmis of game (a brown ragoût) made frequent appearances. The sauce cook was considered the linchpin of the kitchen and, as such, was held in high esteem and regarded as number three to Monsieur Avignon and his sous-chef (deputy), Monsieur Cahouet, who later became Head Chef at the Hyde Park Hotel, Knightsbridge.

Monsieur Lorduron, 'rotisseur' (roast cook), had Bobbie Bonmartin as his first commis and grill cook, and Robert Benveignin was second commis. All the deep-frying was done in fritures – large, oval, black steel deep pans – which, being portable, were carefully moved over the solid-top range. The frying medium was best beef dripping and this was rendered down from minced beef fat and suet in a large black steel pot. By present day safety standards the frying pan was hazardous, for if any food immersed in hot fat was too damp, such as potatoes, and if the fat had been used for too long, then it would rapidly rise and bubble up and over the sides of the friture. If this happened, and it did occasionally, one had to remove the food being fried quickly by using a wire spider and frying basket. If, however, any of the fat got onto the stove, the degree of heat was such that it immediately ignited.

On one occasion I saw Monsieur Lorduron, who had lank, black hair and a large, drooping moustache, frantically working to remove some fried potatoes from the friture; a large quantity of fat had bubbled over, ignited, and was spreading and, of course, with solid-fuel ranges there was no question of turning the heat off. He looked like a devil emerging from Hades, and his language matched perfectly.

Roasting large joints in coal-fired ovens had to be done with great care, for there were no oven thermostats; one used the back of the hand placed in the oven to gauge the temperature. This was a technique I had gained experience of during my time in the pastry where we had a double-decker, solid-fuel oven. We always kept the oven very hot so that when large joints like ribs of beef were roasted, a thick crust of damp-ened rock salt was placed around the joints in order to protect them. The roasts were many and varied: large joints of beef, lamb, veal and pork, turkeys, geese, chickens, ducks, pheasants, grouse, partridge, woodcock and snipe.

Almost all the grills – which included chickens, steaks, chops and cutlets – were cooked on the charcoal grill. A favourite was double black and blue cutlets, which were double-sized lamb cutlets with two rib bones, rapidly cooked on the fiercest part of the grill so that they blackened on the outside yet remained almost raw, or 'blue', in the centre. Fish – whole sole and herring, slices of turbot and salmon – and sausages, kidneys, mushrooms and tomatoes, were placed on oiled metal trays and cooked under the salamander. Pommes frites (chips) were cooked, initially, with a minimum of colour in a moderately hot fat prior to service, and then plunged into very hot fat when required. This had the effect of making a crisp outside and a floury inside – delicious! Soufflé potatoes were always available, and a hundredweight sack of special Dutch potatoes was kept for these alone. Grilled fresh herring with mustard sauce was a lunchtime favourite, as were devilled whitebait.

Shortly after my first meeting with Letty, we decided to spread our wings and attend a special dance at the Hammersmith Palais de Dance which ran from eight until twelve o'clock. I asked permission of Mrs Boyle (Letty's widowed mother) and promised to see her daughter safely home by midnight. We were enjoying ourselves so much that time raced away and we had to leave hurriedly at eleven-thirty, only to find a large queue for the No. 11 bus. Quickly assessing the amount of money I had on me, I called a taxi. It was the first time for both of us in a cab, and whilst making the most of the privacy, my ardour got the better of me and I slid off the seat and finished up in a large heap on the floor. No wonder the cabbie had an amused look on his face when I paid the fare!

Very occasionally, after dancing class, we would adjourn to Nick's Diner just past Shawfield Street and, if the budget would allow, have a supper of egg and chips followed by waffles with butter and maple syrup. Once a year, on either one of our birthdays, we booked a floorside table for a dinner-dance at the Regent Palace Hotel and stretched the evening to the full, being seated at our table as the band struck up, and remaining until the National Anthem at eleven o'clock. This evening consisted of a four-course meal costing three shillings and sixpence, to which we added one drink, and made that last the whole evening. On leaving the hotel we would then walk from Piccadilly Circus to Green Park before taking the bus home, as that saved us a couple of coppers fare.

The Regent Palace Hotel was one of the J. Lyons Company chain which made such a contribution to the catering scene in the 20s and 30s and included the Strand Palace Hotel; the tremendously popular Corner Houses at Oxford Street, Marble Arch, the Strand and Coventry Street; the Trocadero (one of London's best restaurants and the training ground for J. Lyons management trainees); the Popular Café in Piccadilly (now Simpsons) where Letty and I would sometimes go tea-dancing, and, of course, innumerable tea-shops. The Corner Houses in particular offered so much – the ground floor contained a high-class delicatessen, pastry and bakery goods, sweets and confectionery and a florist. I well remember, as a young boy, being taken by my mother and Pop to my first one, and looking around the ground floor seemed to be like exploring an Aladdin's cave. All the foods were attractively displayed and looked so appetising that I couldn't stop my mouth from watering. In the base-ment, or lower ground floor, and on each of the other three or four floors, were inviting-looking restaurants, each of a different character or nationality, with menus to match and an orchestra playing suitable light music to fit the theme of the room.

One of the key-notes of any J. Lyons establishment was that the cus-tomer received value for money, which was obviously why they prof-ited. I, for one, felt sad and am certain that many Londoners shared that feeling when they gradually closed down after the war.

By now I was working on the vegetable partie with 'entremettier' Phil Cornet, first commis Stan Regnaud – who, years later, became Head of Department of Professional Cookery at Westminster College, and two others whose names have escaped me. Here were prepared the potato and vegetable dishes, egg dishes – omelets, scrambled eggs, soft-boiled eggs, hard-boiled eggs, poached eggs, eggs in cocotte and eggs sur le plat – and pastas such as raviolis, cannellonis, gnocchis (romaine (semolina), parisienne (choux paste) and italienne (potato)), spaghetti, macaroni and many more. It was one of the busiest parties in the kitchen because as all the vegetables were so small, they took us hours of prepa-ration. During the summer, when asparagus was in season, Phil Cornet would often be back a half to three-quarters of an hour earlier in the afternoon in order to make a start on the large number of portions required for dinner. Very few customers failed to order asparagus when in season. During busy luncheon services I was often working over the stove for one-and-a-half to two hours with hardly a break, wearing nothing under my white jacket, and by the end of service in summer I could take off my coat and wring out the perspiration. The pancakes on Shrove Tuesday were made in this corner, and we were expected to be able to keep six to eight pans on the go at one time. The pans were small, no more than 4–5 inches in diameter, which helped, and also made them easy to toss. A favourite dish was eggs Chimay, which was hard-boiled eggs, the yolks of which were removed, sieved, mixed with an equal amount of duxelle (chopped mushrooms cooked with shallots), piped back into the whites, coated with cheese sauce and gratinated. Bill Paine, the staff cook known as 'Vauxhall' (which was where he lived), operated in this area. He was a down-to-earth, vociferous cockney with a droll sense of humour. On one particular day everything that could go wrong had gone wrong, and he was in a bad-tempered mood. At lunch-time (staff ate at eleven-thirty, before the service), a chambermaid came to the hot plate (which was steam-heated to a very high temperature) to collect lunch for herself and her colleagues who ate in a separate room, and called out, 'What's for lunch to-day Bill?' Bill came dashing up to the hot plate with his arms full of hot dishes, placed them on her tray, lifted up his apron (he neither wore underpants nor fastened his fly buttons) and replied, 'Sausage!' At that precise moment someone brushed past behind him causing him to sway forward, which caused his appendage to swing forward and touch the hot plate. His face contorted in agony and his language was unprintable. Those around him showed appropriate sympathy by laughing their heads off. To add to his discomfort, Monsieur Avignon emerged from his office, eyes blazing, and soundly told him off. Eavesdropping on the dressing-room conversations afterwards, we gathered that the incident forced him to enter a state of celibacy for a month.

We managed to find something to do most afternoons during our break; we swam at Marshall Street baths, kicked a football around in Hyde Park behind Knightsbridge Barracks, and there were several news theatres that ran a one-hour show consisting of Laurel and Hardy, Harold Lloyd, cartoon films and news gazette programmes. During this period I saw the legendary snooker player, Joe Davis, in action twice, once in the afternoon at the Leicester Square Hall, which occupied a comparatively small space in a large building on the west corner of Leicester Square. It was a fascinating afternoon. The hall was so small, with seating on all four sides, that one could hear all the remarks and asides passed by the players and as these were many, and often laced with humour, it added to the enjoyment. Joe was in good form and scored a century break, which made the afternoon complete and memorable. I also saw him give his stage turn at the London Palladium as part of a variety bill. He had a slanted mirror over the table so that those in the stalls could see. Sitting in the cheapest seats in the gallery I could see the complete programme of trick shots, complete even though from that distance it was a distinctly miniaturised view.

It was now time to move from the vegetable partie to the 'garde-manger' (larder) where John Querico was 'chef d'oeuvrier', Michael Marley, his first commis, and the 'hors-d'oeuvrier', Gachet, had a cubby-hole in the far corner. In between the kitchen and larder was a room under the direction of Monsieur Banderet, who prepared the numerous joints and small cuts of meat and poultry. He was assisted by two men, one who prepared the fish ready to be cooked when called for by the poissónier or the grill chef, and the other, named Pinot, who feathered, cleaned, eviscerated and trussed the poultry and game. In the first corner was a tank in which a dozen or so live trout, ready to be prepared for truite au bleu, were kept, because this is one fish dish for which the fish has to be freshly killed before cooking.

In the larder we prepared all the cold buffet items fresh daily – two 4–5 lb dressed crabs, lobsters, crawfish and oysters when in season, York ham, roast wing rib of beef, dressed ox tongue, liver sausage, game pie, chicken galantine, lamb cutlets in aspic, portioned roast chicken in aspic, poached eggs in aspic – the variety of dishes changing as foods came in and went out of season. Poularde Rose-Marie consisted of a large poached chicken from which the breasts were carefully removed, and each divided into three even portions. A quantity of chicken velouté (basic white chicken sauce), generously finished with cream with a few leaves of pre-soaked gelatine added, and chicken aspic jelly, both made from the stock in which the chicken had been cooked, were made and allowed to cool. Ham mousse, made from finely minced lean trimmings of ham added to the chicken velouté, with sufficient gelatine to allow it to set lightly, was used to replace the space on the chicken left by the removal of the breasts. This was carefully shaped using a palette knife dipped in boiling water and wiped. The re-moulded chicken and the six suprêmes would be coated with the chicken velouté (one, two or three coats to give a smooth but not over-thick finish), left to set, and decorated, with each piece of decoration being dipped in aspic before it was placed on the chicken in order to set it in place. Then the chicken would be given two, three or four coats of aspic, left to set, trimmed, neatly set on a large, oval, silver, flat dish and finished with a light piping of ham mousse.

By a similar method we prepared roast pheasant, using a foie gras mousse, cutting each breast into thin slices, fanning them out in a curve from the dressed bird using a light-brown, game aspic jelly, omitting any velouté and decorating simply with thinly cut lines of truffle to give a silhouette effect.

Again, Duck Montmorency was prepared in a similar way, using a duck or chicken mousse, light-brown aspic jelly, omitting any sauce and decorating with quarter-inch overlapping rounds of cherry and truffle. Chicken galantines were made by completely boning 5 lb chickens without breaking the skin. The best part of the breasts would be kept aside and the remainder of the chicken flesh would be thoroughly chopped and pounded, then passed through a fine mesh sieve, placed in a bowl on ice, several egg whites would be added and the mixture thoroughly mixed until cold. Double cream and seasoning were slowly added whilst continually beating the mixture until it was a light smooth texture. The chicken skin was laid out flat, trimmed to a rectangular shape, and an inch-thick layer of the chicken mixture neatly piled in the centre. Along the length would then be placed, in neat rows, pistachio nuts and neatly cut lengths of tongue, ham, truffle and raw chicken fillet. This was carefully covered with another inch-thick layer of chicken mixture, a repeat of the garnish and topped off with an inch-thick layer of mixture. The skin was carefully folded over, and the whole gently formed into a roll, wrapped in greaseproof paper, a pudding cloth secured with string, and gently simmered until cooked. When thoroughly cold, after the cloth and paper were removed, the galantine would be placed on a wire grid over a tray and coated two or three times with a rich, creamy, chicken sauce to which a few leaves of gelatine were added, and allowed to set. Then it was artistically decorated with thin strips of truffle and, finally, coated with chicken aspic jelly.

Afternoon tea sandwiches were prepared before we went off duty. 4 lb sandwich loaves were used, the crusts of three sides were removed lengthways, together with one end crust. Then thin slices were cut with a very sharp knife horizontally, each being buttered before cutting and stacked in front of the loaf. Six different fillings were prepared, one buttered slice put back onto a crust base, filled and covered with the second slice. This continued until all the slices were converted into long sandwiches, crusts were put back on all sides and the whole wrapped in a slightly dampened cloth. When required for tea, they would be cut into one-inch fingers vertically down the loaf, neatly trimmed to give a curve on all four corners, dressed on lace doileys on silver flats, sprinkled with mustard and cress and served. I remember many years later watching Clement Freud give a demonstration on television, announcing that he would show how professional chefs cut sandwiches in bulk. As he used a 2 lb loaf, which was very fresh, and a blunt knife, he only succeeded in cutting three uneven slices. As he put the knife to the bread it shrank back like a block of soft foam rubber. The resultant sandwich was about three inches thick.

Our knives were kept constantly sharp by frequent use of a steel, and the knife grinder called weekly to collect any knives that had lost their edge. He kept his cart outside the back door in the street where he would sit turning his grindstone by means of foot pedals, sharpening our knives, and returning them all within thirty minutes or so.

Having only one day off a week didn't allow much time for evening social pleasures. I met Letty every evening after work, usually at about ten o'clock, when we would sometimes go for a stroll down the King's Road and window shop. We still enjoyed our dancing when the opportunity arose, and would occasionally attend tea-dances at the Astoria, Charing Cross Road, where a young Joe Loss and his band were extremely popular, or Lyons Popular Café in Piccadilly.

Opposite Chelsea Town Hall was Chelsea Palace, one of London's numerous variety theatres where we saw many of the old-timers like Max Miller; Ernie Lotinga; Flanagan and Allen; Naughton and Gold; Nervo and Knox; Gracie Fields; Paul Robeson; Wilson, Keppel and Betty; Will Hay; Elsie and Doris Waters; Max Wall; Rob Wilton; Tommy Trinder; Tessie O'Shea and many others. A seat on a backless bench in the gallery cost a few pence and, as we queued up outside the theatre, buskers would entertain the queue and peanut vendors sold bags of roasted peanuts in their shells for a halfpenny or a penny. Needless to say, from time to time during the performance as peanuts were cracked open and eaten, some of the shells 'accidentally' fell into the pit stalls, particularly if bald-headed gentlemen were sitting below. They always seemed to be a popular target.

Saturday night was the night of the week for most people, but as I never had a Saturday or Sunday off whilst at the Ritz, I was unable to indulge. Most of my old school chums thought that I was mad working those hours for the amount of money received, but I enjoyed what I did and was reasonably content.

In the 1930s Oswald Moseley's blackshirts were based near the Duke of York's headquarters – a Territorial Army station. At the other end of the King's Road was the World's End pub, which was located in what was then a poor working-class district. A stone's throw from the pub was a meeting hall which housed a branch of the Communist Party. On more than one occasion each organisation planned a march along the King's Road on the same evening and, as they marched towards each other and came abreast, invariably a fight would break out. As this could become ugly we kept well away.

Back in the larder I worked occasional days on the hors-d'oeuvre section and felt very pleased when, on the hors-d'oeuvrier's day off, I was entrusted with the total preparation for both lunch and dinner. We prepared a wide variety of interesting foods in the larder and as my proficiency increased, so did my weekly wage, to seventeen shillings and sixpence a week. At this time my day off was Fridays, which fortunately coincided with Freddie Bridger's, and during the good weather we would cycle to Windsor. Usually we used our solo cycles, but occasionally we would borrow a tandem from a friend, I would put my saddle (a Brooks B17) on the back, and off we would go, endeavouring to beat our time record which was one-and-a-quarter hours from Putney. We would cycle to Windsor Bridge arriving at about eleven-thirty, call in the pub near the river for half a pint, and then walk along to Romney Lock and along the river bank, where we could find a quiet spot. Here we sunbathed, swam in the river, ate our sandwiches, lounged in the sun, had another swim and then tore back to London in time to change, put on our best suits and find a dance somewhere.

During the warmer months we wore shorts and alpaca jackets, and as the weather cooled, we changed into plus-eights, sweaters and lumber jackets. One late-autumn day, wearing our cooler weather gear, we cycled to Windsor and decided to take out a double canoe on the river for an hour. Being well co-ordinated as a result of our tandem cycling, we achieved a good speed and were enjoying ourselves when a large pleasure boat approached leaving a considerable wake which speedily rolled towards us. Putting our knowledge of seamanship (virtually nil) to the fore, we headed our craft on to the waves and rode them triumphantly. Unfortunately, we didn't realise that as the waves hit the concrete bank they came back off the wall underwater in a reverse direction – the first we knew about this was when we found ourselves tipped into the river! We scrambled to the bank, managed to haul the canoe out and got it back to the landing stage. I cannot remember a more uncomfortable hour and a half than the one that followed, cycling home in heavy sodden clothes.

It was around this period that King George V celebrated his Silver Jubilee, and London prepared for a day to remember. Most of the hotels and restaurants put on special gala dinners and, as the procession came along Piccadilly, the Ritz got ready for a bumper day's business. Because of police regulations governing the crowds we were issued with special passes and had to be in the hotel by 6.30 a.m. Starting work shortly afterwards we continued without a break until late in the evening, finally clocking out of the hotel around eleven o'clock. From Green Park to Piccadilly Circus, down to Trafalgar Square, and in many of the side-streets, Londoners and visitors were embroiled in one huge carnival, with *ad hoc* musicians and buskers playing on many street corners. The mood was infectious and encouraged many couples to dance, sing and make merry until the early hours. It seemed only a comparatively short time afterwards that we sadly watched the King's funeral cortège from the hotel roof.

It was also around this time that, over a period of a few weeks, I made several requests for a pay rise from Monsieur Avignon who, to my discomfort, sternly refused on each occasion. After the third request had met with no better success I took my grievance to Poppa Fritz, who suggested that I consider going to work for an old friend of his, Charles Abry, late of the Waldorf Hotel, who was now head chef at a private gentlemen's club in King Street just off St James's Square, named the Orleans Club. I attended for interview, took a liking to Monsieur Abry, wondered about the smallness of the kitchen with six staff and the completely different atmosphere to the Ritz, but went home to think about the move.

Looking back on my time at the Ritz I had taken most things for granted, as is often the way with the young. It wasn't until years later, as I gained a wider insight into the industry and the wide variation in standards, that I realised what a fortunate start I had made to my career, acquiring not only a wide repertoire of classical cuisine, but also a knowledge of the discipline necessary to achieve such high standards. Initially, I thought that Monsieur Avignon had missed his vocation, and that he should have been a colonel in the French Foreign Legion, such was the standard of discipline he rigorously imposed. However, that was the way in which many top-class French kitchens were organised in those days. In fact, a popular form of gossip among young chefs would often be swopping stories about the regimes of some of the holy terrors they had worked for – Monsieur Latry of the Savoy and Monsieur Perrin

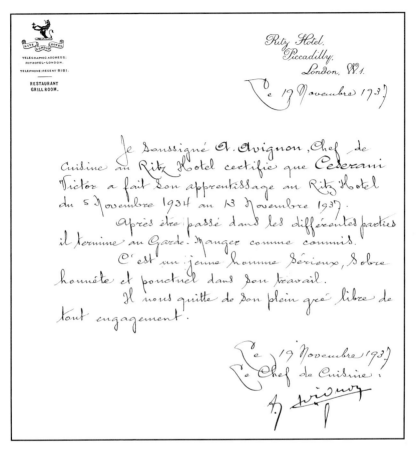

Certificate of apprenticeship, 1937

of the Park Lane, for example. But, equally, these men and many others like them were regarded as peers in their calling.

After a great deal of heart searching I handed in my notice to Monsieur Avignon. When he asked me why, I told him that I had obtained a post elsewhere for two pounds a week, whereupon he turned on his kitchen clerk, John, and severely upbraided him for failing to inform him that I was not earning sufficient money!

CHAPTER 3
1937–1940

Orleans Club, St James's

I left the Ritz in 1937 clutching my certificate of apprenticeship to join Monsieur as his number two. Marie Kellett from Yorkshire was the vegetable cook, Bridget from Ireland was the pastry-cook, Arthur, the kitchen porter, and George, the washer-up.

Monsieur Abry came from Alsace, he was trained in the classic French mould, and was a man with a gentle, helpful disposition. Marie Kellett was a large, buxom, florid-faced, grey-haired lady who had cooked in private service for many years, and worked in several other clubs including the Oxford and Cambridge. In addition to cooking the vegetables she prepared the staff meals and took over the pastry on Bridget's days off. Marie was a blunt, forthright individual and you thought twice before crossing swords with her. Bridget was a quiet, diligent, softly spoken woman of about thirty years who carried out her work without fuss, but could, on rare occasions if roused, display a remarkable temper. Arthur was a treasure among kitchen porters – neat, clean and reliable. His job was to keep the kitchen clean, scrub the wooden tables and chopping boards twice a day, sweep the floor and sprinkle down fresh sawdust twice a day, wash and peel vegetables, chop parsley, and to carry other basic routine tasks. He also cleaned the coal-fired range regularly and lit and kept it fired during the required periods. George was an ex-regular soldier in his late fifties. He still retained his military

28

bearing and proudly tended a pointed-ends waxed moustache. He was responsible for all the washing up, and he and Arthur doubled up for each other during their respective time off. George loved to tell a tale and could be found most nights after work in the local pub, enjoying a pint and regaling his cronies with gossip from the club and elsewhere. Although we had only one day off a week, it was arranged that each shift (mine being with Bridget and George) had alternate weekends from after lunch on Saturday on one week, and a half-day off the following week. Weekends at the club were generally quiet as many members went to the country.

Since the kitchen was in the basement and the dining-room was two floors up, all food was conveyed to the table via a creaky wooden lift, and verbal communication was by means of a speaking tube. To operate the tube it was first necessary to remove a plug on a chain. One then blew down the tube, which caused a warning whistle to sound at the other end, the plug at the other end would be removed, and an ear put to the tube to receive the message.

We operated on split duties daily – from nine to two-thirty, and from five to nine – and, during the better weather, Letty would occasionally come to meet me outside the club. She was a little wary about this at first because walking from Green Park station down St James's Street and along King Street she would be propositioned by one or two gentlemen. In those days ladies of the oldest profession strolled freely along many London streets offering their wares to any seemingly interested party, and in the better parts of town it was not always easy to distinguish a street lady from a passer-by. However, as Letty was never approached by anyone saying other than a hopeful 'Good evening?' she was able to cope without embarrassment simply by ignoring the implied question and walking briskly on.

When we met we would usually take a stroll, sometimes along Piccadilly through to Leicester Square and down to Trafalgar Square, and sometimes walk back home to Chelsea. On summer nights we would stroll through the park to Victoria and home that way. Walking was one of our favourite pastimes. We enjoyed window shopping, gazing at articles in shop windows that were hopelessly out of our reach and wondering if one day we might be able to afford them – and yet, I can never recall us being truly envious or disgruntled. Like so many people in those days, we had very little in material possessions, yet we were happy and reasonably satisfied. Undoubtedly, the fact that we enjoyed each other's company so much was the major reason for this – we didn't get bored, so we didn't require large sums of money for the many extra pleasures of life that so many young people today seem to be continually seeking.

Having said that, there were two occasions when I ventured to gain some extra money; the first was a competition in a daily newspaper for 'an interesting recipe'. Using my mother's name, I sent in a recipe for snow eggs. It was a simple dish, consisting of four egg whites and eight ounces of caster sugar which were whipped to a stiff meringue, then moulded using two dessert spoons, into a shallow pan containing one pint of milk flavoured with two to three drops of vanilla essence. The milk gently simmered for a few minutes, the meringue shapes were carefully turned over until the cooking was completed, and removed onto a teacloth to drain. The milk was made up to one pint, re-boiled, lightly thickened by the addition of the four egg yolks mixed with an ounce and a half of caster sugar, strained onto a shallow serving dish, cooled, and the snow eggs sat neatly on top. It is a light delicate sweet, variations for which are to sprinkle the eggs with toasted sliced almonds and, additionally, or alternatively, some threads of sugar and water cooked to a golden-brown caramel. Gratifyingly, the following week the newspaper carried the result showing that Mrs Ceserani of Chelsea had won first prize!

The second occasion took place some time later. I had noticed that the newspaper regularly carried an advertisment asking, 'Do you want to earn five pounds a week at home?' I sent for details and found that, by sending five pounds, one became enrolled as a member of the National Confectionery Association and received a membership card enabling certain specialist commodities and equipment to be purchased wholesale as well as a book of recipes. I decided to expend five pounds of my Post Office savings, and after studying the recipes, purchased two copper saucepans, a saccharometer (used for measuring the temperature of a solution of sugar, water and glucose), some moulding trays, wrapping paper and paper bags. My range of confectionery included glacier mints, pink and white coconut ice, treacle toffee and butterscotch. Before leaving for work in the mornings, I would put sugar, water and glucose into a saucepan on the stove with instructions for my mother to light the gas at two-thirty. By the time I got home the sugar was well under way. I completed the recipe, poured the mixture into trays, allowed it to cool, turned it out onto my marble slab (scrounged from an old wash-basin stand) and cut it into portions. When glacier mints were made, peppermint oil would be added to the hot syrup, and a strong but pleasant sweet odour of peppermint permeated the whole house. By this time I had to return to work, so my mother and Letty would wrap and weigh the sweets into quarter-pound bags which I sold at a fair price. The sweets were pronounced very good, the word soon got around and business was such that I covered all my outgoings and made a modest profit within a month. By that time I tired of working all day every day, and called a halt.

It was around this period that Pop applied for, and was granted,

British naturalisation, something that my mother had been urging him to do for some time. Shortly afterwards, I received calling up papers for the Italian Army, which I tore up without any qualms of conscience as I did not feel that I owed my allegiance to Italy. I had been born and schooled in London, spoke only English and a little French, and had visited Italy once as a very small boy on two weeks' holiday with my parents. Many people ask why I do not speak Italian, but I saw little of my father as a boy because of the long hours he worked, his knowledge of English and his method of expressing himself was very poor, and as my mother did not speak Italian, I really had little opportunity to learn. This is why I use a soft 'c' when pronouncing my surname as opposed to the correct pronunciation, 'ch'. I also pronounce the first 'e' as in 'eggs', but at school the majority of teachers sounded the first 'e' as a double 'ee', as in 'see', which made it into a languid 'Seeserarni'. My school chums speedily reduced that to 'Seeser'. Throughout my schooldays I was known as 'Caesar' and a much overplayed joke in the playground would be for some wag to come up to me crying, 'Julius!' and to then grab me by the unmentionables shouting, 'Caesar!' Some forty years later I was being interviewed for a Radio 4 food programme by Derek Cooper, and completely spontaneously he addressed me as 'Caesar'. He apologised afterwards, but I was delighted.

Work at the club seemed strange at first after the hurly-burly of the much larger Ritz kitchen, but I soon readjusted and adapted to the new working environment and its responsibilities, for when chef was off, I was in charge. I quickly found that the work discipline on which I had been brought up did not go down well on certain occasions among my new colleagues. One evening, just as we were clearing up after dinner service, a member arrived a few minutes late and ordered a dinner of soup and roast partridge, vegetables and sauté potatoes. The soup was served, I got the partridge in the oven and I heard Marie say, 'I'm not starting to make sauté potatoes at this time of night!' I could not believe my ears – this was akin to mutiny on board a man-o'-war! 'Marie,' I said sternly, 'you *will* prepare some sauté potatoes.' She drew herself up to her full height (which was more than my five feet six inches), folded her arms across her ample bosom and, with eyes flashing like steel, she replied in broad Yorkshire, 'If you want them lad, you must do them yourself as I'm going up to bed!' which she promptly proceeded to do. This was the first challenge to my newly found authority which I resolved by cooking the potatoes myself. I later learned, following that and similar skirmishes, that Marie privately christened me 'Little Tom Noddy'.

On another occasion, one weekend, I was on duty with Bridget who, for Sunday lunch, over-baked a fruit pie and camouflaged the slightly charred pastry by liberally sprinkling it with icing sugar. When I observed this leaving the pastry I upbraided her in no uncertain terms, and told her in the authoritarian tone that I had grown up with at the Ritz, 'You will not serve that while I am in charge. You must bake a fresh pie!' Without a word, she slapped me soundly round the face! As that was the first (and last) time I had had my face slapped by a female I crimsoned up to the roots of my hair, and was at a complete loss for words. Fortunately, it was a storm in a teacup that blew itself out within an hour. Bridget stomped back into the pastry and, within forty-five minutes, produced a delicious looking pie with golden brown, perfectly baked pastry.

These proved two salutary lessons in human relations – Bridget was twice my age and Marie three times, and reflecting later I realised it wasn't so much what I'd said but how I'd said it. However, our working relations improved after those incidents, so all parties learned from the scuffles.

Chef Abry worked in the larder doing all the cold preparation, and I cooked almost all the food: soups, fish, entrées, roasts and savouries – which was good, all round, versatile experience after the partie special-isation at the Ritz. All food was of the finest quality – fresh salmon was sent by the Tay Salmon Company from Scotland by overnight express and we used only free-range chickens from Surrey, plump tender birds of good weight, with full breasts and the faint blueish tinge to the skin which is a mark of quality. Fresh fruit and vegetables came in daily from Covent Garden (a stone's throw away). Meat, poultry and game came from Smithfield, and fish from Billingsgate.

Club members liked good, correctly cooked, well-served food with a varied selection of traditional British dishes and interesting inter-national favourites. A typical menu might feature a roast bird or joint daily, wing rib of beef, leg of pork, stuffed shoulder of lamb, saddle of mutton, chicken, goose or duck. Other favourites included jugged hare; braised ox tongue with madeira sauce; salmis of game; devilled kidneys; curried beef, lamb or chicken; fricassée of chicken or veal; hot veal and ham pie; boiled mutton with caper sauce; wild duck with orange sauce; plover with port wine sauce; partridge braised with cabbage, bacon, sausage, onion, carrot and herbs (delicious!); roast pheasant; grouse; woodcock and snipe. These last two long-necked, long-beaked birds were trussed with their own beaks after cleaning.

Most members had a sweet tooth, especially at lunch time, when we would offer a tempting range of traditional British puddings, the reper-toire for which is so vast that there was never any problem finding variety. There was a different milk pudding every day of the week, suet puddings (blackberry and apple, rhubarb and gooseberry), fruit tarts and pies (raspberry and redcurrant, with a feather-like pastry crust – a favourite), spotted dick, treacle sponge, fruit fools and trifle.

In the evenings, whilst we served a few sweets, hot savouries on toast were popular: oysters or chicken livers wrapped in bacon, haddock and bacon (strips of finnan haddock the size of a forefinger cleaned of all bone and skin were wrapped in paper-thin rashers of streaky bacon, grilled and dusted with cayenne pepper), curried prawns or shrimps, soft roes and mushrooms, creamed haddock sprinkled with grated cheese, chopped ham in cream or curry sauce with a grilled mushroom on top, Scotch woodcock, devilled kidneys, sardines (skinned and boned) and the club specials – Welsh rarebit and beef marrow bone.

For the Welsh rarebit we grated or finely sliced Cheddar cheese and gently melted it in a little white sauce until smooth. An egg yolk was added and a good measure of ale, which was reduced in a separate pan to a teaspoonful. Two to three drops of Worcestershire sauce, a dash of English mustard and a snuff of cayenne pepper completed the seasoning. The mixture was then poured into the inner part of a small, rectangular double silver dish, the outer part of which contained a heated metal block. The ornate silver lid was put on the dish and sent to the dining-room where, in the adjoining pantry, fresh toast was made, buttered, crusts removed and served on a hot plate. The club member then proceeded to help himself to the rarebit. I wondered at first why Marie usually swiftly volunteered to prepare Welsh rarebits until I realised that of the bottle of ale drawn from the bar for every order, only a fraction went into the pan. The remainder was considered chef's perks.

For the beef marrow we used whole beef shin bones, sawn into halves and placed in a large covered pan with a little stock and steamed. One of these would be served wrapped in a white serviette on a silver dish and the member, using a special long-handled narrow spoon, would spoon the marrow onto a slice of fresh buttered toast, season it with salt and pepper, and consume it with relish.

Cheeses of the finest quality were purchased from Paxton and Whitfield of Jermyn Street (about 200 yards away), and we always were required to have a large Stilton in prime condition which, as the justly named 'King of Cheeses', had a trolley all to itself. Members served themselves with a special Stilton spoon (a practice frowned upon by some today), and once an inch of the cheese had been chiselled away a bottle of good port was gradually poured into the cheese (another practice also now frowned upon). Once the Stilton was within an inch of the bottom it was sent to the kitchen and replaced. When the old cheese arrived in the kitchen (which wasn't very often as a large Stilton contains a great mass of cheese) we would cut it into four and scrape away a considerable amount of very ripe, strongly port flavoured cheese which swiftly disappeared between the staff.

The club, in common with most establishments of its kind, practised a no tipping rule, but annually a staff Christmas list would be posted in the front hall on which members indicated a sum of money which was intended to be a Christmas gift and gratuity for the year. As a sizeable sum was collected, club policy was to pay one-quarter of this to the staff in their weekly pay packet before Christmas and the remaining three-quarters in the pay packet before the summer holidays, for which the club closed the whole month of August – a very sensible and beneficial arrangement.

As a result, when I saw the amount of money in my Christmas pay packet my eyes opened in glee and I quickly joined the celebration party being held at the bar counter along the passage from the kitchen. Here for the first (and last) time in my life I drank unwisely, finally leaving the club feeling slightly tiddly. But when I got out into the fresh air, I felt decidedly intoxicated! I wove my way from side-to-side up King Street and St James's Street and somehow managed to scramble onto a No. 19 bus – I had left my bicycle at the club after falling off it twice within the first few yards! I sat on top of the bus with my head spinning, and it seemed an eternity before the bus stop in the King's Road. The conductor helped me off with a cheery grin and a few words of unprintable advice. I staggered down Radnor Street, up the steps of 9 Tedworth Gardens, opened the front door with great difficulty, and promptly fell on my knees moaning, 'Mum!' As it happened my mother was out, so I crawled on all fours along the passage, up the stairs to our flat, opened the toilet door, put my head over the toilet – and was promptly sick. There I remained for some time until my mother came home. She speedily assessed the situation, cleaned me up and got me into bed, all without one word of complaint.

Next morning (my day off) I found myself to be the sorry possessor of a prize hangover, and decided to stay in bed. At eleven o'clock Letty called to collect me and reminded me that we had arranged to go out with friends for the day. I groaned at the thought but washed and dressed with difficulty, shuddering at the thought of breakfast. We emerged from the house to take a bus to Piccadilly Circus where we were meeting our friends. When they arrived and saw my plight they marched me into a nearby chemist's where I was given a draught of a mixture which, within twenty minutes or so, put me back into reasonable form again. This experience was a chastening lesson indeed.

As I now had every other weekend off, Letty and I started attending the Saturday night dances at Chelsea Town Hall and spent many a pleasant evening dancing to an eight-piece dance band. One week it was announced that a young blind pianist from Battersea would be making a guest appearance with the band shortly. This turned out to be George Shearing, who had recently started his professional career. The individual style and touch of genius was apparent even in those early days; he was a great man.

By now I was in my nineteenth year and considered that I looked far too young for my age. To combat this I grew (with difficulty) an apology of a moustache, and decided to buy a pipe. Not long after I had started work I had bought my first packet of cigarettes – ten for 6d – but found that they stuck to my lips making them sore and that they made me cough. Apart from thinking that they made me look more grown up, they gave me no pleasure at all and, worst of all, 6d was a lot out of my week's money – I gave them up.

I shopped around for the smallest pipe that I could find, bought half an ounce of Philips Sweet Cut, and started to experiment. After the usual teething troubles of packing the tobacco too tightly, then too loosely, using untold boxes of matches and dribbling like fury down the pipe so that every once in a while a filthy tasting blob of tobacco-laden spit would return up the pipe stem into the mouth, I managed to get a reasonable smoke going, and proudly displayed this by keeping the pipe in my mouth for longish periods. This was the summer of 1938, and one very hot afternoon I was at home reading (my parents had moved to No. 32 Smith Terrace), when looking up with a start, realised that I was late setting off back for work. Hastily filling my pipe I lit up and set off at a sharp pace for the bus stop. (Letty was coming up to meet me after work that evening, so I wasn't cycling.) I climbed aboard the top deck of a No. 19 bus, smoking continuously, and came down the steps at the double on arrival at Green Park still puffing away. I trotted along Piccadilly, down St James's Street and along King Street to the club, jumped down the stairs to the basement two at a time into the kitchen, to find a message from Marie (who was off that evening along with Chef Abry) asking me to see her in her room. Marie lived in a room in the staff quarters on the top floor to which one ascended by a circular stairway. Up and round to the fourth floor I trotted, smoking furiously, received the message, trotted down and round back to the kitchen still smoking, and changed into my kitchen clothes.

By this time the accumulated forces of heat, haste and tobacco began to take effect, my head started to spin, and I could feel nausea taking hold. It was now six o'clock, so I staggered into the kitchen to get ready for dinner which started at seven and spent an uncomfortable hour preparing food and teetering on the brink of being sick. At seven o'clock I could contain myself no longer, and was violently ill in one of the four sinks we had in the kitchen.

In an adjoining sink, swimming around in a large container covered by a wire mesh, were a dozen live rainbow trout which were on the menu that evening as blue trout (truite au bleu). We did not keep a live trout tank at the club but, when on the menu, they were delivered by the fishmonger during the afternoon. He tipped them into a container in the sink, turned the cold water tap on, covered them with an old sieve wire mesh, and put a weight on top to stop them jumping out. They would then be killed fresh to order, cleaned, passed through vinegar on both sides, gently cooked in a little white wine, carrot, onion and herbs in a covered container, and served with a melted butter sauce. When cooked immediately after being killed the skin of the trout assumes a pleasing, delicate pale-blue colour and the trout does not remain whole, but breaks in one or two places; it is therefore served slightly misshapen. These two distinctive features are the means by which a discerning customer can tell whether the trout was perfectly fresh and alive just prior to being cooked. Concerned at my plight, George went next door to Mr Harris, the chemist, to see if he could obtain a cure for my condition and came back with the sole advice, 'Make him drink pints of water.'

Time was passing and the whistle on our intercom blew indicating that the first members were in for dinner and had ordered. Needless to say, the first order was for a blue trout. I staggered to the trout sink, caught a plump fish in my hand, took one look at it, and simultaneously the trout flew out of my hand onto the freshly sawdusted floor. I returned to my sink in misery. Up piped George, 'Don't worry chef, I'll catch the little bleeder!' He grabbed at the trout with both hands, but because he wasn't used to handling live fish he grabbed too tightly, and the fish shot out like a bullet back onto the floor. Again he grabbed, and again, going round and round the kitchen table, muttering expletives against the non-cooperative trout's unwillingness to submit to the pot.

Meanwhile, I was following Mr Harris's advice, swallowing as much water as I could and promptly bringing it up again, but the wisdom of the advice was becoming evident as my stomach was slowly being cleansed. By this time the intercom whistle from the dining-room was blowing furiously, and impolite remarks were travelling down the tube concerning the non-arrival of the members' fish. All in all bedlam reigned for what, at the time, seemed an eternity but by now I was sufficiently recovered to take up my duties and restore order to the chaos, sending apologies to the dining-room for the delay and managing to complete a (thankfully) not too busy evening without further major incident.

By the time service was over I felt decidedly washed out and regretted the fact that Letty was coming up to meet me, but after washing and changing and emerging from the club into the fresh air, I began to perk up. So much so that we decided to walk across Green Park, on to Victoria, to Chelsea Barracks, where in the Guardsmen's Café a few doors along I demolished egg and chips, apple pie and custard, followed by a large cup of coffee, and felt on top of the world! The next time I smoked a pipe was four years later.

Those of us on the staff who were keen on sport used to pair off with the staff of another club, the Athenæum, and managed to play a semblance of an occasional game of cricket, either in Battersea or Regents Park, where pitches could be hired. Most of these games were played from three till five and one hour's play was allowed for each side. This was not completely satisfactory by any means, but with such a severe ration of time it encouraged most players to 'have a dip' and some quite remarkable scores were set up from time to time. I remember on one occasion we were batting last and I was due back at work fairly promptly as we had a special party on that evening, which meant I should have left the park at four-thirty or four-forty-five the very latest. Batting number five, I strode to the wicket at four-twenty-five with my mind made up to have a quick dip at every ball, get out, and hurry off back to the club. Alas! I swung my bat ferociously at every ball irrespective of speed, direction or height, and by a large measure of luck plus a small modicum of skill, made contact with almost every ball and notched up fifty runs in twenty-five minutes before being caught off a skyer on the boundary.

I came charging off the field to the gratifying sound of appreciative applause from both teams and the spectators (two or three old-age pensioners) feeling like a cross between Don Bradman and Len Hutton, and hurried euphorically back to the club. Here I was promptly brought back to earth by being soundly told off for being late.

Football was easier. Here, again, we combined with the Athenæum to form a team and played in the Catering Trade's Football League and Cup competitions. Most matches were played in Hyde Park where we also used to go for a kick around during many afternoons. One never to be forgotten year we reached the Cup Final, and as the chairman of the Catering Trade's Football Association was Mr Bracewell-Smith, who was a director of the Ritz and Park Lane hotels and also chairman of Arsenal Football Club, he arranged for the final to be played at Highbury which, in those days, had a ground capacity of over 60 000.

It made a strange sight to see our teams battling it out before a crowd of 100, all seated in and around the directors' box. We made up for our lack of numbers by the volume of noisy support we produced and finally emerged happy, hoarse and gallant losers to a superior team by three goals to one.

Summer of 1939 came and passed. Letty and I had arranged a fortnight's holiday with two friends outside Climping. The girls shared a bedroom in a bungalow, and Ray and I slept in a substantial hut at the bottom of the garden where we also cooked and ate our meals. We fed simply, did not smoke or drink, and spent the days on the beach and evenings walking and playing games in the hut. We didn't buy a newspaper or listen to the radio the whole time we were away, and at the end of the holiday when we arrived back in London, were amazed to see hoards of young children clutching gas masks, parcels and cases, milling around and embarking on trains out of London. Evacuation had begun, and I was back at work the following morning, a Sunday in September, when Marie came downstairs with her portable radio listening to a special news bulletin which included that momentous announcement, 'His Majesty's Government has declared war on Germany'. Shortly afterwards the sirens blasted out their screeching whine, the noise that was so frequently to alert and alarm Londoners and the population of many other towns and cities for a considerable time to come. The mood amongst the staff was quiet and sombre as we discussed possibilities for the future – all of us were completely wrong, needless to say.

The following week I went to the local recruiting office and volunteered for the Army, but when they took my particulars and noted my age I was told to go back to work and await my call up, which would shortly be implemented. In fact, the call-up date was 15 February 1940, and in-between times we all carried on with our jobs and daily lives in a fairly normal way.

A strict black-out was imposed throughout the country and, although difficult at first, it was surprising how quickly we adjusted and got about in the pitch black of night without too many scrapes. Only one night in November gave me a problem, when a real pea-souper fog enveloped the city. I left the club at nine o'clock on my bike. The headlamp was hooded, leaving the merest chink of light and, of course, all street lamps were turned off; you could hardly see your hand in front of your face. Progressing at a snail's pace I navigated carefully down St James's Street, turned right between St James's Palace and Marlborough House down to the Mall, and gingerly turned right. Cycling almost blindly along the wide expanse of the Mall was nerve-racking, but I had managed to locate the near-side kerb and used that as my guide after the last right turn. The night was eerily still, no lights, no sounds of traffic, no sounds of pedestrians, and although progress was painfully slow I felt increasingly confident – too much so. My front wheel hit the kerb, almost pitching me over the handlebars and, to my horror, I realised that it was the off-side kerb I had hit! Anyone who has walked across the width of the Mall will realise the distance I had travelled off course, and when I considered the oncoming traffic I might have collided with, I hastily dismounted and walked the remainder of the way home.

So, the autumn of 1939 passed. As we entered into winter, I wondered whether I would be at home for Christmas. I was, but in common with the majority of other families, we spent a quiet, thoughtful Christmas and New Year, hoping for a speedy end to the war.

CHAPTER 4

1940–1946

Once a Fusilier, always a Fusilier

In January 1940, a letter from the War Office arrived informing me that I should report to Hounslow barracks on 15 February to join the Royal Fusiliers. Continuing at work after that was rather an anti-climax, but in order to earn as much money as possible, I carried on working until the last moment before joining the ranks at two shillings a day.

The day I enlisted, my mother and Letty were tearful. I had mixed feelings of anticipation and excitement but after saying goodbye, as though for the duration of the war, I was back home again before six o'clock that evening, looking as uncomfortable as most new recruits in an ill-fitting uniform complete with civilian gas mask in a cardboard box slung over my shoulder. Letty, who was a most competent needle-woman, took my khaki blouse in hand and performed wonders on it by altering it to fit me, while my mother cooked a nice meal. So passed a pleasant evening.

Nobby Clark, an ex-regular soldier who had served with the Royal Fusiliers in India in peacetime, was sergeant of our thirty-strong platoon. He 'marched' us around the barracks to collect our kit from the Quartermaster stores, then on to the barrack room where we were allotted double bunk beds and dumped our kit, then back to the armoury to collect rifles, which were Lee-Enfields as used in World War I. Nobby took each rifle from the QM storeman and threw one to each of us in turn. As soon as I grabbed mine I automatically went through the motions of the arms drill learnt at school. When we fell in outside, Nobby gave us our first lesson in arms drill, and I was put at right marker. He then informed us that the Royal Fusiliers were known as the 'Baby Guards of India' because of the smartness of their drill and turn-out, and that was what we were going to be like by the time he had finished with us! 'Once a Fusilier, always a Fusilier,' he said with pride. The rest of the morning was spent folding up kit and bed blankets (three), filling palliasses and pillow cases with straw, and receiving general instructions.

At twelve o'clock we heard the bugle call, 'Come to the cookhouse door boys, come to the cookhouse door,' and we joined the long line for the first Army meal which consisted of a fatty, gristly meat stew; boiled potatoes full of eyes; cabbage which was a similiar colour to our battle dress and which looked as though it had been cooked immediately after breakfast (which, in fact, it probably had been, because the barracks and the cookhouse were very over-crowded); and prunes in a thick, lumpy, watery custard. I managed to get a look inside the cookhouse, shuddered, and was determined to keep quiet about my training as I didn't fancy the idea of working in that sort of environment. Little did I know that my 'toffee-nosed' West End attitude to the kitchen would soon be knocked out of me!

The afternoon was spent on marching and arms drill. The bugle blew for supper at five o'clock when training finished for the day, and we could leave the barracks (properly dressed in uniform) to be back before 23.59. Any latecomers would be 'put on a charge'. Those who lived within a reasonable distance hastily made tracks for Hounslow West Underground station and home, but we were all back well before mid-night and into our bunks.

When reveille sounded at 6 a.m. it seemed like the middle of the night, as my normal rising time was two hours later. Mine was a bottom bunk, and my upper bunk mate was Ginger who lived too far away to be able to get home at weekends, and most evenings played a successful Romeo role in and around Hounslow. I soon became accustomed to the sight most mornings of a thick wrinkled rubber sheath hanging out to dry from the underside of the top bunk. This was usually followed by a dawn chorus of ribald remarks from the rest of the platoon concerning Gin-ger's adventures and conquests.

Primary infantry training at the barracks lasted six weeks. Nobby, in typical Army drill sergeant fashion, marched us up and down to hoarse bellows of, 'Eff, oight, eff, oight, eff, oight, eff, smarten up you shower, shoulders back, keep that rifle straight, it's a weapon not a — umbrella! Eff, oight, eff, oight, ALT! Stand still! You're swaying like a load of — pansies! Roight turn! Properly at attention now! Fumbs in line with

the seams of your trousis! Stand-aaaat eese! Pick your — feet up and
stamp them down, don't worry they won't drop out they're in a — bag!'
The parade ground was full of platoons all undergoing the same drill,
and the noise and bedlam reminded me of my first day in the kitchen.

Nobby knocked us into good shape and became proud of his platoon
by the sixth and last week when we were given pride of place in the
commanding officers' marching-out parade. We soon found he had a
warm and generous nature under his military veneer, and were genu-
inely sorry to say goodbye as we moved off for the next phase of training.
During this time I was asked if I would sign a paper signifying that I
understood that, if captured by the Italians (who at that time were allies
of the Germans), I was liable to be shot. I signed without giving the
matter a great deal of thought, and although I could never be sure, I
surmised that that was the reason I never received an overseas posting
whilst hostilities continued, although shortly after VE day I received my
first overseas posting. The unit then moved a short distance to Hounslow
Heath and was billeted in accommodation condemned in the First
World War, whilst undergoing six weeks' field training.

During this period we were taken to Pirbright Guards depot for firing
practice on the ranges with rifle and bren-gun. After the first day,
cleaned up and on our way to the NAAFI, chatting away, six of us
innocently took the obvious short route across the barrack square
whereupon we were blasted by a guard sergeant major who bellowed
out the information that anyone found on the square outside of parade
hours would be 'put on a charge' without ceremony. Just to make the
point he doubled marched us twice around the square in case we forgot!

When firing practice was completed all companies were ordered to
march in battle order back to Hounslow, a distance of approximately
twenty miles. This news brought a mixture of response, chiefly groans
of anguish, but grumbling in time-honoured 'Tommy' fashion we prepared ourselves as ordered. I had been given the tip by an old soldier to
anoint my feet with Vaseline and lemon juice, start with a clean pair of
socks, and change socks from one foot to the other at every break (we
marched fifty-five minutes and rested five in each hour). I followed the
advice and completed the march with feet aching but without a sign of a
blister, which was more than could be said for a number of the platoon
who had developed a sizeable collection amongst them. After about
fifteen miles, some of the lads, finding that we were marching down a
main road along which buses were running towards the camp, had
hopped on, hoping they would be unobserved. They hadn't reckoned
with our new Platoon Sergeant Dusty Miller's eagle eye, however, and to
add to the discomfort of their blistered feet they found themselves 'on a
fizzer'. When they appeared on company commander's orders the following morning they were each given seven days confined to barracks,

plus 'jankers' (fatigue duties to be carried out each day, usually consisting of the dirty jobs around the camp). When they returned to the hut with the news it received the normal allocation of sympathy – hoots of laughter and ribald remarks. Ginger's night sorties were unaffected as he had given his feet the same treatment as mine. No fool was our Ginger!

During our time on the heath there was an occasional alert that enemy paratroopers might be dropped and we were confined to camp with guards posted at the entrance. We were allowed out one evening for four hours; Letty came over and we went to the cinema to see Judy Garland in *The Wizard of Oz*.

To get back into camp you were halted at the gates by a sentry and required to give the password before being allowed in. Inevitably, a group of youngsters would mill around outside the gate. Their sharp ears soon picked up the password so that when the next incoming soldier was ordered by the sentry to give it, he did so in concerted chorus with the audience!

Included in our issue of clothing were long-sleeved, high-necked woollen vests and long johns, but these had been greeted with scorn and derision and we preferred to wear civilian singlets and short pants. That was until we had spent hours crawling all over Hounslow Heath on field training wearing denim uniform. It was now mid-winter 1940, particularly cold, and it only took one bad day with the temperature well below zero and all of us, to the man, took the woollies out of our kitbags – and were we glad of them!

Towards the end of field training, six of us were detailed off for a special course on the 3-inch mortar. We had a 15-hundredweight truck, a driver and a training sergeant, 'Chalky' White, who informed us that there wasn't a 3-inch mortar bomb available so that we would learn 'going through the motions'.

The mortar consisted of three parts, all heavy and clumsy to lift: a base plate, bipod and the barrel, one man being allocated to each piece. The driver would take us to a position selected by Chalky who then gave the order to assemble the mortar. Number 1 on the base plate placed it in position, number 2 stood the bipod up, and number 3 slotted the barrel into its groove in the base plate and secured it to the bipod. We then knelt in position awaiting the order to fire, and as firing was carried out (by going through the motions of dropping imaginary bombs into the barrel) which, with live bombs, would cause a kickback pushing the base plate into the ground, Chalky would stamp on the base plate to give a similar effect.

When firing ceased the order was given to dismantle and the three pieces, in reverse order, were quickly manhandled onto the truck while we scrambled aboard. Chalky emphasised the need for speed by informing us that at the end of the course we would be given ten seconds from the order to dismantle, and the truck would set off whether we were on board or not. As he intended selecting a site some distance from the camp, anyone not on board would walk back to camp carrying his piece of equipment.

We practised continuously in order to build up speed and efficiency, and on each occasion were allocated a different piece of equipment. As the base plate was always the first piece down and the last up, we wondered who would be allocated number 1 on the last day. As it turned out, Ceser drew the short straw. It had rained ceaselessly the previous night and Chalky picked a particularly muddy spot for us to assemble. When I put the base plate down in a muddy patch (his choice not mine) he jumped his thirteen-stone weight on it several times before numbers 2 and 3 added the bipod and barrel.

Mock firing continued then, with a stop-watch in his hand, Chalky gave the order to dismantle the mortar. Numbers 3 and 2 moved at speed and scrambled safely on to the truck with their equipment, but I lost time because of difficulty in dislodging the base plate from the mud. I finally managed to heave it on board as Chalky gave the order to drive off. In desperation I stretched out my arms towards the truck, my two mates, numbers 3 and 2, grabbed an arm each and I was dragged along behind the now swiftly moving truck, finally piling on board with some difficulty. Chalky gave us a grin, said, 'Well done lads,' and we drove back to camp.

So we all qualified as mortar men, and awaited instructions for our first posting to a unit. Postings were pinned up on a notice board outside the company office and the word spread like wildfire when they appeared. '6467558 fusilier V. Ceserani promoted to war/substantive rank of lance/corporal – posted to the mortar platoon of the 2nd Battalion Royal Fusiliers in Germany.' We were pleased to read that the mortar team were going together, and we went off home on forty-eight hours' leave.

On returning to camp I went straight to the notice board to read 'Fusilier V. Ceserani – promotion and posting to 2nd Battalion Fusiliers cancelled. New posting – officers' mess cook, 19th Battalion, Northwich, Cheshire'! My initial reaction was one of disappointment but when, several months later, the news filtered through that the 2nd Battalion had suffered severe casualties in action and that the mortar platoon had been almost completely wiped out, I was sad at the loss of good friends, and inevitably felt, 'There, but for the grace of God, go I.'

In company with about one hundred men from the barracks we drove to a golf course not far from Northwich where we prepared to receive 40 officers and 900 men direct from 'civvy street' who were to be trained as the 19th Battalion. Bell-tents for sleeping and marquees for messing were soon erected. Bluff ranges (long ranges with a channel for fuel down the centre which heated rows of ovens on each side and boiling plates above) were provided, along with long lines of Soyer stoves, which were invented by the famous chef Alexis Soyer – one time of the Reform Club, London – for use during the Crimean War. These latter consisted simply of a large boiling pan set into a stove fired by solid fuel from below, with an L-shaped chimney jutting out from the back.

I was taken by the Quartermaster Sergeant to a corner of the camp, shown a thicket and told, 'This is your cookhouse.' I couldn't believe my ears. Where was the stove? What if it rained? What was I expected to produce? 'You will have forty officers in mess in forty-eight hours' time. They will expect breakfast, morning coffee, lunch, afternoon tea and three-course dinner, seven days a week. Build your own stove and shelter – You *might* get permanent ones built eventually. Daily rations will be issued at three o'clock.' With that, the Quartermaster Sergeant marched smartly away. I set about rescuing my heart from where it had sunk in my boots, and set off on a scrounging foray. Sixty old bricks placed in two rows with metal plates and bars set across the top was my first effort at building a makeshift oven under which a fire could be lit and for which there was plenty of wood around. Three Soyer stoves plus dixies, trays, mixing spoons, knives and a wooden table completed the officers' mess inventory of equipment. I drew the first day's rations for the handful of officers and batmen who were setting up the mess, and produced a well-received meal. So began the start of a six-year stint of a phase of cooking which was to be a complete contrast to my previous comparatively sheltered and pampered life at the Ritz and Orleans Club. It was hard going at first, with so much to learn; resourcefulness was a very important quality to possess. I shall never forget cooking the first morning's breakfast of sausages. Having got a good fire going, and a tray of fat in which the sausages were to be cooked, the rain came down. I managed to make a ledge of two sheets of corrugated iron to protect the fire, and then sat on an up-turned dixie wearing a gas cape and steel helmet, prodding away at the bangers with a fork. On that occasion 'bangers' was the appropriate name, for every now and then a drop of water got into the hot fat causing a minor explosion and raining the surrounding area with hot beef dripping. In retrospect, however, there is no doubt that the sharp contrast in method of so much that I was required to do here, in comparison with the way I had worked in London, helped to broaden my mind and experience, and left me a much more rounded and adaptable cook and person.

The ration scale in 1940 for the forces was generous provided that care and economy was employed. The meat ration was ample, and by trimming off and rendering down beef fat, there was always a plentiful supply of good beef dripping available. A dixie half full of this set on a

Primus stove that was 'borrowed' made an excellent deep-fat fryer, and gave the opportunity to add variations to the menu.

Fried potatoes in different shapes and sizes were always popular, as were potato fritters (quarter-inch slices of raw potatoes passed through batter and deep-fried), and when bread and jam fritters and sultana fritters were introduced they were greeted with much praise.

Bread and jam fritters consisted of a sandwich of two slices of bread, butter and jam from which the crusts were removed (to be kept for bread pudding), cut in halves, passed through a light batter and deep-fried until a crisp golden brown. On removal from the fat they were drained and tossed on both sides in a mixture of caster sugar and cinnamon and served hot.

Sultana fritters consisted of a thickish batter to which was added a generous quantity of sultanas (or raisins) which had been soaked the previous evening in a measure of brandy. Spoonfuls of the batter were fried in hot fat, drained, generously coated with sugar to which a little mixed spice was added, and then served hot with warm golden syrup or treacle. Also produced from the deep-fryer, when issued on rations, were fritters of corned beef, spam, ham, cooked meat, luncheon-meat, sausage and apple and, of course, fish and chips.

Officers were issued with the same rations as the men, but all officers paid a mess fee which was controlled by the president of mess committee (the PMC). The mess committee would decide on the allocation of the money to various sources in order to improve the standard of messing, and an amount was voted for the purchase of extra commodities to boost and add variety to the daily rations. The PMC acted as my daily contact with regard to this money, and any particular likes or dislikes of the members. This was similar to the London club system when daily contact was made between the club secretary and head chef for the same purpose.

Once I had readjusted and got into my stride, I found this new challenge interesting and enjoyable. As a result, a good varied standard of food was produced which was appreciated and gained me a measure of respect among both the officers and their batmen.

A number of officers' batmen would be on daily duty in the mess for laying up, serving at table, serving drinks, washing up and cleaning the mess tents and area. They would feed in the mess when on duty and, because I looked after them, they reciprocated by doing any odd jobs that helped, such as peeling vegetables and washing pots and pans. Thus I got rid of time-consuming chores and was able to spend more time cooking.

I coped with the open brick fire, Primus stove and Soyer stoves for over three months and had erected a crude but stable shelter using several sheets of corrugated iron and a number of thick wooden poles. I had learnt that the way to handle Soyer stoves to get the best results was by lifting the boilers out daily, thoroughly removing all accumulated soot from the stove, boiler and chimney, and to always face the fire box towards the prevailing wind when lighting. In this way five gallons of water could be brought to the boil from cold in twenty minutes. Alexis Soyer did the Army a great service when he conceived such a simple but effective stove. Fresh soup was made for dinner most nights using vegetable water from any potatoes or vegetables boiled during the day as stock. Meat was issued daily and would be either beef, lamb, pork, offal, bacon or sausages. Fresh vegetables were also issued daily. A reasonable variety of sweets could be provided from rations, added to which were commodities purchased with the mess allowance. A favourite was steamed suet or sponge pudding, for which I found empty, large rectangular spam tins opened at one end made useful moulds. The pudding could be varied with the addition of currants, sultanas, raisins and mixed spices, and cooked by steaming in a Soyer stove. Two nights a week I prepared a mainly cold buffet meal which the batmen could serve, and this gave me a break.

So the summer of 1940 came and passed, and in September a semi-permanent cookhouse was built and a coal-fired solid range with two ovens was installed, which made life considerably easier. I celebrated my 21st birthday laying on the bed after dinner had been served, with the noise of an air raid a few miles away, reading Letty's birthday letter by the light of a shaded hurricane lamp. For almost the whole of my service Letty wrote daily, and this became legend in my unit as no one else that I ever heard of was blessed with such a regular and unfailing correspondent.

In November I attended a six-week cook's course at the Army School of Cookery, Aldershot, in order to qualify as a Cook Class III, Group B Tradesman, which would give me a few pence a day extra pay. I had to travel with all my kit as the battalion was due to be posted shortly, and so bade farewell to my first Army kitchen.

On the first day of the course we met our cook sergeant instructor (an old sweat), who informed the class in no uncertain terms, 'I'm — fed up with — young squaddies with — foreign names who have all — worked at either the — Savoy, the — Dorchester or the — Ritz! Nah then, call out yer — names and where you have — worked!'

In the group were two others with similar pedigrees as myself, and their announcements were greeted with heavy sarcasm. As it happened, I was the last one to speak and no sooner had I given my name, than the reply came, 'Ces what?' After dutifully repeating the name, he guffawed, and promptly christened me 'Sidi Barrani, ho, ho, ho!' The mention of the Ritz brought forth the expected expletives, but once he had got that out of his system, he settled down and gave us a useful informative course.

The irony for me was that, having learnt how to cook in the field and to build a variety of stoves and ovens, I never had occasion to put that knowledge into practice. However, the course was interesting, I learnt many new things, qualified at the end by passing a trade test, and shortly afterwards was transferred to the newly formed Army Catering Corps as a private – so much for Nobby Clark's, 'Once a Fusilier, always a Fusilier'!

After the course I went home on forty-eight hours' leave with full kit, including small pack, large pack, steel helmet, rifle, gas mask and kitbag, to find on arrival in London a heavy air raid in progress. On reaching South Kensington station I found the platforms and stairs were crowded with local residents lying on makeshift beds, preparing to stay until dawn (this was a nightly occurrence during the blitz). After struggling through the crowds to the lift I came upon a notice which said, 'Lifts not working, use stairs', so up the spiral stairway I clambered to be greeted by an air-raid warden who said, 'I should stay under shelter, if I was you, son.' It was only ten minutes' walk to Letty's home where Letty's mother and my parents were in an air-raid shelter, so I decided to chance it, which gave me my first experience of London under air attack. It was an unforgettable experience, and when one considers that Londoners and the population of many of our towns and cities had this to contend with night after night, for long periods of time, it is a reflection on the guts, determination and resilience of the British people of that era. It is a pity that severe hardship and adversity had to be the catalyst for bringing out the best in so many people, and a spirit of patriotism and togetherness, so often missing in long periods of peace. It makes me sad to see and hear how 'love of country' is ridiculed by a large number of the younger generation who, I sometimes think, are spoilt by 'having it too good'.

Following the forty-eight hours' leave, I had orders to report back for attachment as officers' mess cook to Battalion headquarters at Shorwell, Isle of Wight, where HQ officers' mess was billeted in the largest house in the village.

The 19th Battalion, along with two other battalions of infantry and one battalion of light infantry, were engaged on coastal defence and we remained on the island for almost the whole of 1941, moving around every few months to Ryde, Sandown and Rookley in turn.

The NCOs and men of HQ company were billeted in bell-tents at Shorwell amidst a field of wild garlic, which wasn't noticed when the tents were pitched, but in the spring when the bulbs started shooting everyone wondered where the strange smell was coming from!

One night whilst billeted at Rookley, a number of German bombers flying homewards after a bombing raid dropped a few remaining incendiaries which fell on and around the field where HQ company's bell-tents were sited. Fortunately there were no casualties, but it made a strange sight to see the men hopping out of bed, some with underpants on, some with nothing on, frantically dashing buckets of water on the numerous fires. Prompt action extinguished all the fires, but by now everyone was fully awake. One bucket of water thrown by a playful soldier over another, who was starkers, was sufficient to set everyone off into a mad frenzy of water sports.

Certainly, Army life was not all hard work; all the beaches around the island were heavily protected by barbed wire, but at Sandown we were allowed to clear a small section during the afternoons in order to be able to swim in the sea. The battalion also had a keen cricket team that summer, and was fortunate in being able to arrange matches which were sometimes played on the Hampshire county ground at Newport, and on Ventnor Cricket Club's ground, which was surely one of the most attractive in the country. I kept wicket and, mainly through the team comradeship, made a good friend of one of our opening bats. Lou was an ex-regular who had spent seven years in India where, being a gifted sportsman, he had represented the battalion at cricket, hockey and soccer. Listening to him recounting his experiences the period of his regular service sounded idyllic!

We often wondered why Lou never attended weekly parade to draw his pay. The only time he drew money was before going on leave, when he would draw three months' pay in one lump sum. It emerged that Lou ran a weekly low-key lottery, for which he sold forty tickets costing sixpence each (2½p). The one prize was a ten-shilling note (50p) which left him with 100 per cent profit on his investment.

When the battalion left the island towards the end of 1942 it went under canvas at Denmead near Portsmouth, and there being no establishment for promotion in the officers' mess, I requested transfer to the men's mess. Here I joined a team of cooks under a regular peacetime cook sergeant with a thousand men to cook for in one mess. Early morning duty started at 3.30 a.m. in order to get all the fires cleaned and lit, and my first morning job was to make twelve dixies of porridge, or 'burgoo', as it was called. The twelve dixies were three-quarters filled with water and placed on top of a bluff range to boil. Porridge oats were stirred into the water which was then brought back to the boil, covered and left on the side of the stove. Just before breakfast-time a pinch of salt, sugar and tinned evaporated milk were added. I added two tins of milk to each dixie, sweetened it to my own taste (there were no Scots in the battalion) and was gratified to see it all consumed.

When cook sergeant came on duty he had his breakfast, went into the stores and, with a loud bellow like that of an elephant in pain, called my name.

'Where's all the — milk gone?'

'I put it in the burgoo sarge.'

'How much did you put in for — sake?'

'Two tins in each dixie sarge.'

'You stupid —, we only put in half a tin!'

'Sorry sarge,' I said, and off I went.

In due course I realised why one of our swill bins was always kept spotlessly clean. Each time the local pig farmer called to collect the swill, in the clean bin would be a case of milk, corned beef or some other item from the rations. The sergeant then got his pay-off that evening in the local pub!

I was somewhat relieved when, shortly afterwards, a posting came through for me to go back to Aldershot on a corporal cook's course. Here, to my surprise and pleasure, I met Bill Sandys who was now a sergeant instructor at the Army school. We spent two convivial evenings over the dinner table in his quarters discussing 'the old days at the Ritz', and I met his charming wife. Bill did very well in the Army, signing on after the war, gaining a commission and becoming a well-liked and respected member of the Army Catering Corps.

After successfully completing the course, I returned to the 19th Battalion only to find that overnight they, as had many other infantry battalions, had become Royal Artillery anti-tank regiments. All the fusiliers became gunners, and corporals became bombardiers. We were now '243 Anti-tank Regiment RA' and intensive retraining began. When the regiment was split into companies, each company moved to a different location and I was attached to HQ company men's mess as corporal in charge, with two cooks to assist.

Towards the end of February 1942 the regiment moved to Southampton where, shortly afterwards, we were put on forty-eight hours' standby for overseas posting.

Letty and I had become engaged some months previously and had now decided that we wished to wed. Along with two other members of the regiment we were granted a special seven-day leave in order to marry. We came home with a full kit, including rifles, prepared for a recall to the unit at short notice.

I had been brought up as a Roman Catholic, but had not practised my religion since starting work. Letty was a member of the Church of England, so we arranged for the wedding to be held at Chelsea Registry Office on Monday 16 March 1942.

Churcher of Radnor Street was booked as the photographer, but he was called up two days before the wedding. The reception was arranged in The Commercial (now The Chelsea Potter) on the corner of Radnor Walk and the King's Road. The food allowance for the reception on the wartime ration scale was two shillings and sixpence per head (now 12½p), the spirit allowance was one bottle of whisky and gin and the beer whatever the pub could manage. The one-tier wedding cake made by a local baker contained no dried fruit, a minimum amount of sugar and fat, and a little dried egg. There being no icing sugar, cardboard shapes were fashioned which fitted over the 'cake' and a formal decoration was secured in the centre.

Wedding reception bill, 1942

But although this was wartime, it was a family occasion and a good time was had by all. Letty and I spent our first night in the back room of my parents' house, 32 Smith Terrace, to which we retired at midnight, only to be interrupted by knocks on the door by the still celebrating wedding guests until the early hours of the morning. They made continual enquiries about our health, and asked whether we wished to purchase various useful items for the home, such as a second-hand battleship or a lawnmower.

During the next few days, we visited the cinema and took in two West End shows. Like all service men, I had to carry rifle and gas mask at all times, and as there were a number of troops on leave, the clatter made by the collection of rifles in cinemas and theatres was a noticeable feature of this period of the war. I had apologised for not having a honeymoon and promised, 'Never mind, we'll go to Paris for our twenty-fifth anniversary.'

I returned to Southampton and Letty followed the next weekend to stay with the Kirk family nearby, about ten minutes' walk from our billet. When she arrived Peter Weddell, the CO's batman and a good friend, told me, 'There's nothing doing this evening, Vic, go and spend the night with Letty.' I was somewhat dubious, but he reassured me, saying, 'I'll come round for you if we get the signal to move off.'

Mr and Mrs Kirk were splendid and laid on almost a second wedding reception for us. Around midnight after a most convivial evening we went up to bed. It was sometime afterwards we discovered that an assortment of empty tins and cans had been loosely tied to the underside of the bed springs and a large portion of liver salts sprinkled into the chamber pot!

Around 2 a.m. I stirred out of a heavy sleep to the sound of pebbles being thrown at the window. Leaping out of bed in the altogether, I opened the window and popped my head out to find Peter down below dressed in full battle order. 'Vic!' We're off! Come on, hurry!' he explained in a loud whisper, and with that turned and set off at a sharp trot back to the billet.

In frantic haste I three-quarter dressed, and set off smartly back to the house in which I was lodged, completing my dressing with difficulty as I ran. On turning the corner into the long road in which the regiment was billeted in houses on either side, my heart sank. There was not a lorry, truck or gun to be seen. Entering our house, which was deserted, I began to feel a distinct chill in the stomach and wondered what on earth I should do!

After a period of around thirty minutes (which seemed more like three hours), the sound of heavy transport came nearer and nearer. Peeping out of the window I saw, to my great relief, the transport returning, and then the troops came stomping back to the house. By this time I had locked myself in a toilet, and I could hear a great deal of cursing and swearing going on outside – a senior officer had decided on a training exercise, had turned the regiment out and taken them to the point of embarkation before breaking the news. After five minutes or so I left the toilet and went back to my room to discover that I had not been missed other than by my room-mates who had covered up for me.

The regiment did not receive an overseas posting whilst I was attached, but continued training and moved, from time to time, around

England. We spent time at Southend, Clacton and then at Bury St Edmunds during sugar-beet picking time, for which large numbers of troops were employed.

Along with three others I was billeted over a pub in the centre of town. One of our number was an earthy old sweat, 'Smudger', who had a vast capacity for beer. As the American forces were now in England, with considerable numbers based in East Anglia, the pub was frequented nightly by groups of US troops. They were amiable characters on the whole, who prevailed upon us to show them how to play darts, shove halfpenny and skittles, in return for which they insisted on paying for the beer.

Smudger was in his element, and would stagger up to bed most nights well 'tanked-up'. Occasionally, in the early hours he would be aroused by a needy call of nature, whereupon he would lean out of bed (we slept on the floor), pick up a boot, relieve himself in it and promptly go back to sleep. All our remonstrances and threats to make him stop this practice fell upon deaf ears. 'It's good for the leather – keeps it soft, he would reply amiably. One morning, however, the landlady of the pub called me into the bar and pointed to a damp patch on the ceiling saying, 'What is that?' 'Oh, that was Smudger. He spilt a mug of tea!' She glared at me in obvious disbelief but, looking on the bright side, I thought that this would put a stop to Smudger's nightly caper. It did have partly the desired effect, although he still would not leave the room. Instead, he lifted the lower window at the back of the pub and, whistling softly, he would spray the outhouse roof.

Some time afterwards the regiment was re-formed and I received a posting to a Royal Army Medical Corps Unit where for a while I worked under a most genial cook sergeant, Billy Holmes. Billy, a delightful Friar Tuck-ish character, came from Derbyshire. He spoke with a gentle, soft accent and possessed a fine singing voice. Frequently during the day, when all was going well, his melodious tones could be heard sounding out 'Jerusalem' or one of his many other favourites.

The unit had short spells at Yarm, Yorkshire, then on to Ambleside in the Lake District where we stayed only seven days (it rained the whole time), before proceeding to join a larger unit at Kimnel Camp in North Wales. The CO here was a rugby fanatic and the unit had one of the most successful teams in the north of Britain. It was later revealed that the CO had intervened personally in a number of postings over the previous two years in order to keep the squad intact. However, from records at the War Office it was eventually discovered what was going on and in one large posting, virtually the whole of the rugby squad moved out, leaving the colonel a chastened man.

The unit remained in North Wales until early summer so we were able to swim occasionally off the magnificent beaches which were usually deserted. Because they were deserted, after a while we dispensed with swimming trunks and enjoyed bathing as nature intended. This practice was brought to a speedy halt one day when a group of nurses came trooping down to the beach in swimsuits just as we were preparing to leave the water. Looking at each other in consternation we decided to make a run for it, and in one straggling file, sprinted up the beach to the sand-dunes using our hands as modesty shields with our cheeks crimson. From the peals of laughter that went up from the nurses they thoroughly enjoyed the impromptu spectacle.

It was around this time that a zealous duty officer decided that HQ admin staff were getting out of condition and needed some exercise. As a result, we were ordered to negotiate the local assault course at the double, dressed in battle order. Since it was in North Wales, the course was fairly demanding, but at least it was a pleasantly warm midsummer afternoon as we set off with the duty officer trotting alongside to keep his eye on us.

Most of us were in reasonably fit condition and were quite enjoying the challenge. At the three-quarter stage I found myself in the lead as we approached a fairly wide pond covered in green slime, over which was slung a rope. If I had been wiser, I would have laid low for a few seconds to gain my second wind. Instead, I galloped straight to the rope and started to monkey climb along it. Half-way across I ran out of puff. My legs dropped off the rope, my grip slowly loosened, and I sank down into, and under, the evil-smelling pond.

I emerged slowly, crawled to the bank, completed the course and set off back to camp, feeling damp and miserable, and smelling abominably. It was now almost tea-time, and the troops were lining up outside the mess-hall which we had to pass on our way back to the billets. Needless to say, our condition (and mine in particular) made an amusing diversion.

My next posting was to No. 36 Casualty Clearing Station, RAMC, who were stationed on Swindon Town football ground. Nissen huts had been erected around the pitch which was made smaller at one end only, by the installation of a hut, so we had virtually a full-size league football field at our disposal in leisure time. The cookhouse had been fitted at the back of the grandstand and, as the invasion of Europe was not far off, the unit were preparing to receive casualties. Transport aircraft towing troop-laden gliders were based in large numbers in the surrounding areas, and were busily occupied on training flights for many hours of the day.

We all possessed tremendous feelings of excitement and expectation on 6 June 1944, the fateful day of the invasion. We awaited each news bulletin eagerly in order to follow the progress of events, with sadness and grief at news of casualties and excitement at proclamations of successes. After over four years of war, which often seemed to be never-ending, hope began to form in people's minds that the end might be in sight.

There was, however, a long, gruelling period of eleven months ahead, with many set-backs. The civilian population, having been terrorised for so long by German bombs and then VI flying bombs, were now faced with the much greater terror of the V2 rockets. Many bombs were still to be rained on our cities in the Germans' last fling in desperation before that long awaited day, 8 May 1945, when the Germans finally surrendered. Victory in Europe was proclaimed and duly celebrated.

By this time, my unit was stationed in huts in the middle of a cherry orchard at Barming, Kent. A grand party was organised, and Letty came down to join in the festivities and stayed the night with a local family. Letty, at this time, was working at the Duke of York's HQ, Chelsea, where she was petrol controller for the whole of the Home Guard. To help with the fun she brought along six thunderflashes, which were large firework bangers used in troop exercises to simulate gunfire. Towards the end of the party these were ignited, and the young boys, in particular, were highly delighted. Someone had the bright idea to put the last one into an empty dustbin and to cover it with the lid. To the surprise of all present, the force of the explosion sent the dustbin lid soaring about twenty feet into the air. Luckily no one was injured.

Sometime after VE day I was posted to France where I worked on the 'Medloc' run. This was a train service shuttling back and forth between Toulon and Dieppe, bringing home troops from the Mediterranean.

On 2 September 1945 Japan surrendered. At last the war was finally over, and we became impatient for news of demobilisation. This was to be a slow, protracted affair, and we had to curb our patience for some time yet.

Several months later, I contracted a severe attack of jaundice which put me in hospital for two weeks. On discharge, the MO ordered six weeks' convalescence for which I would be sent to a home in Belgium. As this home had recently closed I was sent instead to Richmond Park, Surrey. On discharge from convalescence in June 1946, for my final six weeks' service I was attached to a Military Police unit stationed at the Duke of York's Headquarters, Chelsea.

On 23 July 1946, a group of four of us proceeded to the demob centre where we handed in our kit, and were issued with a complete set of civilian clothing. So ended my Army service.

CHAPTER 5

1946–1950

Boodles Club

Back home, after several days readjusting to civilian life, I began to look for a job. The Orleans Club had been destroyed by enemy bombs and subsequently was to amalgamate with two other clubs of similiar size. In order to retain all three names, the new club was called the Marlborough-Wyndham, and was situated in premises known as Orleans House, just off Pall Mall. I had started to look for a position in the City of London, with the idea of being able to work a straight shift now that I was married; I did not want to return to the pre-war split-shift system which most West End establishments still operated.

As Chelsea residents almost since birth, Letty and I applied to the borough council for accommodation, but from our position on the housing list it would obviously be a very long time, if ever, before we had any chance. By a huge stroke of luck the Radfords, old family friends for many years, were able to sublet a first-floor flat for fifteen shillings a week in a large house they rented in Wandsworth.

As Letty had worked at Peter Jones before the war she was able to arrange for sufficient carpeting from our furnishing coupons to be fitted in the lounge. When we married in 1942 we were entitled to a basic allowance of seven furniture coupons, which was sufficient to purchase an occasional table and four dining chairs, cheaply made in what was known as a 'utility range'. We had received a three-piece bedroom suite, a bed and an oak gate-leg dining-table as wedding gifts. Later in 1942 we had rented a second-floor flat, at a very low rent, in a large house just off Chelsea embankment, five minutes' walk from Stamford Bridge, and I spent the next four leaves redecorating. We ordered our fuel ration – a ton of coal, which was tipped through a hole in the pavement into a cellar, and had the furniture delivered. We were all set to move in on my next leave, but a week before I was due home, the house was bombed, it had to be evacuated, and our furniture, fortunately only slightly damaged, was put into store.

There remained the problem of the coal in the cellar which, if left, was inevitably going to be stolen. I called on Mr Jones, the milkman in Radnor Street, told him the problem, and he kindly loaned me an old three-wheeler, hand-pushed milk-cart with the proviso that I returned it thoroughly scrubbed and clean.

Off I went with two buckets and a shovel, pushing the cart to our blitzed flat, I descended the stone steps to the cellar, unlocked the door, filled the buckets with coal, took it up the steps and deposited it in the barrow until the barrow was full. I locked the cellar door and pushed the cart back to Smith Terrace, unloading by the same method, this time carrying it through my parents' house to the shed in the bank garden. I then went back again for the second batch – it took me almost ten hours before I had completed the task, exhausted, but satisfied that none of the coal would be wasted. We didn't possess a bathroom so, after scrubbing the cart clean and returning it to Mr Jones, I went to the public baths at Chelsea Town Hall and almost fell asleep lying in the comfort and ease of the hot water.

So the furniture came back out of store and we set up our second home. The only method of heating the flat was by coal fire, and to store the coal I placed a 2-hundredweight bin on the landing. Whenever the coalman delivered, it would be two hundredweight sacks tipped into the bin, which left a film of coal-dust all around the immediate area.

In the meantime I had attended several job interviews in various establishments in the City, but as none of them appealed to me (most of the kitchens were in a dreadful state), I decided to look again at the West End.

I finally gained the position of second chef at Boodles Club, St James's Street, where Monsieur Antoine Gervais was in charge. Although back on split duties, it was worth it for the opportunity of working with such an experienced man. Monsieur Gervais was a first-class chef who had been in charge of the kitchens at the Adelphi Hotel in Liverpool, and the Queens Hotel in Birmingham in their golden days before the war. A charming combination of a French gentleman and a confirmed anglophile, we struck up an excellent working relationship from the outset.

Food remained on ration for several years after the war and catering establishments were only allowed to spend a certain amount of money on meat – in our case, four pounds ten shillings a week – which in 1946 would buy one whole lamb and a wing rib of beef. The club was open seven days a week for lunch and dinner, and the staff also had to be fed. The meat allowance barely covered two days, but occasionally it would be supplemented with a few sausages or some offal. For the purchase of groceries, eggs, fats and tinned foods, an allocation of points was made which was very tight, so that we had to organise and plan with great care and economy.

Inevitably, a flourishing black market existed, and if you were prepared to pay the price, almost any quantity of any commodity could be purchased. Respectable clubs and establishments frowned on this practice and we were never allowed to buy food other than the legal entitlement.

The club was more fortunate than most establishments, as members who farmed, hunted or fished would send in surplus requirements. British Rail vans were regular callers, bringing large hampers of assorted game from Scotland and salmon in a wide variety of sizes in long, woven rush containers. Salmon would vary in weight from 7 to 50 lb. All 14-pounders were sent to a salmon-smoking company in the East End of London who, after smoking them, would keep the sides in store until required.

Whole carcasses or sides of venison wrapped in sacking would be dumped unceremoniously on the floor of the larder. These would be butchered, keeping the haunches marinaded in red wine, vegetables and herbs for forty-eight hours, before being roasted and served with a sharp, peppery sauce. The tender fillets were kept for steaks to be fried or grilled and served with a variety of well-flavoured sauces and garnishes. The remaining meat was trimmed, diced and left under running cold water for forty-eight hours, which made the meat much lighter in appearance. After blanching and refreshing, it was then used for a variety of stews, pies and curries, or minced for cottage pie, pasties, steaks and casseroles. The bones would be chopped and browned, along with any other game carcasses, and made into rich well-flavoured stock with the addition of herbs and vegetables. This stock would then be made into an ever popular game soup, to be finished at the table with the addition of a glass of port, madeira or brandy.

One club member reared pedigree turkeys in Norfolk and, in addition to the excellent birds he supplied for roasting, we were also able to purchase turkey eggs, one of which in size roughly equals two hens eggs. Another member had a large estate of prize-winning fruit trees, specialising in English apples. At the beginning of the season, a large wooden box containing 56 lb of Beauty of Bath, together with a typed card giving all relevant information, would arrive. Some time later would follow the Worcester Pearmains, and so on, right through numerous varieties of the very best of dessert and cooking apples, ending with Cox's Orange Pippins. All the apples were packed with loving care, and on opening each box, it was like looking at the gold medal winner at the autumn Royal Horticultural Society show at Vincent Square, Westminster. His Charles Ross were magnificent, often weighing a pound each, a splendid cooking apple that can be eaten or cooked. If I was a painter, it is one I would dearly love to put on canvas.

When Christmas puddings were prepared, a week before mixing we would put all the dried fruit – raisins, currants, mixed peel, sugar, mixed spice, ginger, chopped almonds, prunes, dates and apples – into a large wooden barrel. Next was added twelve bottles of ale, six bottles of stout, and one bottle each of sherry, rum and brandy. The barrel was securely covered and left for seven days, and stirred occasionally so that the fruit became thoroughly impregnated with the liquid. Flour, breadcrumbs, butter and eggs were added and the mixture was then put into basins and steamed in the traditional way. We would make thirty-five 2 lb and twenty-two 3 lb puddings annually, and usually served them with brandy butter or brandy sauce.

It was in the late 1940s that Princess Margaret, holidaying in Capri, was served scampi which she enjoyed very much. On her return, she started to ask for scampi in her favourite restaurants of which Quaglinos was one and the entrance to which was opposite the staff entrance to the club. That started the fashion, and scampi have remained popular ever since in restaurants at all levels.

By now I had settled down to a routine, with half a day off one week and the weekend, from after lunch on Saturday, the other. I would leave home at eight-thirty in the morning, returning at about ten in the evening. The journey home was too far to be made during the afternoon break, but Letty continued working anyway three days a week until I had settled back to work by the end of January 1947. With so little leisure time we found we were able to save some money and build up the Post Office account. My weekly wage was seven pounds ten shillings.

When we married in 1942 we agreed that we would like children fairly soon, and hoped for two boys and two girls. By 1947, however, as there appeared little likelihood of any little ones, we went to consult our doctor. Dr Chandler was a real family practitioner of the old school, married with six children, a gentle, helpful, friendly man, he listened to our problem, offered what advice he could and recommended us to the fertility clinic.

We underwent numerous tests, saw various specialists, faithfully acted on all advice offered, but all to no avail. Finally, after a considerable period of time when the clinic had exhausted all possibilities, they declared that we were both perfectly fit to have children, they could find no fault at all with either of us and, furthermore, could not suggest any reason why our marriage had not been blessed with a family. The final thought the consultant left us with was to consider adoption. We came home somewhat despondent to discuss the situation fully, and decided to start adoption proceedings, by which time several years had passed since 1947. Dr Chandler promised us every support with the application. The procedure for adoption was, quite properly, lengthy, slow and thorough, and here I will leave this matter as this episode was not to be completed until 1954.

I made peace with my old headmaster, joined the school old-boys' association, playing badminton in the hall on Wednesday evenings and adjourning to the Cranleigh in the Fulham Road afterwards. On Sundays we played cricket, which made for pleasant days out and about, with Letty keeping the scores. Match days finished with convivial evenings in the nearest local, where we had no worries about drinking and driving as only one member of the team could afford to run a car.

Bill Janes, the pre-war wine waiter from the Orleans, looked me up one day. He was now working as a barman at the Army and Navy Club in St James's Square. As we enjoyed a game of snooker we joined the Empire Club, situated underneath William Paige's kitchen equipment shop in Shaftesbury Avenue. The club had a resident professional – a Canadian, Conrad Stanbury – and as we played regularly from three to five on Tuesdays and Thursdays, he suggested we buy our own cues. A Joe Davis endorsed cue complete with metal case and a lock cost a fiver. A number of entertainment personalities were members. Lew Grade frequently played on an adjoining table, unfailingly smoking the largest cigar available firmly clenched between his teeth. Ronnie Carroll was another regular.

At the end of 1949 we decided to put a deposit down on a car, a Ford Prefect (for which there was a waiting list of 145 names ahead of us), and I enrolled for a course of driving lessons with the British School of Motoring in the Fulham Road. After passing the test we began to look forward to owning our first motor car, which was to be a big event in our lives.

Life in the flat was pleasant, and we appreciated and enjoyed being in our own home. Letty was a highly talented needlewoman who could turn her hand to making almost any article of clothing. Her training was in fine lingerie at Bradleys, one of the most exclusive houses of its kind, where she learned how to make delicate well-cut underwear of the finest silks and lace. I enjoyed modelling old galleons, and we passed many an hour, each occupied with our piece of work in hand, listening to the radio, quite content with each other's company.

The Radfords, who occupied the ground floor, were very quiet, with the exception of the occasional Saturday night when they would spend a lively evening in the local. Ten minutes or so after returning home merry and bright, we would hear a 'tap, tap, tap', as though a light hammering was taking place. After several occurrences when we sat puzzled, wondering what on earth they were doing at that time of night, curiosity got the better of us and we asked. Outside the local was a shellfish stall that did a heavy trade on Saturday night, and by the end of the evening, as they were closing down, they offered for sale carrier bags half-full of small crabs' claws. Mrs Radford would buy a bag, and on arrival back home, Mr Radford got a light hammer and a small plank of wood, and they sat around the kitchen table cracking open and extracting the crab meat.

One year we were invited to spend Christmas with friends, Tom and Babe, in Liverpool. On our last visit to the butcher's before the holiday we bought a raffle ticket, tucked it away in a drawer, and promptly forgot all about it. We spent a most enjoyable yule-tide experiencing northern hospitality at its generous best, and the day after our return, went shopping. In the butcher's shop-window was a notice. 'Unclaimed raffle prize, ticket No. 126'. We could not remember our ticket number, but on returning home and checking, to our delight we found ticket No. 126 in the sideboard drawer. In all haste I returned to find that the prize was a 20 lb turkey.

Our small gas oven could not cope with a bird that size, so I took it to work and stuffed and cooked it in the club kitchen. After pondering what we were going to do with such an amount of turkey meat, we decided to throw a party, for which the size of our 27-foot-long lounge was ideal. Cold ham was added to the bird, plus a variety of salads, cheese, cold sweets and fruits, and I carved the turkey at the table, taking the wishbone out of the bird before cooking to facilitate carving. We had borrowed tables and chairs, put a barrel of beer on the coal bunker on the landing, and eighteen of us had a good 'tuck-in'.

I had also prepared a programme of party games, estimating roughly how long each would keep the company amused and, at around midnight when the party was in full swing, we started 'horse-racing'. A bookie and clerk were appointed, six of the company were recruited as 'horses', and the bookie was given a board and invited to chalk up odds on each runner. The course was marked out along the length of the room, the horses lined up on the starting line while the company were backing their fancy (to the accompaniment of ribald comments), and all was ready for the 'off'! The horses numbered one to six moved by the throw of two dice, these being thrown by each member of the company in turn. As a horse's number was called, so it would move one foot over the other, progressing towards the finish.

Needless to say, as the horses 'raced' slowly down the room, some in a straight line, others in a gentle waver, excitement mounted as the finish came in sight. Following each throw of the dice, a chorus would echo each pair of numbers, 'One and six! . . . Two and four! . . . Three and three!. . . Hooray!' from those who had backed number three. By the time the leading horses were almost at the finish the volume of noise was deafening and the room was getting hot, so we opened two bottom windows and drew back the curtains to get some fresh air.

The race ended, the bookie paid out, the horses changed, fresh bets were made and the second race began. I had allowed for three races in my games schedule taking about half an hour, but everyone wanted to continue and the race meeting kept going for two hours, providing much fun and laughter for the company.

The following day I met our neighbours from the house opposite who told us that they had been lying in bed listening and envying us all the fun and merriment that was taking place. 'We were trying to work out what was going on. All we kept hearing was, "One and two!. . . Five and four! . . . Three and six!. . . Come on, come on, Hooray!"' So we explained, much to their amusement, and heard later that they tried it out at a party with equal success.

Some months later, while spending Christmas with wartime friends at Swindon, we introduced the game at a large family party, again with success. Because the room was too small for human horses we substituted playing cards numbered one to six which were moved end over end along the shortened course to the throw of the dice in the same way.

Monsieur Gervais was a keen fly-fisherman and an inveterate card player. One of his best friends visited him from time to time at the club when they would have a drink and gossip for ten minutes or so. This friend was a keen coarse fisherman, and the arguments they got into on the respective merits of one sport against the other often made interesting and amusing listening. It would usually take place in the larder where chef and I worked, so that I could not help but overhear.

Monsieur Gervais would sometimes leave on a Saturday for a weekend off, start playing cards on Saturday night and play all through the night and most of Sunday. On Monday morning he would return to work looking heavy eyed, declaring he had had a good weekend! His idea of a perfect holiday was to go off on a fishing trip with a friend to Ireland. Each morning after a hearty breakfast, armed with a bottle of whisky and a snack lunch, they would go off to fish, delighted if it poured with rain all day. Their return in the late afternoon or early evening was followed by a hot bath, drinks in the bar around the fire telling fishermen's stories, a good dinner, coffee and cognac and bed where, in his own words, he 'slept like a top'.

Monsieur Gervais was always a popular man and one who could mix and communicate easily with all levels of people. In his days at the Adelphi and the Queen's he was on the best of terms with most of his directors and was frequently invited to socialise with them. As part of this friendship he received sound advice regarding investments and prospered accordingly.

In the summer of 1948 he began to look and complain of feeling unwell and decided to see his doctor, who advised him to consult a specialist. He returned to work one evening in June and said, 'What do you think my doctor has told me Victor? He has told me that I should retire!' I started to commiserate with him, but he merely smiled and said, 'I'm not worried Victor. I shall return to France to relax, fish and enjoy life. There will be sufficient income from my block of flats to keep me in comfort.' He was then fifty years of age, and up to 1985 I continued to receive a New Year's card from him written in a firm hand from his home in Polliat département Ain, not far from his native town of Annecy, Haute-Savoie.

I was deeply sorry to see him go, having enjoyed his company as a man, and he was an excellent master to work for. When he informed the Club Secretary, Major Dicks, of his retirement, he recommended me as his successor. I duly accepted and, in July 1948, took up my first post as head chef at a substantial increase in wage.

My first task was to hire a reliable second to be able to take charge when I was off duty, and was delighted to be able to recruit Cecil Bill, whom I had worked with at the Ritz before the war. He proved a first-class man, completely reliable, so much so that when I left in 1950 he took over and remained there until his retirement in 1984.

Major Dicks would come down to the kitchen every Monday morning regularly for a chat about business, usually finishing up with the current cricket gossip. One morning he told me that he had been to see his son at Haileybury play an annual needle match against a rival school. He was enthusiastic about an outstanding young batsman he had seen, called Colin Cowdrey, who he was sure would be playing for England one day!

I relished the challenge of my new responsibilities and tackled them with enjoyment and interest. Altering the morning journey, I would alight at Leicester Square and, walking through Soho, called on some of the suppliers whose shops were *en route*. Slater, Cooke, Bisney and Jones, butchers in Brewer Street, were the last stop where I called daily in the hope that there might be a little something not on rations.

A surprise awaited me one morning, when the manager replied to my usual question, 'Anything going this morning?'

'Yes, I've got something for you.' With that he opened the door of his large cold room and removed a tray on which lay a skinned animal resembling a short fat rabbit.

'What's that?'

'It's a beaver.'

'A beaver? What am I supposed to do with that?'

'Don't ask me,' he replied. 'I'm only the butcher, you're the chef.' On close examination, the animal looked clean and plump. There was a fine grain to the meat and it looked good quality.

'All right, I'll have it,' I said. 'Send it in.'

When the butcher's delivery boy arrived an hour or so later, Cecil and I had a discussion about how it should be prepared and cooked. We made a tasty herb and onion-flavoured stuffing for the inside, covered it with thin slices of fat bacon and pot-roasted it slowly on a bed of vegetables and herbs.

Around eleven-thirty as usual, Mr Sharp, the club steward, came down for the day's menu. When I said roast and stuffed beaver he thought I was pulling his leg, whereupon I took him out to the kitchen, Cecil opened the oven door, slid out the tray, removed the lid and basted the animal. 'We can't put roast and stuffed beaver on the menu, the members won't eat it!' he said. I replied, 'I can't call it anything else, that is what it is and that is how we shall have to put it on the menu.' Somewhat reluctantly Mr Sharp finally agreed.

The club had one or two members who lived in grace and favour residences in St James's Palace, from which at twenty-five past twelve daily one elderly knight would totter up St James's Street in order to be first in for lunch. After seating himself in his customary chair, he perused the menu, called for the head waiter, and said in a loud peppery voice, 'What the b — hell is this?'

'Exactly what it says, sir,' replied the head waiter.

'What the blazes is the club coming to? They'll be serving cats and dogs next! I'll have the escalope, I like a bit of veal.' Little did he know that the escalope (which was not called veal on the menu) was prepared from the cut of meat from one side of the saddle of an imported frozen rabbit.

Two members ordered the beaver and ate it without complaint. I had some for my lunch and found it acceptable, but the remainder went through the mincer and ended up in the staff rissoles for supper.

Occasionally, we were able to obtain a case containing twelve frozen rabbits, which made a useful variation as they could be prepared in a variety of white or brown stews, curries, pies and pasties. The saddles were always used by boning out the two cuts of meat and soaking them well in cold water in order to whiten the flesh. Then, by cutting lengthwise three-quarters of the way across, opening out, and carefully beating using a little water, they could be made into thin slices about the size of a dessert plate. Covered with flour, egg and crumbs shallow-fried and served with a wedge of lemon or a variety of garnishes, they were very popular, and on more than one occasion brought forth the comment, 'Nice piece of veal!'

Towards the end of 1949 I started to experience digestive problems which gradually worsened and began to give cause for concern. The doctor prescribed a white chalky medicine and advised that I watch my diet. The treatment began to take effect and I felt some relief, but at the turn of the year it flared up again and progressively worsened, so much so, that the doctor arranged for hospital tests to be taken.

A duodenal ulcer was diagnosed and I was admitted to St James's Hospital for surgery. After the operation the surgeon informed me that as my appendix needed attention he had removed it at the same time. It sounded to me as though his watching students had applauded his skill, and he had cut out the appendix for an encore!

The first morning in hospital that I was able to take breakfast, when the trolley came round I asked for a plate of porridge. A young nurse said porridge was not allowed, but I could have a kipper. For at least two years previously I had not been able to face a kipper for fear of the subsequent discomfort, and was more than a little surprised to hear that two days after the operation I could have one. However, I have great faith in human nature. Somewhat gingerly I tackled the kipper, bread and butter, and a mug of tea, and settled down optimistically for my digestion to flaunt its newly found freedom. Two hours later my stomach felt as though on fire, and when Sister J — came on her rounds, I complained bitterly of severe pain in my stomach. Sister J — was a magnificent specimen of womanhood, six feet tall, an ample bosom and a sergeant-major's manner. The ex-servicemen in the ward automatically 'lay to attention' when she approached their beds. She fixed me with a stern glare and said, 'What have you eaten this morning?'

'Only a kipper, sister.'

'A kipper! You stupid man. You shouldn't be eating anything like that so soon after the operation!' When I started to explain what had happened, she cut me off half-way, gave me a withering look, and continued on her round.

It wasn't funny at the time, but later on I could see that episode in a *Carry on Doctor* film, with Hattie Jacques playing the role of Sister — and Kenneth Connor the patient.

On leaving hospital, having been ordered to take three weeks' convalescence, I informed the club of the situation and settled down to rest and relax. As it was mid-June, Letty and I passed a pleasant three weeks, and it also gave me time to lie back and think.

I found myself going back over life since entering the industry. I had realised by now not only how lucky I had been to receive such a sound training in my chosen career, but also how comparatively few chefs had received the opportunity to experience the standards and variety of work within classical cuisine. Army experience had added a new dimension of resourcefulness, and I had gained confidence to deal with almost any given emergency situation at short notice. It was while counting my good fortune that the idea of teaching those skills to youngsters coming into the industry first began to formulate. By the end of convalescence my mind was made up and, on my return to the club, I requested an interview with Major Dicks.

Boodles had been very good to me during the six weeks' absence and kept me on full pay, which in those days was quite exceptional. On informing Major Dicks of my plans he was kindness itself, and said that he would be sorry to see me go. I recommended Cecil Bill for the post, which recommendation he was happy to act on. He then offered to introduce me to Basil Edwards, who was then secretary of the Hotel and Catering Institute which I had joined shortly after its formation in the late 1940s, and whose office was above Jacksons of Piccadilly.

I formally handed in my notice, to take effect from September, wished Cecil all success in the post, and wrote to Basil Edwards for an interview. He was most helpful and suggested that I apply to the Technical Teacher Training College for a one-year course. After brief consideration I thought this would be an excellent first step, particularly as I had never stood up in front of a group of people to speak, let alone teach.

On hearing this, Basil telephoned the College (it was only three weeks before the start of their academic year and the year's intake had already been interviewed and accepted), briefly told them of my situation, and the Principal, Mr Jameson, arranged for a one-off interview for me in two days' time.

The interview panel consisted of the Principal, Deputy Principal, Mr Skinner, and His Majesty's Inspector for Catering Education, 'Dickie' Bird. It was an interesting interview, and although they questioned me at length, their attitudes put me completely at ease.

Mr Jameson asked why I wanted to teach, which led to a good discussion. Mr Skinner explored my background, reading and hobbies while Mr Bird questioned me on various technical matters, throwing in a question or two in French which I fielded quite happily. In reply to one of his questions, 'Can you name the joints in a side of beef?' I replied, 'I'm not really sure, I could attempt to bluff, but as I don't believe in that I'd prefer not to answer!' Three days later, notification of my acceptance arrived by post, seven days before the start of term.

CHAPTER 6
1950–1951

Teacher Training College

So, in October 1950 I made my way via Camden Town Underground station to the North-Western Polytechnic, Prince of Wales Road, for a full-time course at the Training College for Technical Teachers, which subsequently became a college of the University of London.

The course included:

(a)	Education	Principles and aims of education, Educational psychology, history of education
(b)	Teaching method	General and special methods in catering subjects
(c)	Teaching practice	To take place in technical institutions over a period of twelve weeks
(d)	Social and industrial studies	
(e)	English language and speech training	

On arrival at the college reception I was directed to a hut in the grounds (which was to be the catering group's class-room for the duration of the course). As I walked past the side of the hut making for the door, thirteen pairs of eyes swivelled as one towards me, and I realised I was probably the last member to join the group.

Our tutor was Mrs Holes, a friendly extrovert and ex-domestic science teacher, and the class consisted of ten ladies (all trained in either domestic science or institutional management) and two men – Jim Russell, ex-RAF, and John (Jack) Cooper, ex-RN, who had both trained as Westminster College chef students.

The first morning was spent in outlining the course in detail, giving us an insight into what would be required, explaining the college timetable and routine, and general administrative details. Over lunch we began to get to know each other, and quickly settled down to become a helpful, friendly group. Jim, Jack and I found that we had a great deal in common, despite the fact that Jack supported Blackburn Rovers (his home team), Jim, Arsenal, and me of course, Chelsea. The afternoon was spent on Special Method with Mrs Holes which I found interesting, and I went home at the end of the first day feeling reasonably comfortable about what lay ahead for the next few months.

I had applied for, and been given, the maximum maintenance grant allowed, which was thirteen pounds a month, until the end of June 1951. This was about four-and-a-half times less than my earnings at the club. On learning this, Letty and I blessed our prudence in having built up a small sum in the Post Office which we calculated, with careful management, would see us through the course.

About 100 students were enrolled and were sub-divided into groups according to their respective industrial experience: engineers, painters and decorators, business people, accountants, and so on. Students studied general and special methods of teaching their respective subjects in their own groups but came together in a main lecture hall for general lectures on educational topics, most of which were delivered by the college Director, Mr Jameson (Jamie). Mr Skinner, Deputy Director, gave all the lectures on psychology and soon had us scratching our heads! All group tutors gave at least one general lecture to the whole college so that we had a variety of teaching styles and mannerisms to observe, criticise and discuss.

The most formal member of staff was the tutor of the business studies group, Dr O. G. Pickard, who always set an example to his group by being meticulously dressed in a dark suit, white shirt and sober tie. The student body were assembled one day ready to receive a general lecture from Dr Pickard. No lecture title had been announced but we thought it would probably be a bit of a bore. As the starting time of two o'clock came and passed we wondered what was happening, as punctuality was generally respected. At eight minutes past two the door burst open, and in strode a man wearing a light sports coat, loud-checked shirt, bright red tie, and with his hair standing out from both sides as though he had received a fright or been out in a gale.

We couldn't believe that this was Dr Pickard! Without a word he went to the blackboard, picked up a piece of chalk, and started to write. After three words had appeared he put down the chalk and, still with his back to us, vigorously scratched his backside. He then put one hand in his trouser pocket, and jangling the loose change, he strode over to the window and stood gazing out.

At last he started talking, moved away from the window, took his hand out of his pocket and, continuing to talk, he strode up and down the platform alternatively looking at the floor and the ceiling. Then he removed a rubber from his jacket pocket and started throwing it in the air and catching it whilst continuing to pace up and down like a caged lion.

The whole performance lasted a full five minutes, at the end of which he went to the lectern, paused briefly and then said, 'How many of you could tell me what I have been talking about since I entered the room?' Not one hand was raised.

He then went to the blackboard, completed his lecture title and proceeded to deliver an interesting talk on 'Teachers' bad habits in the class-room and the effect on students' concentration', which raised praise and much amusement from his class who likened his performance to an Alistair Sim headmaster's cameo. He assured us that every mannerism he had used at the beginning of his lecture he had observed being used by a number of teachers.

Our group then met Miss Arnott who was to take us for speech training. She was an experienced teacher with a strong personality, who set an example by delivering impeccable English in a clear, well-modulated voice. At the end of our first session we were told to prepare to speak for five minutes on any subject to the remainder of the group at our next class.

Almost all the students had varying experience of standing on their feet and addressing a group, with the exception of Jack Cooper and myself, and neither of us were relishing the idea, particularly as we had problems thinking of something suitable to talk about.

A few days later we each found ourselves on our feet facing the remainder of our group with Miss Arnott at the rear of the room. As we each completed our talk, Miss Arnott gave an immediate comment and constructive criticism in full. The girls on the whole were good, and Jim Russell was pronounced very good (Jim had been teaching at the Borough Polytechnic) and he also possessed a strong commanding personality.

It was then my turn, and I had unwisely chosen to talk about a rather too light-hearted topic, a wartime Wembley cup final when Chelsea had won. I also brought in the unforgettable incident at half-time when the crowd (almost all in uniform) were being entertained by an American Air Force band who gave one of their faultless, slick marching displays to a variety of music, including jazz numbers, and gained richly deserved applause for their entertainment value. They were followed by a large band from the Guards regiments, and as they marched on, the crowd were saying, 'Now we'll see some real drill and precision!' The band marched on in true Guards style to traditional British military music, and as they passed the half-way line, the officer in command gave the order, 'About-turn!' Well, seemingly because of the tremendous din and excitement, half of the bandsmen failed to hear the word of command, but as the other half did, the resulting shambles had to be seen to be believed and the crowd went completely silent in embarrassment!

There was a similar silence in the room when I sat down, and without uttering a word about my effort, Miss Arnott turned to Jack and said, 'Mr Cooper'. Jack got to his feet, as embarrassed as I had been, but at least he had chosen a more serious subject. When he'd finished and sat down, Miss Arnott said, 'Oh well, Mr Ceserani and Mr Cooper, as you will be teaching cookery for most of the time you may not be called upon to do much formal lecturing – just as well!'

Not a very confidence-inspiring beginning, but we felt slightly better when we learned later that many fellow craftsmen in other groups had fared just as badly on first impact with the redoubtable Miss A. If I had been a play or film casting director I would have chosen Peggy Mount for her part!

Special teaching method sessions with Mrs Holes were gaining momentum, and after two weeks we were each told to prepare a fifteen-minute practical demonstration. Once again Jim and the girls gave reasonable performances. Jim's was very good, and Jack also gave a passable show.

I, unfortunately, was floundering again, for although I'd made a reasonable choice of subject, leek and potato soup, I had no idea how much previous preparation to do. Consequently, I spent too much time at the sink washing vegetables with my back to the class and running out of words to say when cutting up vegetables. It was obvious that I was going to take twice the allotted time, so Jim and Jack came up to give a hand and it ended as a successful, if uproarious, affair.

After those two false starts I couldn't help but think back to the words that Poppa Fritz at the Ritz had said to me within a month of my starting work. 'Vicky, when you do something for me for the first time and you do it wrong, I won't mind, within reason, as long as you find out why it went wrong and take more care in the future. Because often, if you do a thing right the first time, you may think it easy and become careless when you have to repeat it.'

We were kept fully occupied during the course and in our spare time were given reading, note writing and various assignments to fulfil.

Preparations were now ready for the first three weeks' teaching practice and we were told that the main purpose of this period was to sit in and observe as many classes as possible, taking note about the various teaching styles and patterns of student behaviour.

I was allocated to South-East London Technical College, Lewisham, and on the Monday morning of my arrival was given a timetable which spread over a variety of classes and teachers. Miss Griffin, head of department and a brisk, cheery lady, welcomed me in and always found time for a few words when we met. At our first meeting Mr Goode, senior lecturer in cookery, pointedly informed me that in his opinion no one should be allowed to teach cookery until they were at least forty years of age, as they wouldn't have sufficient experience. I was the oldest member of our group, at the age of thirty-one!

Mr Goode was a strange man who seemed to spend endless hours in and out of practical classes making and decorating Christmas cakes, which he kept in a large locked side-room off the main training kitchen. On more than one occasion when I went into the kitchen, the students would be working away on their own, and when I asked for Mr Goode they would reply, 'He's in his cake room, as usual!' I never did find out what happened to the cakes!

Mr Van de beken was a cultivated gentleman, a lover of good music and the fine arts. Impeccably groomed, he would use his expressive hands by gently waving them around as he was discussing various items of food. His voice and diction were of the highest quality, and on the first occasion I walked into his class-room he was describing a herring, holding it on high between a gently curved forefinger and thumb of one hand, whilst waving the other hand around like an orchestral conductor. All his teaching was carried out in a calm, unhurried sedate fashion, and I frequently wondered what would happen if he had to take a really busy practical class on lunch preparation, but as these sessions were not on his timetable I never found out.

When I first met Miss Swinton she greeted me, 'Ah! Just the man I'm looking for. I shall give you all the topics in my classes [practical cookery] that I'm not too happy with.' Miss Swinton was a large, pleasant lady with a forthright manner who always spoke her mind and brooked no nonsense from anyone. She was later to become Head of the Hastings Hotel and Catering School. I took to her from the outset, we developed a good understanding and relationship, and I did more teaching in her classes than in almost any other.

John Vigurs was the man who helped me most of all. An ex-Westminster Hotel School student, he was also experienced in industry, and was a most useful member of staff in the department. His students thought

highly of him, although he chased them around unmercifully in practical sessions when the occasion demanded. The larger part of my timetable was with John, and he was always ready to discuss problems and
offer what advice he could.

This period of teaching practice proved a fascinating three weeks'
experience that passed quickly and left my mind and notebook full of
ideas, experiences and situations, and I looked forward to the following
term for the final nine weeks of teaching practice.

On returning to college we all had many experiences to relate and
notes to compare, much of which was carried out as useful class-room
sessions under the chairmanship of Mrs Holes. We were surprised to
learn of the variation in colleges regarding their attitudes to student teachers. Some were properly inducted, given full meaningful
timetables with more than plenty to occupy ourselves, whilst others
were virtually ignored and left to their own devices to glean what information and experience they could. Fortunately, I was one of the lucky
ones, and had been warned by Miss Swinton that on my return I would
have plenty of teaching to do for her, which suited me fine. Miss Griffin
also offered me the opportunity to teach a part-time City and Guilds 151
cookery class on two evenings a week for which I would be paid! John
Vigurs had assured me of all possible help and advice, so I left SELTEC
well pleased.

The end of autumn term followed soon afterwards, and we went
home for the Christmas break during which, as well as passing a pleasant time at home with the family, I was able to carry out some reading
and studying for the course.

In January 1951 I went back to college for the second term which
consisted almost completely of teaching practice. The few course members who had unsatisfactory colleges for their teaching practice had been
switched to more suitable locations, and we spent most of the first two
weeks in special teaching method sessions with Mrs Holes, discussing
class-room and student attitudes and behaviour, and each in turn giving
practice lessons and practical demonstrations to the remainder of the
group. We were also advised to read the situations vacant columns of the
Caterer and Hotelkeeper and the *Times Educational Supplement* to begin
to acquaint ourselves with potential situation openings for the start of
the new academic year in September.

Jim Russell had a job to return to at the Borough Polytechnic and one
or two of the girls had jobs in prospect, but the remainder of us had to
start from scratch. Jack Cooper hoped for a post up north, and I was
looking for a situation in London.

Before the end of January we were back on teaching practice, and in
the first week I had to give my very first lecture demonstration, followed
by class practice on puff pastry. This was for one of Miss Swinton's

classes and I was pleased at the choice of a subject for which I had ample experience and confidence. I was also fortunate to be able to enter the kitchen well before the start of the lesson and was able to prepare the demonstration table to my satisfaction and weigh up all the ingredients for the class to follow.

The class were a good bunch of students. I demonstrated with confidence, enjoying what I was doing, and we soon established a satisfactory rapport. Finishing off the making of my slab of pastry with a flourish, I said, 'That's it, are there any questions?' Up popped one hand.

'What is the lemon for sir?' Untouched on my table lay a lemon, the juice of which I had intended to squeeze in with the liquid.

'Oh! I'm sorry, I forgot to put it into the pastry.'

'What's the lemon juice for, sir?'

'I'm afraid that I don't know. I was taught always to put lemon juice into puff pastry, but I don't know the reason why. I will find out and tell you next week.'

That was the first, but not the last, occasion on which I realised the truth in the old saying, 'In teaching others you teach yourself.' I found out that the reason for adding a little acid to puff-pastry dough is to help strengthen the gluten in the flour, making the dough elastic. A more elastic dough lessens the risk of the fat oozing out when giving the paste its numerous turns.

Two important lessons were learned from that episode: never try to bluff students, and if you can't answer a question don't be afraid to say so, they will respect you all the more for it in the end. As well as saying that I would find out the reason, I should have told the class to do the same, as we could then have had a brief discussion on the topic to reinforce the learning.

By now I was in full swing with my timetable, giving lecture demonstrations of varying lengths three or four times a week and really beginning to enjoy classes in the practical situation. I was less happy with pure lecturing, particularly if I had to work from prepared notes which we were required to write out for every lesson. From time to time on teaching practice tutors from the training college would visit, sit in on classes and assess our performance. Properly prepared teaching notes had to be available for inspection.

On Tuesday and Thursday evenings from six until nine o'clock the City and Guilds part-time class met. They were a good bunch, all working in the industry in a variety of establishments: hotels, restaurants, hospitals or industrial canteens. I particularly enjoyed taking this class because, being adult, they had a mature attitude; they were eager to learn and their attendance was invariably one hundred per cent. Moreover, there was no one else in the room other than a cleaner and, also, I was earning a little extra money!

The system in use by the London County Council was that the cost of food used by the class was totalled, a percentage added towards overheads, and the total then divided between the number of students in attendance for that class. This sum was payable at the end of each lesson, but students could then take the food home (in their own containers).

Time on teaching practice passed rapidly as it was full of interest, with a variety of students whose ages ranged from sixteen in full-time classes to sixty in part-time classes. One afternoon a week John Vigurs had a two-hour class on pub food and snacks for publicans' wives who were a jolly, lively group that we both enjoyed taking. Although nine weeks is a very short time, I nevertheless found it invaluable because of the many opportunities it gave to study, and be part of, a busy hard-working department.

In discussion with Miss Swinton one day, I learned that she was attending a course one day a week on trade cookery for domestic science teachers taught by Gerry Hudswell at Acton Technical College. She was thoroughly enjoying the course, gaining a great deal of knowledge from it, and made a point of discussing with me the work they covered week by week.

Towards the middle of March she informed me that an additional lecturer in cookery and related subjects was required at Acton, and strongly advised me to apply for the post. It was about the same time that John Vigurs mentioned that there could be a post for me at SELTEC if I was interested. On reading the Acton advertisement in the *Times Educational Supplement* and noting that the wording stated specifically 'a woman with institutional management qualifications', I showed it to Miss Swinton. 'Oh, ignore that! Put an application in,' she said. Somewhat puzzled I went home to consider which of the two posts to apply for.

I soon reached a decision and applied for the Acton job on the grounds that a different college would broaden my experience. In addition, there was the appeal of starting fresh as a full-time teacher in a department where I had not previously worked. If my application was unsuccessful, there was the SELTEC post to fall back on. So off went my first teaching job application form, and shortly afterwards I was invited to attend for interview for the post.

I reached Acton Town Underground station and after a five minutes' walk down Mill Hill Road I entered the Woodlands Annexe of the college, where I passed a large hut on the left which housed a small training restaurant and the main training kitchen fitted with commercial type equipment, both recently built. Half a dozen paces beyond was an older building which had been converted from a school gymnasium into a training kitchen fitted with domestic-type cookers, sinks and tables.

The main building was about thirty yards away on the right, and as I made my way across, a lady came bustling down the steps heading towards me. As she approached her face broke out into a delightful, friendly smile and she asked, 'Mr Ceserani?'

'Yes, that's right,' I replied, 'Miss King?' and that was my first meeting with Mary King, the head of department, who immediately put me at ease and showed me to the waiting room for the interview.

I cannot remember any details about the interview, conducted by the College Principal, Mr McAdam, Gerry Hudswell and Miss King, other than it was relaxed, friendly, and that I took to all three of them at once. Subsequently, on being offered the post as a lecturer grade A to commence on 1 September 1951, I accepted by return of post. Whilst chatting after the interview I said to Gerry Hudswell, 'I nearly didn't apply as your advertisement specifically stated a woman.'

'Oh,' he replied. 'Miss Swinton put in a special word for you!'

I returned home to tell Letty the good news, my enthusiasm tempered slightly by the fact that my starting salary was to be considerably lower than at Boodles, and I would not receive the first monthly payment until the end of September. In the excitement of a new start to a fresh career we shrugged off financial matters, and I went back to training college to complete the course and prepare for final examinations. The fact that I had a permanent job awaiting acted as a further incentive to effort in the remaining course work which I tackled with enthusiasm and successfully completed by the end of June.

Looking back, I am certain that the teacher training course was well worthwhile as it opened my mind to so many aspects of education. Without it I would have been a less effective educationalist.

So, the course dispersed. Jack Cooper went to a post at Hollings College, Manchester (he was later appointed head of department at Hull) and Jim Russell went back to the Borough Polytechnic (later to become Head at Llandrillo Technical College, North Wales). Almost all the girls had gained appointments by this time, and Margaret Todd subsequently became Head at Worthing and Pat Cannon, Deputy Head at Croydon. Jack and Jim stayed at their respective headships until retirement in the mid-1980s. Jim had one son who developed into a keen Chelsea supporter. How does the only son of a lifelong follower of Arsenal living in North Wales become a Chelsea fan? When he was quite young, on rummaging in our loft one day, I came across my original box of Chelsea programmes going back to the 1920s which I sent up to him.

Acting on advice received at college, I then did something for the first time in my life which I had never done before and have never done since – signed on at the Labour Exchange in order to receive dole money and, for some strange reason, I felt ashamed at doing so. When the clerk at the exchange interviewed me he asked me what job I could do. 'A lecturer in cookery,' I replied. 'I have a job to start in September.'

'Can't you take a temporary job as a chef?' he asked.

'No, I will only take a job as a lecturer.' With that, he dismissed me rather curtly.

I confess to feeling more than a little guilty at what I had done, until I received my timetable from Acton and realised how much written preparation and reading I needed to do over the next two months.

CHAPTER 7
1951–1963

The Acton Years

As a grade A lecturer, my teaching timetable was twenty-four hours a week, with the addition of 2 three-hour evening classes which were paid overtime. My full-time class, a first year chefs' group, were with me about eighteen hours a week on practice and theory of cookery. The remainder of the timetable was made up with other groups, full and part time, teaching subjects such as commodities, kitchen and personal hygiene, and calculations, in addition to practice and theory of cookery.

The only syllabuses available were those issued by City and Guilds. There were no recognised textbooks and consequently this meant a considerable amount of reading and writing (including all recipes) for each meeting of every class. I spent several hours daily over the next two months writing out more detailed syllabuses, schemes of work, lesson notes and recipes, and enjoyed being able to do this work quietly at home without any major interruptions. It was time well spent as it gave a good solid foundation for the first term in September.

The student body began college the third week in September and the teaching staff returned two weeks earlier, giving me the opportunity to meet my new colleagues.

Paul White, ex-RAF, had joined the same day to start a new one year full-time course in hotel bookkeeper reception. Nancy Brien taught a nursery nurses course and hygiene and nutrition to full-time students, as did 'Bully' Bradley (Mrs). Jean Bowes taught French, Kate Witchell, food service and related subjects and Alfie Liebold, restaurant service. Gerry Hudswell, a captain in the Army Catering Corps during the war, was deputy head of department and taught cookery to the senior students. Freddie Sharman, formerly non-commissioned officer ACC; Stan Gray, ex-civilian instructor ACC School of Cookery, Aldershot; and Eddie Jonckheere, ex-civilian instructor RAF School of Cookery, Halton; all taught cookery.

Acton Hotel and Catering School started in the domestic science department of Acton Technical College in 1948. One class-room in the main building was converted into a training/production kitchen with four commercial cookers and was used by a class every morning as a production kitchen for student lunches. Another class-room opposite doubled up as a dining-room, and there was one small domestic science kitchen. The food store, six class-rooms and the school offices completed the accommodation. The main kitchen, restaurant and the converted kitchen were situated away from the main building.

Full-time students numbered between sixty and eighty and were studying on one of three courses: chefs, hotel and catering operations and bookkeeper receptionists. A similiar number of part-time students attended either on day-release or one or two evenings a week.

Mary King, a dedicated educationalist, had a domestic science and institutional management background. She was ably assisted by her right-hand man, Gerry Hudswell, a hard-working dynamic personality with a sound knowledge of the commercial industry. Under their leadership the school buzzed with activity, and it soon became apparent that I had joined a truly professional organisation.

Mary King's style of management was firm, gentle and kind – I can never recall her ever *telling* me to do anything. She would always ask with a pleasant smile, and an explanation if necessary. Gerry had a more direct, brusque style, but one that was completely acceptable. Although Mary and Gerry were opposites in many ways they complemented each other perfectly, and enjoyed a sound working relationship. On reflection, I consider that a large part of their successful leadership could be attributed to the hard-working example they set together with the consideration shown to others. I, for one, learned a great deal from them.

Although the staff were on duty two weeks before the start of term to deal with preparation and administration, nevertheless, the tempo of work during this period was comfortable, and I went home on the last Friday feeling quite excited at the prospect of welcoming my first full-time class on the Monday morning.

In they came, ten girls and six boys all aspiring to be chefs or cooks, looking as many first time students do – a little bewildered. My class!

We spent the whole day together, the morning on general administration, and after lunch they wore their 'whites' for the first time. The girls were comfortable as they had several years of domestic science behind them, but the boys looked embarrassed, particularly as the chefs' hats, when new, were not starched. Some flopped one way, some the other. One lad's hat was only prevented from falling over his eyes by a stout pair of ears.

We soon started work. I demonstrated briefly and they followed, back and forth throughout the afternoon, with the emphasis on knife drill. I quickly realised the necessity of ensuring the first-aid box was well stocked with sticking plasters and subsequently had cause to be grateful for the nearness of Acton Hospital at the end of Mill Hill Road for more serious cuts or burns.

Time flew on the first day, and I went home pleased and satisfied with 'my little family' and eager to see them again. We met on three days a week, and although food rationing was easing gradually, it was July 1954 before all restrictions were ended.

As the week progressed I met my other groups and completed a record of work after each session for every class, a practice which I found invaluable. When, in following years, I taught the same subject to a similar group, the detailed record of work with comments on how the lesson had progressed was helpful when preparing a new scheme of work.

At six o'clock on Friday evening I arrived home at the completion of the first week's full-time teaching, changed, sat down, and suddenly felt very tired and weary. This puzzled me, particularly as it was twenty-four hours before I began to revive. This same pattern persisted in varying degrees for about the next two years, then gradually eased. Although my teaching week was hard work (I had been brought up all my life to work hard, so that did not bother me) I thoroughly enjoyed it, and on waking in the morning looked forward to each day. However, the work was almost completely mental as opposed to the physical work which I was used to, and I presumed that this took time for readjustment and explained my pattern of weariness.

Not long after I started at Acton, Nancy Brien, who was teaching a class of young ladies in an adjoining kitchen, came into my class of first-year chefs. She was looking slightly flushed, holding a cooked lobster, and said, 'Could you show me how to deal with this?' I cut it in halves, removed the gravel sac in the head, cleaned out the trail (the intestinal tract), and she left, leaving me feeling slightly superior!

The following week at the same time at the finish of a demonstration which included the use of yeast, a student asked the question, 'What is yeast?' I paused, thought for a moment and replied, 'I don't know: I can tell you how to handle it, what and what not to do with it, but I don't know what it is!' I went into Nancy's room for help and she gave me the answer immediately. This was when I realised that domestic science and trade teachers could often be of help to each other.

By the end of 1952 our adoption procedure was progressing, and Letty and I started to consider the accommodation position in the flat, with an infant and no garden of our own. We didn't care for the idea, began to wonder if we could afford a house, and arranged for the adoption to be deferred for a short time. Thankfully I'd now been upgraded from lecturer grade A to B, with an improvement in salary, which helped.

Out walking one day we came across a 'For Sale' board on a property two streets away. It was the last of four new terraced houses built on the site of four pre-war houses which had been flattened by enemy action. The cost was £2 600, and we were able to obtain a loan from the borough council at a fixed rate of interest of 4½ per cent.

At the same time the Government introduced purchase tax on motor cars. As a result, the waiting list for Ford Prefects shrunk rapidly and we received notification that we now headed the list!

The decision to buy a house or a car was 'no contest' – we cancelled the order for the new car, scraped together the deposit for the house and moved in March 1953.

Once the house was ship-shape we set about the small garden, which seemed to be four parts rubble, one part soil. We decided to build a paving wall half-way along the garden to contain the rubble, put a thin layer of soil on top and sow grass seed. To build the wall, paths and a patio I ordered a ton of broken paving in May for fifteen shillings from the borough council which, when delivered, was tipped on the road outside the house. As I was on evening class and not due home until after dark, Letty took one look at it blocking the roadway and decided to carry it piece by piece through the house into the garden. As some of the pieces were large, heavy and awkward she was quite weary when I arrived home.

Letty was also worried about her weight, which was increasing, and had been taking PLJ lemon juice to see if it would help. Shortly afterwards, feeling unwell, she went to see Dr Chandler only to come home with her face beaming and the news was that she was pregnant. Needless to say, PLJ has been a family joke ever since.

In June, as part of Her Majesty Queen Elizabeth's coronation celebrations, Gerry Hudswell had arranged to carry out an ox roast on a green in Charlwood, Surrey. At almost the last moment he was unable to travel and he asked me to take over. Letty and I went along, I donned whites and wellies and surveyed the scene. The fire was going steadily and a group of local Scouts were on hand to assist and rotate the wheel on the spit (which was rather high to my thinking). I borrowed a long-handled dusting brush for basting the ox, and by dusk the party began.

The ox was lifted down onto a table in front of the fire, I dissected it into joints and passed them forward to three tables occupied by two local doctors and the dentist, who assisted in carving the joints. The local ladies then put the meat in between slices of buttered bread and sold them to the, by now, hungry onlookers, who washed them down with copious draughts of ale or Coke according to their age.

Letty was being given every care and attention to assist with a successful pregnancy and from July to August was sent to hospital for four weeks complete rest.

This was the time of that excellent pair of Surrey spin bowlers, Laker and Lock. The Australians were over and the results were level, with the final test match at the Oval to decide who held the Ashes.

Our good friends from Liverpool, Tom and Babe, came down for a holiday in London and the day before the fifth test match Tom decided he wanted to go to the Oval, could I get tickets? I told him that he must be joking, as tickets were as scarce as gold-dust. He then talked me into going with them on the morning of the match, as he was sure we would be able to buy tickets outside the ground. He was correct in his assumption but had not realised the amount of money that was being asked for, and in many cases paid, for precious tickets. At times like this some sport lovers get so carried away with excitement and anticipation that it resembles a type of fever. They lose all sense of proportion and will, in fact, pay grossly inflated sums to satisfy the anticipation they have built up.

We hadn't got the amount of money being demanded, Tom and Babe were looking fed-up and I suddenly had an idea.

'Follow me,' I said, and led them into one of the large blocks of council flats close to the ground, up to the third floor where I knocked on the front door of one of the flats overlooking the ground. A lady came to the door. I apologised for disturbing her, explained our problem and asked if we could possibly pay her for the use of three seats by an open window.

'Of course you can, my dears,' she replied. 'Come in and make yourself comfortable and I'll make you a cup of tea.' With that, we settled down with a splendid, if slightly distant, view of the historic scene and enjoyed England's triumph and Australia's discomfort to the full. The lady of the house was pleased to have our company (she was a widow living on her own), and she beamed with delight when we generously rewarded her on leaving.

An eventful two years had passed. My first batch of students had completed their courses and left for various jobs in the industry, and I now had a different timetable for the following academic year with a full-time class of eighteen hotel and catering operations students.

Once again I was able to spend a great deal of time on lesson revision and preparation during the summer break as Letty was resting as much as possible. We walked most days on Wandsworth Common and at week-ends, if the Old Oratorians were not playing, would often take a snack lunch or tea and watch cricket at The Sinjuns (Walter St John School old boys) or Grammarians (Battersea Grammar School old boys) ground in Trinity Road.

In September 1953 I went back to college where my new full-time class were mainly youngsters aged sixteen to eighteen with higher academic qualifications than the chef students. The course was designed to prepare for entry into various sectors of the industry as prospective supervisors or management trainees. The school philosophy at that time (and for many years to follow) was for potential management students initially to be given a firm foundation of practical and theoretical knowledge in the skills of the kitchen, dining-room, reception and housekeeping departments, together with the discipline required for the operation of those key areas effectively. Management orientation of these subjects plus pure management and related studies such as accounting, economics, law and personnel would be studied at a later stage in the course.

One highly intelligent young man in my group who was in his middle twenties did not possess a practical bent and experienced difficulties with acquiring manipulative skills involving the use of knives. He was shaping carrots using a small knife one day when I took one look at his work and said, 'I'm going to christen you "Chippy". You'd make a good carpenter!' He was a pleasant lad, popular with the group, and it was all taken in good part, but the nickname remained with him for many years after leaving college – even when he became a hotel manager. Whenever I met an ex-student from this group and we started talking about the old days or where members of the class were now working, if this lad's name came up he was always referred to as 'Chippy'.

I found the experience of taking a different level of student refreshing and challenging and, as with most young people, provided they found the course enjoyable they accepted a sensible code of discipline and worked well.

Those of us on the staff with trade experience knew that the industry was generally hard-working and demanding in terms of unorthodox and unsociable hours. We therefore did our best to work our students hard, and bring them up to that code whilst in college. In the great majority of cases this philosophy worked well, resulting in a busy, industrious department which, on the whole, enjoyed good personal relationships between the student body and teaching staff.

January 1954, and our first offspring was due. Letty and I shared a mixture of excitement with a degree of anxiety. Daily, people would enquire, 'Any news?' Even my full-time class got into the act and on entering the class-room I would be greeted with, 'Any news, sir?' January passed, we entered February and finally, on the sixth, son John decided to grace us with his presence. We were delighted as were all members of the family, particularly the two grandmothers and my father.

John was a fine healthy boy, full of energy, who seemed to require very little sleep and for the first eighteen months of his life never gave us a full night's rest. It wasn't that he cried a lot, but rather that he wanted to play or be amused which was fine during the day, but as a regular occurrence in the early hours of the morning became very wearying. I was becoming more and more tired and my patience both at home and in class was wearing thin. Then at 3 a.m. one morning after eighteen months, he was lying in our bed playing and fidgeting around, and my patience snapped. I picked him up and tossed him into his cot by the side of the bed. As I did so, I had the horrible nightmare of instantly thinking, 'Supposing he catches his head or neck on the cot bars – I could have killed him.' Fortunately he came to no harm, but that incident taught me a salutary lesson.

We counted our blessings when this phase ended and we were able to enjoy a full night's sleep. He would wake early, but we could bear with that. John loved to get out of his cot on waking and come into our bed where we would amuse him until getting-up time. One morning, feeling extra tired, we decided to keep our eyes closed and pretend to be asleep. We heard 'his nibs' clamber out of the cot, say, 'Mummy,' and 'Daddy,' several times and made no response. He went for a little toddle around the bedroom, rummaged on the dressing table and then climbed into our bed. His little fingers then started tracing patterns first on Letty's face and then on mine, but he was quiet, so we remained 'doggo'. A few minutes later Letty opened her eyes, took one look at me, and burst out laughing. At which I opened my eyes and looked at her, and did the same. Both our faces and the sheets were smeared with liberal streaks of lipstick, giving us the appearance of a pair of inebriated Red Indians who'd made-up with shaky hands for a ceremonial dance!

Our next problem was one of religion. Neither of us had practised our religion for many years, but Letty had been brought up as a regular member of the Church of England, and me a Roman Catholic. Although legally married according to the law of the land, according to the teaching of the Catholic faith, I was not. We considered it a parental duty to bring up our son in accordance with a Christian faith and, to assist with the problem, Letty agreed to undertake instruction for conversion to the Catholic faith. Following that we arranged for a marriage service in the local church. Dicky White, a fellow Old Oratorian and my badminton doubles partner, was godfather, and the three of us were the only ones in church for the ceremony. We took John in his pram (to attend his parents' wedding!) and left him asleep in the porch. Half-way through the service he awoke, started to cry, and one elderly lady on entering the porch asked, 'Where are the parents of this baby?' only to be informed that they were inside getting married.

In the 1950s the three services were cutting down on personnel, resulting in an unwanted surplus of officers. A scheme was offered by the Government whereby officers who were to be 'bowler-hatted' could take specialised short courses at colleges of further education to aid with resettlement and assist them with finding suitable employment in civilian life. We planned a number of intensive courses for those wishing to start a small catering business or run a pub. The first group, twelve in number, had representatives from the Royal Navy, Army and Royal Air Force, and were such a congenial bunch of characters that they soon became firm favourites with the teaching staff.

Half-way through the course a visit to the Guinness brewery at Park Royal (a short distance away) was arranged, and it included lunch. The group was due back for an afternoon class at two o'clock but at five minutes past two there was no sign of them. At two-fifteen three cars pulled up about twenty yards from where they had to go for the afternoon class. The car doors opened, and in varying degrees of unsteadiness they clambered out (all in full uniform), put on their caps, and walked away in what was supposed to be a brisk service fashion. The discipline of years in the service kept their shoulders square and backs straight, but the generous Guinness hospitality was too much for their legs. The sight of the thin straggling line, weaving gently from side to side with slow but steady progress, made the onlookers of this cameo from a nearby window burst their sides with laughter, and we couldn't wait to hear the results of the afternoon lecture.

The lecturer concerned came out smiling, saying that it was the most hilarious class he had ever taken, that is, for the ten members who had managed to stay awake. The other two had dozed off and spent the period slumped in their seats, snoring gently, as he described it, 'like bees gently buzzing on a hot summer's afternoon'.

On the Woodlands extension site opposite the main building was a field large enough for a fair-sized football pitch which was put to good use by the students. A decision had been made to increase the number of colleges of advanced technology, and this site was earmarked for the building of the Brunel College of Advanced Technology which was later to move to Uxbridge and be designated a university.

The initial work of Brunel College was formed partly from the advanced courses being carried out at Acton Technical College, but the work of the catering school was not included. Nevertheless, the demand for hotel and catering courses was increasing steadily year by year, additional staff were recruited, and all class-rooms and training kitchens were occupied morning, afternoon and evening on all five days a week. We were literally bursting at the seams and something had to be done.

Sufficient space was available at the rear of Ealing Technical College and School of Art, St Mary's Road, Ealing, for an extension, and a decision was made to apply for approval to add on a purpose-built building and transfer the school from Acton to Ealing College. Even if approved, this would take time, so extra temporary accommodation was sought and eventually found at Norwood Hall, Norwood Green, Southall.

This was a splendid house, set in spacious grounds, which had been acquired by the council some years previously. It served both as the horticultural studies centre for Middlesex, under the direction of Frances Perry, and for the study of the husbandry of small animals such as rabbits and chickens.

The house had a largish kitchen in the basement, with a sufficient number of domestic-type stoves and a big room on the first floor. This allowed for two classes to operate daily (when not in use by the Hall), one on practical work in the morning, the other on theory in the afternoon, and vice versa. The morning class planned its work to supply lunch for both classes, and the products of the afternoon class would be sold, always making sure that the head gardener who lived in a house alongside had a good helping for his large family.

We soon made friends with the head gardener and his colleagues for, to our delight, we discovered that they grew a wide range of vegetables, fruits and herbs, and were quite amenable to supplying us with surplus produce. An added bonus was the fact that they grew many unusual varieties which we had difficulty in obtaining from our supplier.

Although not an ideal teaching set-up at Norwood Hall, nevertheless it helped us over a difficult period, and those required to teach there came to enjoy it because of the pleasant house and surroundings.

One part-time course offered by the school was the City and Guilds Advanced Cookery for Hotels and Restaurants 152 (later to be renumbered 706/3) with Gerry Hudswell taking the second year, and I the first year. Although there was no textbook as such designed for the course, the recommended book was *A Guide to Modern Cookery* written by the master chef, Auguste Escoffier, and published in 1907, a copy of which had been given to me on the day I entered the trade.

I found this course a delight to teach, as it covered a range of cookery at the highest level, and we were fortunate in having sufficient money to buy all the necessary ingredients. All the cooking was carried out in the classical manner, and the level of student work expected to be produced in the final six-hour practical examination was that of a chef de partie in a first-class West End establishment. Two examples of practical tests would be to prepare and cook for four covers the following menus:

Potage Germiny	*Crème Agnès-Sorel*
* * *	* * *
Homard Américaine	*Turban de Fillets de Sole et*
* * *	*Saumon Villaret*
	* * *
Poularde Albuféra	
Fonds d'Artichauts	*Caneton Braisé aux Navets*
Florentine, Pommes Mireille	*Subrics d'Epinards Pommes Anna*
* * *	* * *
Charlotte Royale	*Soufflé Rothschild*
* * *	* * *

In addition, a three-hour theory paper was set, but to achieve a pass result success in the practical exam was mandatory.

The chef examiner for many years was Jean Vincent, Head of Professional Cookery, Westminster Hotel School, who was (rightly) a hard, demanding taskmaster. He endeavoured to conduct all the practical examinations personally, and only when this became physically impossible did he allow a very small number of hand-picked colleagues to assist. Pass results were difficult to achieve, the annual rate usually being in the order of thirty to forty per cent. Consequently, the standard of successful candidates had to be high.

I taught the course, which ran from 3 to 9 p.m. one day a week, for almost ten years, rated it as one of the most enjoyable on my timetable and would happily spend two to three hours preparing for the initial demonstration and practice class to follow.

A number of well-known names passed through my hands on this course, including Michael Guthrie, Chairman of Mecca Leisure; Bob Leighton, Head of Swindon Catering School; Brian Price, Chef of the Year and former Principal Lecturer at Ealing; Ian Nutbourne, Senior Lecturer at Salisbury; Dave Oliver, Senior Lecturer at Crawley; and Mary Martin, Head at Ipswich. George Ingham, Senior Lecturer at Southfields College in Leicester, attended in the early days, travelling back and forth from Leicester regularly, and I can never recall him ever being late or missing a class. George Bennett, Head of Worthing Catering School, was working at Derry and Toms roof-garden restaurant in High Street, Kensington when he took the course. George was an exceptional craftsman who always wore an impeccable set of whites, including a tall, perfectly starched and pleated hat which his wife, Shirley, laundered and pressed for him regularly.

On the day of his final exam George was unlucky, as one or two things did not go as planned. His confidence began to suffer and, under Jean Vincent's eagle eye, this was noted and he duly failed. Understandably disconsolate and disappointed, he declared that that was his last exam. We let him cool off for a few days, and then started to persuade him to look upon the exam as experience and retake the following year, not necessarily attending every class. He then had the summer break to think it over, and we were delighted when he returned the following September to re-enrol. Everything went well on the second practical exam the following June and quite deservedly he gained a pass with credit, a considerable achievement in the tough days of Jean Vincent. When the directors at Derry and Toms heard the news they gave a small cocktail reception to mark the occasion, at the end of which George was invited to go into the store and select any men's suit of his choice with the compliments of the Board of Directors.

By now, having become thoroughly established in teaching and gaining so much satisfaction from it, I firmly believed it to be what I wanted to do for the remainder of my working life. I began to question the content of the City and Guilds syllabuses and examination papers. As a result I was invited to join the Catering Advisory Panel, which was the beginning of a twenty-year association during which time I sat on a variety of committees and panels concerned with the content of courses and examinations.

In 1957, much to our delight, Letty became pregnant again and on 11 August was delivered of our second son, Michael. Because of post-natal problems Letty had to stay in hospital for some time and I visited daily.

While passing our local off-licence I noticed a sale of wines, which included an Entre deux Mers at 5s 9d per bottle. With a mad rush of blood to the head, elated by the fact that we now had two sons, I purchased six bottles. They were individually wrapped in sheets of white paper, carefully put into a bag, and I returned home. The cellar of the old house remained. I had acquired a wine rack, and I went down to unpack the initial instalment of my first wine cellar.

Unwrapping each bottle carefully I placed them in the rack until the last one, which slipped out of my hand, fell on the concrete floor and smashed. Because this bottle was still in its wrapping paper, only about a quarter of the wine escaped. I went to the kitchen, got a basin, a funnel, a piece of cloth, and strained the remaining wine. I was due to visit Letty in half an hour, took one look at the wine, decided to drink it and set off for the hospital, five minutes' walk away. On arrival in the ward I leaned over the bed, kissed Letty and expressed the hope that she was well. 'I'd be a lot better if I'd had half of the wine you've drunk!' she replied, at which I related the tale and we both had a good laugh.

Before the war in Britain, the only college offering courses in catering subjects was Westminster. In 1946 the college at Brighton began, then in rapid succession colleges at Acton, Portsmouth, Birmingham and most other large cities and towns followed suit. In most cases, catering courses and schools grew out of existing domestic science or institutional manage-ment sections, and had to prove themselves in far from suitable accommodation before new purpose-built buildings were sanctioned. By the late 1950s the number of centres had increased rapidly to around 100, and there was evidence of continuing growth for years to come.

Towards the end of the 1950s during a summer conference of catering teachers organised by HMI 'Dickie' Bird, the suggestion was made that an Association of Catering Teachers could be a useful organisation for the furtherance of catering education. Eric Stevenson, head of catering at Croydon and a member of the well-established Bakery Teachers Associa-tion, Paul White from Acton and Frank Hussey from Brighton, sat talking one day at the conference and, helped by Eric's experience of the Bakery Teachers Association, started the ball rolling. About twelve willing vol-unteers formed a steering committee at which, to my surprise but consid-erable pleasure, I was elected chairman.

The Catering Teachers Association was launched in 1959 and was greeted with enthusiasm by the majority of teachers, many of whom, because of the rapid growth of catering education, had come into the teaching profession with little or no experience. There were still no text-books available because the best textbooks emerge from a teacher's actual teaching experience over a period of time; in my view a minimum of ten years.

I held chairman's office for four years, and found it most rewarding. Paul White and Frank Hussey gave excellent support as treasurer and sec-retary, and all the committee were keen and eager to work on behalf of the members. We arranged meetings on as many Saturdays as possible up and down the country, always in a catering department of a college (which took care of our inner needs for the day). The business of meetings (never political) in the early days would consist of experienced teachers talking briefly on how they taught their subject, followed by questions and dis-cussion, backed up by visiting lecturers from City and Guilds and various sectors of industry. The attendance on most Saturdays was around 100, and it was obvious that delegates welcomed the opportunity to listen, question and discuss with colleagues common teaching problems.

I can remember four of us meeting at Gerry Hudswell's house at Henley at 4 a.m. consuming bacon sandwiches and coffee on arrival, then driving in his Humber Hawk to Manchester for a full-day Saturday Conference, and arriving back home around 10 p.m. feeling quite elated at the success of the day's business.

The Association has kept going over the years, continuing not only to serve its members, but also to assist them to help each other. The silver jubilee meeting was held at the Westminster College annexe, Battersea, which formerly housed an institutional management department under Dora Seton. When hotel and catering courses were introduced at Battersea they ran under the headship of John Fuller, who also pioneered the first degree course in hotel management. Subsequently, this department moved to the University of Surrey.

Considering that the Catering Teachers Association has always been run by volunteers, all in full-time teaching posts, I believe it has made a sound, if unspectacular, contribution towards improving the standard of catering education. I am proud to be a member and take considerable pleasure in having been the Association's first chairman and in later years, its first president. Its motto is, 'Those who dare to teach must never cease to learn'.

When Michael was still a baby, I acquired my first car in a rather unusual way. Bill and Addie were friends who lived at South Harrow, and had two sons, Colin and Bobbie. Bill owned a 1939 Morris Eight series E which he kept in good running order, and whenever we met, I would say, half seriously, 'Give me first offer on the car, Bill, if ever you decide to sell.' Bill sadly passed away in middle age when Colin, in his early teens, was going through a phase of mischief and unruly behaviour which increased after his father died. Soon after the funeral, Addie rang up one day in a distraught condition and said, 'Vic! Colin keeps trying to start the car and I'm afraid that he will damage it and injure himself if he should get it going. Bill always said that he would sell the car to you for £100 – please come and take it away and pay whenever you can!'

I arranged to go the following Sunday morning. It was a hot day and John, aged about three-and-a-half, accompanied me. Although I had passed my driving test almost ten years before, fortunately I'd renewed the driving licence. On the way I realised that in those ten years I had only driven a hire-car on two day-trips to the coast, and mentally began to practise car drill.

When we arrived at Addie's, luckily Colin was out. Addie unlocked the garage, handed over the keys and car papers, and thanked me profusely for taking a large load off her mind. John and I climbed in and, needless to say, he was full of excitement and couldn't stop asking questions!

The car started without too much bother, I found what I hoped was reverse gear, pressed the accelerator, slowly eased the clutch, and the engine stalled. This was repeated six times, with John interjecting an unhelpful comment or question each time. The day was hot, the garage was hot, the car was hot, and my face was getting redder and redder! Finally, I realised that if I took the handbrake off it would help matters!

'Why didn't you do that before, Daddy?' piped up John.

I reversed slowly and jerkily onto the road, waved goodbye and we were off. Then I realised that I hadn't made the journey from Wandsworth to South Harrow other than by public transport. We finally arrived home safely to find Letty nursing Michael and keeping Sunday lunch warm, me a nervous wreck and John chattering non-stop telling of our adventures.

The following weekend I gave the car a thorough clean and re-painted the body with Valspar lacquer using a new, soft two-inch brush, taking a little over an hour. Luckily there was no wind to raise dust, the lacquer dried quickly and as a result, more by luck than judgement, a number of people commented on the quality of the paintwork.

At Acton we were always endeavouring to make our courses as realis-tic as possible with regard to industrial practice, never missing opportunities to take on outdoor catering functions either in conjunction with full-time caterers or on our own. One or two lecturers would take parties of students to agricultural shows and various other functions. For a period of seven years a large number of staff and students worked with John and Dorothy Boon, caterers from High Wycombe, on the Royal Household Staff Association Christmas Ball at Windsor Castle. The caterer would send the raw food into college one or two days before, which gave us an excellent opportunity with the students to prepare and dress large joints of ham and beef, as well as tongue, pork, salmon and pies, and a variety of salads and cold sweets for several hundred guests. On the day the food would be transported to the castle by lorry, and the students followed by coach and car.

We would arrive at Windsor early in the afternoon, prepare all the tables (the buffet was in the Throne Room), then take a break for sup-per. The room had to be ready by 9.30 p.m., with all staff looking spick and span, lined up behind the buffet. At 10 p.m., Her Majesty the Queen and members of the royal family would enter slowly and walk along the front of the buffet, occasionally stopping for a word with members of staff, and finally entering the ballroom where an hour's cabaret took place. The students were allowed to observe from an upper gallery overlooking the ballroom.

At 11 p.m. dancing began, guests started to emerge for food and we started carving. Nothing was carved in advance, every joint was freshly cut to each guest's requirement. The service would usually last for two to two-and-a-half hours, and at 2 a.m. we would start to close. Everything had to be cleared, the room cleaned, and all items of glass, crockery and silver washed, dried and packed in boxes. If all went well we would be away by 3 to 3.30 a.m., finally arriving home between 4 and 4.30 a.m.

Towards the end of the 1950s it was decided to change the format of our three-year full-time hotel and catering operations course into a four-year sandwich course pattern, to include 3 four-month periods of industrial release. These three periods came after Easter, year 1 specialising in the kitchen, year 2 in food service and year 3 in front office control and housekeeping. All three periods were to be spent in three different establishments. This was pioneering work, and we experienced some teething problems, but most of the students had sound potential for the industry, adopted sensible and co-operative attitudes and eliminated many of the doubts in the minds of some staff in industry as to the wisdom of the scheme.

Most of the staff and many students subsequently believed this to be one of the best courses ever offered by the school. Not only did it give the students an excellent foundation for their careers, but because many of the staff visited students on the job it gave us the opportunity to meet and cross-exchange views with colleagues in industry, which is always an invaluable exercise for any catering teacher.

For a sound and purposeful education in catering, college and industry must work closely together, each understanding the other's problems. Heads of departments and lecturers of all subjects should visit industry regularly, talk to people in the industry, and keep themselves fully aware of current and potential industrial practice. Colleagues in industry should also be asked into college regularly, invited to see and comment on teaching curricula and to talk to members of staff and students so that they are conversant not only with what is currently being taught, but also how. Students attending colleges where industry is regarded as a partner in the scheme of things will receive a full, practical and meaningful course which should prepare the young person with confidence to enter the industry.

In December 1958, we moved house from Wandsworth to Cranford, and I can remember laying turfs for my front lawn on Boxing Day. The move more than halved my journey to college, which meant a much-appreciated saving of valuable time.

The extension for the new school at Ealing had been approved, and Mary King and Gerry Hudswell were spending a tremendous amount of time in drafting plans, meeting with the architect and making schedules of accommodation and equipment. This time had to be found over and above their normal timetable which was already demanding, and the strain on them began to show. For administrative purposes the school was then transferred from Acton Technical College to Ealing Technical College and, to my surprise, we learned that our new Principal was Dr O. G. Pickard.

I sat in the staffroom one Tuesday, indulging in a grumble about the length of the teaching day on Mondays that term – ten-and-a-half hours in total, with three different classes all in the one training kitchen. The blackboard occupied the width of one wall, and was completely filled with recipes, which meant a wipe clean at the end of each class and rewriting. With demonstrations to organise, and food for student practice to allocate, I virtually had a non-stop day from 8.30 a.m. until 9.15 p.m.

My grumble was aimed at the amount of time wasted on the blackboard and dictation, and I was pleading for someone to write a recipe book suitable for our use. Ron Kinton was in the room at the time, and when I'd finished my moan he said, 'Well, why don't you write one?'

This took me slightly aback and I replied, 'I don't think that I could face all that writing. Basically, I'm idle when it comes to putting pen to paper!'

'Why don't we have a go together then?' he replied.

I thought for a moment and said, 'Why not?' and that was how we started.

Ron Kinton had trained at Westminster, followed by experience at Claridges, and had been a sergeant instructor in the Army Catering Corps during the war. After this he worked at ICI Millbank under two ex-ACC officers – Major Surtees, who was catering manager, and Major Tom Roberts, who was a well-respected chef. Ron left in the 1950s to take the teacher training course at Garnett College, and subsequently joined the school at Acton.

The fact that Ron started at Westminster and that I started as an apprentice in the trade turned out to be a bonus because we had differing opinions on a number of issues which had to be argued out, often to the benefit of the end result. We would each take a small section of work to write up at home, then exchange our papers, comment critically, and on our next meeting would argue, discuss and finally agree. We met at 7 to 7.30 a.m. most mornings before classes started, half or whole days at weekends, and arranged more frequent meetings during holiday periods. In all it look two years.

We approached Mary King to ask if the college could publish, and Mary enquired of the Principal who informed her that there was no money in college budgets for such a purpose. We then went to the library, and after browsing among cookery books, we agreed on one with a style, quality and lay-out that appealed. We wrote to the publishers who invited us to call and see them. When telling the publishers our intention we stressed the fact that it was a teaching book, and we wanted it sold at a price that all students could afford – not more than £1. They asked us to leave our manuscript and said that they would write in due course. We returned to college full of hope.

Some six weeks later we went back, and the publishers informed us that they were prepared to publish the book. They liked it, thought it had housewife appeal, and they intended it to include colour plates and to have a coloured hard cover.

When we asked what the selling price would be and were told £2 10s, we gasped and said, 'That's ridiculous. Students can't afford that, and, with all respect to the housewives, this book has been designed and written for students.'

At which they replied, 'Then we're sorry, but we cannot help you.'

With that, we took our by now weary-looking manuscript (which had been printer proof-corrected), and sadly returned to college where the first person we met was Ella Ramsay, who taught typewriting and shorthand to the reception students. Ella took one look at our long faces, asked us what the problem was and on being told, took our precious manuscript, impeccably typed it out and made two copies.

In the meantime, Ron's father had given us an introduction to Edward Arnold Publishers and following this, we went to see Mr Morgan, the company chairman, a charming man with whom we had a most cordial interview. Once again we stressed the purpose of the book, and even more strongly our views on its selling price. Mr Morgan then asked for an estimate of the number of copies the book might sell in its first year. Here I had the advantage of my background knowledge of the CTA and after considering for a moment I gave a figure of 10 000, in reply to which he gave a slightly quizzical smile and said, 'We will write to you in due course.'

Within a month Edward Arnold agreed to publish *Practical Cookery*, the first edition appearing in 1962 at a price of £1. It was well received and, encouraged by this, we started on a companion book, *The Theory of Catering*. In this we planned to cover all related theory to provide for chefs and cooks following the basic and intermediate City and Guilds courses (which could take four years). The first year sales of *Practical Cookery* were not far short of my estimated figure and we managed to hold the selling price at £1 for almost ten years.

In later years I said to Mr Morgan, 'What did you think of my reply that first day when you asked for an estimate of a sales figure?'

He replied with a smile, 'I thought that you were another pair of authors with a slightly exaggerated opinion of the value of your work!'

In 1974, we suggested to the publisher that we would like to insert some questions after each section of the book and they considered it a good idea, so we started writing and sent in 1 000. They considered this figure excessive but, as we were reluctant to withdraw any, they suggested what we thought was a good idea – a separate book of questions. This was published in 1975 and a similar question book on *The Theory of Catering* appeared the following year. At present, *Practical Cookery* and *The Theory of Catering* are both in their sixth editions and upon reflection, our false start into publishing was due to the fact that in our inexperience we had unknowingly chosen the wrong kind of publisher.

Encouraged by the way our books had been received, other Ealing colleagues followed suit in becoming authors over the next few years, resulting in an impressive list of helpful, well-structured textbooks including *Hotel Reception* by Paul White and Helen Beckley, *Food and Beverage Service* by Dennis Lillicrap, *Vendange* by Andrew Durkan, *Hotel, Hostel and Hospital Housekeeping* by Joan Branson and Margaret Lennox, *Hotel Law* by David Field and *Accounting* by Reginald Simmerson.

We were informed that the new school premises would be completed and ready for the start of a fresh academic year in September. At this good news the staff spent the last week of term, with the help of all the students, packing and transporting a large quantity of teaching and office equipment to Ealing where we were able to store it in class-rooms in the existing building. Then, after a further week of tidying up, we left the Woodlands site for the last time, ready for our summer holiday and looking forward to working in new custom-built premises in September.

Frank Hussey had resigned from Brighton College and purchased a guest-house at Sandown on the Isle of Wight where he proposed to operate a hotel bookkeeper receptionist course and convert the remaining accommodation into self-catering flats. On mentioning this at a CTA council meeting, he said, 'Come on down fellows, and help me get started.' Letty and I were amenable. I booked a flat for Letty and the boys, and we had a splendid holiday which the boys enjoyed so much they wanted to return the following year. We had been joined by her sister Margery, husband Jack and their daughters, Ann and Sally, who were roughly the same ages as John and Michael, and the eight of us finally spent eight consecutive years of happy holidays together, with plenty of fun and laughter and many amusing and fond memories of the island.

During our first year on the island, Paul and Audrey White with Martin and Valerie, took another flat in the house and we occasionally met up on the beach. One hot, sunny day Paul and I and the four children were playing in the waves while Letty and Audrey sat in deckchairs on a comfortably crowded beach looking out to sea. I decided to attempt to stand on Paul's shoulders and was facing the beach at the time, wearing sunglasses and swimming shorts which had an inner tie-cord which were fashionable then. Upon standing up, I almost over-balanced, my sunglasses began to slip off my nose and because I had forgotten to secure the tie-cord inside my shorts, they started to come down!

Three factors registered in a split second – I was facing a fairly large number of people, if my glasses fell off they would probably be lost, and if my shorts came down I would be embarrassed. The shorts did come down, and as I grabbed for, and dropped, my glasses I fell off Paul's shoulders under the waves of the incoming tide. Paul ran out of the water, scampered up the beach and came back wearing a pair of underwater goggles and handed a second pair to me. I put them on, hoisted up my shorts under the water, securely tied them, made half a dozen dives and was fortunate to find the glasses undamaged. As I surfaced and came out of the water everyone started laughing, as it turned out I was wearing a pair of frames without any lenses. As the rest of the party came out of the water laughing their heads off, the interested audience gave a gentle round of applause. One bystander observed that it was the best show she had seen all day, which only served to increase my embarrassment.

At around this time John decided he would like a pet, and plumped for a white rabbit. We went to the pet shop and purchased a snow-white young animal who was instantly christened 'Snowy', complete with a hutch. Returning home, we went to the local hardware shop and purchased sufficient wire to make a pen which we staked out in the back garden ready to be moved every three or four days. John and Michael were getting excited by this time and couldn't wait to see Snowy out of the hutch and in the pen. When he came out, he sniffed around and promptly hopped straight through one of the loops in the wire. We put Snowy back in the hutch and returned to the hardware shop where the shopkeeper smiled when we told him the story and invited me to select more suitable wire.

This time Snowy smartly shuffled out of the hutch towards the wire and hopped over it. By this time, the boys and Letty were in fits of laughter, but at the third attempt I got it right. After a year or so the boys lost interest in Snowy, and I put him on offer at college where he was eagerly snapped up by Gerry Craven for his two young daughters. On his first evening in the new home, Snowy got out of his hutch, found his way into the next garden, and when Gerry's father-in-law came down the following morning, a large part of his prized vegetable plot was lying comfortably inside the stomach of a self-satisfied white rabbit.

By now, the boys were growing up, their toys were getting bigger, requiring more space, and we decided to board a large area in the loft and install a power point on either side so that they could keep the railway track and racing-car circuit permanently in place.

One Sunday morning, about half an hour before lunch-time, I went into the loft to clear the necessary space. Needless to say, John and Michael had to come to 'help'. I was treading carefully onto the beams and issued dire warnings to them to do likewise (otherwise they would be in danger of falling through the ceiling and injuring themselves). At about five minutes to one (lunch was at one o'clock), one of my feet slipped off a beam and crashed through the ceiling. Simultaneously, the other foot followed suit on the other side of the same beam! I landed with a sickening thud, crashing my nether regions onto the beam and causing excruciating pain. For one brief, agonising moment I thought that the drive-shaft of my engine room was permanently damaged.

Letty came flying out of the kitchen exclaiming, 'I was just taking the Yorkshire pudding out of the oven,' and was greeted with the sight of a pair of legs dangling through the ceiling, and an unholy mess of plaster all over the hall floor. John and Michael were expressing the expected degree of sympathy – they were falling about laughing. I managed to extricate my legs with difficulty and clambered down, clutching the pit of my stomach. Letty sat me down in a dazed condition and gave me a brandy. I rested for half an hour, washed my hands, then carved the Sunday roast and we sat down to lunch. Letty and the boys were trying hard to keep the smiles off their faces, but we all ended up having a jolly good laugh and no damage was done other than to the ceiling.

John was a keen member of the local Cub pack, taking part in all activities with great enthusiasm. He arrived home one day to announce that they were holding an iced sponge-cake competition in a few weeks' time, and that Akela (the lady Cub master) had asked if I would be prepared to judge. I agreed, and John then declared that he was going to enter. This I forbade immediately, telling him that it would be unfair for me to judge a competition in which he was a participant, because if he were awarded a prize people might say the judge was biased in favour of his son. Grudgingly and unhappily he accepted this, and I heard no more about it.

On the Saturday morning of the competition I went to the Scout hut to find an assortment of about sixteen sponges at varying stages of 'lift-off', or rise, all lavishly decorated in varying colours with a thick dollop of icing. The competition was sponsored by a brand margarine who also framed the rules which stated that only this margarine could be used in both sponge and icing. I dutifully cut a wedge out of each, and began to feel positively sick at the thought of tasting that amount of icing which, in most cases, was ghastly. However, the discipline of my calling prevailed, I completed the tasting, made the awards, doused my palate with a large mug of tea and watched Akela turn the award-winning plates over to reveal the winners' names.

To my complete surprise, there was John's name on the third prize. He and Letty had arisen early that morning, he had made his sponge, and removed it from the house before I awoke. Initially, I felt slightly embarrassed, but when the story got around everyone enjoyed the joke. I mildly told him off with a twinkle in my eye, but the sponge-cake plot completely fooled me. John's final riposte was that he considered he should have received the first or second prize. Never one for modesty, our John!

Letty had begun to remind me of my throw-away remark in 1942, that as we were unable to have a honeymoon, we would go to Paris on our silver wedding anniversary, so we decided to make plans. Margery and Jack kindly offered to take John and Michael for a week during the Easter break, when Jack took a week off his annual leave. We went without the car and stayed at a modest hotel, the Derby, where we were greeted by a card of welcome, a bottle of champagne and some lovely flowers from Mrs Thomas (who taught at Hendon College) and her husband.

We walked and walked and walked, which is the only way to explore a big city. The weather ranged from snow to sunshine, and we thoroughly enjoyed exploring the French capital, taking in most of the standard tourist sights: Napoleon's Tomb, Notre-Dame, Bobino Music Hall, the *Folies Bergère*, National Museum, Concert Mayol and Versailles, where we were disappointed to find all the splendid rooms cold and bare without a stick of furniture. We particularly liked Montmartre. By the end of a most enjoyable week we felt as though we had walked ourselves to a standstill.

CHAPTER 8

1963-1968

The Ealing Years – Part I

September, and the staff returned to Ealing eager for the start in new, practical accommodation, only to find the builders present with a considerable amount of work still to be completed. The usual excuses for non-completion were given, together with an assurance that the work would be completed by the end of the year. Some of the training kitchens on upper floors were usable, so all the carefully prepared timetables went into the melting pot and it was a case of making the best of a bad job for the first term. At times like this if staff are of the right calibre, co-operate and work together as a team, any set-backs are overcome with ease. Because the school had probably the best group of teaching staff in the country, the term progressed without any major problems.

It was a help for us to all be in the one building, able to keep a day by day watch on the progress of the unfinished work, particularly as half-way through term it was clearly evident that completion was in sight. We went home for the Christmas break confident that in January the whole building would be habitable, as indeed it was.

It was strange at first to be in new and different accommodation but, by and large, a good job had been made of the planning. Because of the narrowness of the building the layout of the training kitchens was not ideal, with storage space for equipment in short supply, but anything was an improvement on the Acton premises.

We were delighted with the main training kitchen and the public training restaurant, which was designed on two levels with a balcony running the length of one side. It also had the advantage of a drinks licence. In the makeshift dining-room at Acton, students had had to go through the charade of serving water out of a collection of wine bottles into the correct glasses.

One idea that in theory appeared sound, but in practice soon led to problems, concerned the siting of the reception counter used for practice by the bookkeeper receptionist course. On entering the public restaurant from the street, there was a small lobby with cloakroom and toilets. In the restaurant area a space about one third of the total was divided off by sliding doors. This contained the teaching reception desk, frequently manned by a group of reception students with a member of staff. It soon became evident that this class hindered the class operating the training restaurant. We persevered for a time trying out different formulas, but in the end it was agreed by all parties to remove and resite the desk in a large class-room.

The training larder was a good size and well situated, with a large walk-in cold room and walk-in deep-freeze. The pastry room was rather small, with two double-decker ovens which backed onto a baker's oven in the bakery section, which had previously been part of Isleworth Polytechnic. There was a second smaller dining-room intended for staff feeding purposes, a science laboratory and an equipment workshop.

A large room for the teaching of housekeeping was equipped to take the various cleaning machines, and the floor had been divided into three different types of surface for comparison purposes. In addition, there were two hotel bedrooms of different layouts, and a lounge in which a wide variety of materials had been used so that ease of cleaning and wear and tear, for example, could be compared.

On the top floor was a refectory for the whole college. It had a manageress and a permanent staff, but every morning one of our practical classes worked in the refectory kitchen with a member of the teaching staff, learning about large-scale budget catering.

On a rota basis over the duration of a course, the aim was to give students tuition and practice in working in the refectory, staff dining-room and public restaurant in order to keep their minds flexible regarding the preparation and service of food at different levels. All catering students, including potential chefs and cooks, spent time on food service and worked in the public training restaurant. We considered it important for those preparing to earn their living by cooking food to understand the problems of serving the customer.

The annual student intake was steadily increasing and Mary King took a great deal of time and trouble interviewing potential students individually, each interview always concluding with a personally conducted tour over the school. Mary was also an active member of the Hotel and Catering Institute Education Committee, and would often return from meetings fuming at the attitude of some industrial members of the committee. A small number believed that catering colleges should concern themselves only with training specifically for certain jobs, and had little patience for anyone with a liberal educational point of view. Although I was never present at any of these meetings, the news soon spread that Mary made a formidable opponent in committee. Mary King commanded great respect at all levels in our field, and it came as no great surprise when she was honoured by being made a Member of the Order of the British Empire for her services to catering education. We on the staff were highly delighted, and we enjoyed a happy time at a celebration party that followed her award presentation.

Even though the school now had adequate practical accommodation, Gerry Hudswell continued to take on outdoor catering jobs, large and small, so that we had more food for the students to handle and they gained benefit from the experience. One weekend, however, he miscalculated, taking on a particularly large job, the food for which came into college on a Friday, had to be ready by midday on Saturday and included 250 lobsters. No students could be made available to assist, and the chef teaching staff were all fully occupied. As a result, Gerry was working flat out in one corner of the main kitchen. Realising that he needed help, six of us volunteered to come in early on Saturday morning to assist. On the Saturday morning we were working away, completely relaxed, when I suddenly remembered a letter that I'd received in my capacity as Chairman of CTA, from Canada. I introduced this into the conversation.

Bracebridge High School near Ontario was starting a catering option for senior students and required a suitably qualified teacher. Gerry, when he heard this, said, 'I've always wanted to go to work in Canada. Could I have the letter?' Without a second thought I agreed, handed it over, and promptly forgot all about it. Gerry made an application, was offered the post and prepared to tender his resignation from Ealing.

At the next CTA national conference held at Birmingham, on conclusion of the day's business, as usual I invited questions on any matter. Louis Klein stood up and in a typically abrasive manner, proceeded to give me a dressing down for passing on a letter containing a job opportunity which, he said, should have been made available to all CTA members. He was absolutely right, but we were friends so there was no animosity in his remarks.

Mary King was happy for Gerry, but disconsolate at the loss to the school, for not only was he her strong, reliable right hand but also his driving force had been a major factor in the success of the school's evolution. When Gerry finally left, Paul White and I assured Mary that between us we would do our best to replace him, and that she should call on us at any time if she required assistance.

Paul and I were both by now principal lecturers and we shared an office on the ground floor of the new block, two floors below Mary's office. Several months passed and it was obvious that the strain of the last few years were taking their toll as Mary looked more and more weary.

One day after lunch Mary entered our room looking desperately tired, and said, 'I'm afraid that I can't go on!'

'Take Mary home in your car,' I said to Paul. 'I'll follow with her car.' With that we took Mary home, where she remained on sick-leave and sadly never returned. (I am happy to record that Mary King, now well past the age of eighty, is in reasonably good health, quite sprightly and living in a house on the Thames at Bourne End.)

Returning to college I reported to Dr Pickard, who said, 'Hand over all your classes and take charge of the school, Victor.'

I replied, 'I'll take over the school, but I must keep one class. It's a City and Guilds Advanced Cookery 152, and they take their final examinations within the next few weeks.'

'You won't be able to cope,' he replied, 'but I'll leave it to you.' I kept the class going somehow, but realised that Dr Pickard had been right. I was never able to find sufficient time to prepare for the class as I wished, and would have numerous interruptions while I was with them, some of which necessitated my leaving the kitchen for long periods of time.

The day following Mary's departure I called a staff meeting to put everyone in the picture, and informed them that our head of department was likely to be away on sick-leave for some considerable time, and that the best way we could help was to keep the school operating as smoothly as possible in her absence. I said that I would do my best to lead the school, apologised for the fact that I was not an administrator by inclination, but with their goodwill and co-operation I felt sure we could manage.

All colleagues were stunned by what had happened for all, without exception, held Mary in the greatest of respect, not only as our head, but also as a friend. This was manifest in the way they reacted and by the tremendous help and co-operation shown to me over the next few months.

Mary had her full quota of sick-leave plus a further extension, but finally the decision was made to retire. Dr Pickard sent for me to say that the post would now be advertised, that I should feel free to apply, but I should not consider that because I had held the position temporarily for almost a year it would automatically be mine. Returning to the office I told Paul what had been said, and asked him if he would be applying for the post. He promptly replied that he wasn't, whereupon I said, 'Well, in that case I may apply,' and went home to give the matter thought.

Once again, my close connections with the CTA came to my assistance and I was able to formulate a fairly shrewd guess as to a likely list of applicants. Having done this I then considered which of them I would be happy to work with as my head of department, and speedily arrived at the answer, which was none of them!

This left me in a quandary. I had missed the class-room and training kitchen contact with students over the past few months, and did not really want to forgo that for the rest of my career in education. Having prematurely stopped my own schooling because I did not want to spend my life behind a desk, I was facing a decision that might cause me to do just that for the next twenty years.

Finally, because I had gained a great deal of satisfaction from the time spent since 1951, because all my colleagues on the staff had given such help and support over the last year, and because I could not stomach the fact of someone else coming in from outside to take over the school (which by now had built up a fine reputation), I submitted an application.

Two weeks after the closing date for applications, Dr Pickard telephoned down and asked me to go and see him. 'Victor,' he said, 'why have we only received one application for the post other than yours? This is now considered to be one of the plum jobs in catering education.'

I replied, 'I'm not a mind reader, and can't possibly answer that question, but I'll give you a calculated guess, for what it's worth. The catering education field is comparatively small, and many of us teaching in it have a great deal in common by virtue of our industrial background which tends to make us a close-knit community. My guess is that many of those who would under normal circumstances have applied for the position have said to themselves "Victor has held down the job for almost a year, he is well established at Ealing and it should be his job, so good luck to him!" '

Dr Pickard gave a grunt and muttered one or two non-committal remarks. Seven days later I was offered, and accepted, the post. This was now 1963. I invited my colleagues to join me for a celebratory drink, arranged for two jereboams of Lanson Black Label champagne, and the beginning of my headship was well and truly launched.

John had left Cranford School on the advice of the headmaster, and entered Latymer Upper School, Hammersmith, to be followed three years later by Michael. They were both fairly indifferent to academic study and developed the knack of doing the minimum amount of work necessary to get by. When it came to the athletic field, that was a different matter, and they both developed into keen competitors. John had never been interested in soccer, played rugby at school and spent a great deal of time behind the scenes at the annual Jantaculum and other

Guild productions. Michael was a keen and able soccer player, but the school's policy was for all soccer players to play rugby for the first six weeks and vice versa with rugby players. After six weeks they could make their own choice. When Michael was given this order, he came home in a belligerent, rebellious mood stating that he was not going to play that stupid game and that I would have to speak to the games master. He received short shrift from me and was ordered to do as he was told. We didn't hear much about the game after that, and I felt fairly certain that he would revert to soccer when his six weeks were up. To my surprise he not only continued with rugby, but developed into a useful player, playing for the school team year by year up to the first fifteen when in the sixth form. Although I did not understand the finer points of the game, I always went to see the boys play home and away matches, sometimes with them playing in different teams on adjoining pitches.

Letty and I went annually to sports day and gained tremendous pleasure from seeing them both perform so ably. John usually managed to lead the field home in the 400 metres, and one year Michael broke a long-standing school record for the triple jump by a sizeable distance, and we came home very pleased. Parents' evening was another story. We would attend once a year to hear a brief address by the headmaster following which parents circulated among subject teachers to receive first-hand verbal accounts of their offspring's progress. By and large, this was a miserable evening, and we grew weary of the much repeated phrase which was the theme for almost all the reports: 'If only he would work and use his potential, he could do well!'

I returned home most years feeling fed-up, and it would take several days to shake off the bad mood. Friends all said, 'You worry too much, Vic. It will all work out in the end, and worrying about it or nagging them won't make a scrap of difference.' Easier said than done. What really frustrated me, I suppose, was the fact that I seemed to be able to encourage my students to achieve results up to their capabilities but not my own sons.

When John was coming up to his O-level year I'd enquired of his form master what his likely chances of success were and the possibility of his taking A levels to follow. His reply was that I shouldn't worry about A levels, as he was not likely to achieve O-level results to warrant a sixth-form place. That cheered me up no end! In desperation, I offered John a sum of money for each O-level pass he gained, adding that if his form master was correct in his assessment, I wouldn't be paying out very much.

At college, with the added confidence of now being confirmed in the headship post, I tackled the job with renewed energy and vigour. Paul White made an excellent deputy because, although we shared the same wish for the school – to make it into one of the best in the country – we disagreed on a number of matters of policy. This meant we had to discuss and argue many decisions before their implementation and as a result, most policy matters had a sound foundation.

Paul had started his career at the Hotel School, Lausanne, and on completion of the course returned to England to become a J. Lyons management trainee. In those days, the training standards of J. Lyons were considered to be among the best in the country. Trainees invariably commenced their kitchen and restaurant stages at the Trocadero, Shaftesbury Avenue, which was a high quality restaurant. Paul moved around gaining further experience, served in the RAF during the war and gained the DFC with distinction. Before being appointed to the school in 1951, he was working in catering management at the House of Commons. We had completely different backgrounds, and this was another bonus when we sat to discuss school matters, for it gave us a wider experience to draw upon.

One of the problems the school had always faced was that of servicing teachers for subjects such as science, accounting, economics, law and building maintenance and services. In the early days at Acton, a science teacher would come from the science department making little or no attempt to relate his subject to the industry, and consequently boring the students to tears. We gained the impression that they considered it an affront to their dignity to be asked to teach students of catering. As a result, our students received lessons in pure science with its numerous formulae, most of which went straight over their heads.

Mary King had made a start by recruiting a well-qualified young lady teacher of science who was enthusiastic and prepared to examine other parts of the curriculum in order to relate her subject. She would also spend time in practical classes to observe students working. As a result, she was not only able to teach students important principles related to their favourite studies, but also gained confidence herself which she imparted to her classes, resulting in good class-room communication.

With Dr Pickard's approval we now started to recruit our own specialists to the school staff, and made good appointments in the fields of law, economics and accounting. Building maintenance and the services of gas, electricity and water remained a problem. It seemed logical to enlist the part-time teaching help of specialists from the gas and electricity companies and the water board, but they were usually far too technical in their respective subjects and endeavoured to teach at too great a depth.

In desperation, I rang the head of Hammersmith College of Building, explained the problem and he immediately replied, 'You need someone who has had architectural training.' He recommended one of his own part-time teachers who was able to assist for a term. After his first class I deliberately stood outside the class-room as the students emerged and followed them down the corridor. As they were discussing the lecture and talking with interest about what had been covered in class, this told me what I needed to know. As a result we appointed, in due course, a full-time teacher with an architectural background.

An excellent young law teacher, David Field, was recruited, and he so took to our work and the students that he produced an excellent textbook. Then followed a sound appointment in economics, Paul Lock, and much to my surprise and pleasure, I found him one evening in a City and Guilds cookery class, which he successfully completed. He had enrolled as a student in order to find out more about the class and the work of the industry. Dr Pickard continued to be supportive and against strong protests from his vice principal, he allocated the school a few senior posts over and above our establishment entitlement.

I was now spending a considerable amount of time interviewing potential students, initially following Mary King's lead by seeing every applicant and parent individually, although before long this had to be delegated to course directors, for with the continuing increase in applicants it became too time consuming. At first I interviewed the prospective student with the parents, but soon found that a number of well-meaning parents tended to dominate the proceedings. As a result parents were requested to join for the second part of the interview, which gave a better opportunity to get to know the young person. We looked at three things on interview: previous school report, qualifications, and personal attributes with regard to suitability for the industry, the latter, in my view, being the most important.

Two lads from the same school were on interview as potential craft students. Their previous school report was poor and, without putting it in so many words, said, 'Don't accept these two, they have never worked and have frequently been the cause of trouble.'

All prospective students received a tough 'putting off the industry' talk, leaving them in no doubt that unless they were prepared to work hard, accept discipline which must be developed into self-discipline, and be prepared for the possibility of long, unsocial hours, this college (and certainly the catering industry) was no place for them.

The more I talked to the two lads the more interested they became and they eventually joined the course. They developed so rapidly that at the end of the first term both sets of parents came to see us expressing surprise and pleasure at the change in their offspring since September. This was not an isolated case, as we had many similiar examples over the years. In the majority of cases it appeared that students had found little to interest or motivate them in their previous schooling. (Most of the catering craft students came from local secondary modern schools.)

A large number of applicants for management courses came from the public schools. I remember one pleasant lad whose father was a grammar school headmaster. He was terribly concerned at the career his son had chosen and, although meticulously polite, it was obvious that he did not consider the catering industry had sufficient standing to be suitable for his son. 'What can he possibly do in the industry?' he asked plaintively. The young man, David Clarke, turned out to be a model student and has made a successful career as a hotel manager.

A desperate father arrived one day with his son who had a poor school record, and had only achieved two indifferent O-level passes. At that time the external validating body of this particular course required entrants to possess a minimum of three O-level passes, one of which had to be English language. The parent pleaded for a chance for his son, and on pointing out that the lad lacked the required entry qualifications he looked so wretched that I gave the son a rigorous interview. Against the rules he was accepted, provided that he re-took and passed his O-level English within nine months. The boy repaid our faith with interest, successfully passing his O level at the next attempt and all the course examinations, finally emerging with the 'Best Student of the Year' award in the final year. Michael Franks, son of Manny Franks, is now successfully established in restaurant management in California.

We always encouraged potential students to gain employment in the industry for as long a period of time as possible before starting their course. Experience clearly showed that those who had previously worked in the industry displayed more motivation and confidence and made better students to teach because, having sampled the industry first hand, this double-checked their initial ideas of a career and they knew where they were going.

If I could have my way I would insist that no one be allowed to start on a course in preparation for the catering industry without having previously worked in that industry for a reasonable period of time, at least six to eight weeks, and preferably longer.

One of the most successful, yet regretfully short-lived, courses started in Mary King's time was a Dietetics Diploma approved by the British Dietetics Association. The three-year full-time course aimed to produce a well-qualified dietician with some practical knowledge and experience of commercial professional cookery and was taught by one of the school lecturers. An excellent team of staff was recruited, all highly qualified in their respective fields, and the course director, an ex-hospital dietician from one of London's leading hospitals, led with dedication and sincerity of purpose. The quality of students was high, and everyone approved of the type and quality of person emerging from the course.

Unfortunately, the course director, who dealt with the students completely satisfactorily, displayed attitudes with her teaching colleagues that caused resentment, distress and embarrassment. When these same attitudes began to extend to the administrative staff the situation became worse. The course was offered for several years, but in spite of a great deal of effort by many concerned, the situation finally came to an unpleasant head and the course ceased.

Although relieved at the cessation because of the stress and aggravation caused I felt sorry at the loss of what could have been a most rewarding course that produced ideal personnel for the dietetics profession. It was sad to learn, several years later, that an almost identical situation had developed and was terminated with even more distressing consequences at a college in the north under the same course director.

One aspect of the headship that took me a long time to adjust to was the number of committees I had to attend and the hours they took. The college academic board was the largest and meetings would sometimes last for three to four hours. The academic board also had several sub-committees: there was a school board of studies, course committees, examination boards and a weekly heads of schools' meeting.

Once a month following the heads' meeting, we would adjourn for lunch in the public training restaurant and I usually slipped into the kitchen before the meeting to enquire what was on the menu. One day I was informed that braised oxtail was available. Did I think that the heads would like it? I quickly assented, as this is one of my favourite dishes provided that it is well cooked and removes easily from the bones. Our meeting concluded, we adjourned for lunch, consumed the first course (I dislike the term 'starter') with relish, and sat back sipping Jake Drew's home-made rose-petal wine awaiting the main course. (Jake Drew was Head of the School of Art.)

From the kitchen came the piping hot dishes of oxtail, and my gastric juices started flowing as soon as the dish lids were removed. Sitting opposite me at table was John Kenney, Head of the Management School, a quiet, gentle, charming man. As the portion of oxtail was put on his plate I noticed a look of horror on his face. He looked at his plate a second time, glanced over, and whispered, 'What is it Victor?'

'Oxtail, John!' I replied, with the pride of someone who has bestowed a valued gift on a friend.

'I'm afraid that I can't eat it, I am so sorry,' he replied.

I realised how unthinking I had been in agreeing to that particular dish for lunch without consulting my fellow heads in advance. A speedy acceptable replacement was served and lunch progressed smoothly.

Our inveterate teller of tales, Syd Matthews, Head of the Photography School, inevitably had a story for the occasion. A rather pompous dowager duchess, on being served braised ox tongue, declared in haughty tones 'Disgusting, I am not going to eat anything that came out of an animal's mouth! Take it away and fetch me a boiled egg instead.'

Once a year, heads of schools presented their budget proposals to a number of the college governors and a representative from the borough treasurer for approval. Each head spoke in turn, answered questions, and items were either approved, amended or deleted. Observing the two heads who spoke before me I realised that this was a type of sparring match of which I had no previous experience. As a result, when it came to my turn, the first sum of money that was questioned I promptly offered to reduce by a half. Whereupon one of the college governors said with a smile, 'Steady on, Victor. Don't give way too quickly!' I was grateful for his intervention, rapidly learnt the rules of the game, and found this to be an interesting session in subsequent years.

The reputation of the school and its public training restaurant continued to grow, as a result of which I would receive many telephone calls from a variety of organisations, large and small, enquiring whether they could book a function. We would accept as many as could be fitted into the curriculum, endeavouring to take a wide variety in order to further the students' experience.

Many callers would enquire if I was the catering manager, the banqueting manager or the head waiter. Other calls requested a drinks extension until midnight, wanted to know whether there was room for dancing, and could we supply a cabaret? It became clear that in organising the working of the training restaurant closely to an industrial pattern we were being regarded as a fully commercial operation. Most people were by now referring to the room as 'the restaurant', and after lunch one day I received a caller from the *Good Food Guide* indicating that they wished to insert the restaurant in the next edition of their book. Would I agree? I replied that although it was gratifying to hear of so much praise for the students' efforts, nevertheless we could not and would not guarantee that the standard would remain constant. The only way that might be possible was if the teaching staff did the work with the students assisting, and we did not run our classes on those lines. In spite of my remarks, the restaurant was inserted in the next edition where it remained for one year only, being removed the following year, which I considered made my initial point!

We then decided to do something about the name of the room, formed the inevitable sub-committee, and fairly speedily resolved to call the training restaurant 'The Mary King Room', a solution which was received with acclaim throughout the college. At the same time, we had a suitable message explaining the aims and method of working in both the room and the main training kitchen printed on cards. These we would periodically put on tables at meal times and, by and large, this did the trick.

In the mid-sixties the vice principal spent a few weeks in the United States on a study tour of American hotel schools. On return, in his report, he highly praised Cornell and Professor Matthew Bernatsky, who was subsequently invited to spend a sabbatical term with us at Ealing. Matthew was the son of a professor of botany from the university at Budapest, who had decided to make a career as a chef. Following considerable experience on the continent and in the United States he was appointed to the hotel school at Cornell, where he became an esteemed member of staff. Matthew was an interesting man and a good lecturer, and our students benefited by gaining an insight into the American approach to food and beverage operation.

Matthew and his wife, Helen, were keen collectors of old china, and would spend time at weekends rummaging down Portobello Road and other markets. Letty and I took them on a visit to Apsley House at Hyde Park Corner, the home of the Duke of Wellington, where they thoroughly enjoyed seeing the displays of china and many other items of historical interest.

Within a year of Matthew's return to the States we received visits by two more professors from American hotel schools, Donald Lundberg from Massachusetts and Lew Minor, President of the Minor Food Corporation and a part-time visiting professor at Michigan State University. Lew Minor had made a detailed study of food flavours as a mature student, and had been awarded a Ph.D. for his work on chicken flavour. I was later given the opportunity to read some of his papers, and found them fascinating. It was some time after graduating that Lew established the Food Factory at Cleveland, Ohio, where food bases made from natural ingredients were produced, and it developed into a highly successful business.

From the outset, Lew introduced his products to chefs of good standing who were so impressed that they would often give demonstrations using them. Lew was a shrewd man, and when well-known chefs retired, he would invite them to act as sales representatives for his products, which obviously gave the advantage of chef selling to chef. Lew and I had a good rapport during his short visit to London, and when he returned home we both expressed the wish for future meetings.

In 1967, Dr Pickard started talking about the possibility of my taking a degree, and suggested that I applied to Cornell for a Masters course. The idea of returning to intensive study at my age did not appeal, and I reacted strongly against the suggestion on several grounds. Once Dr Pickard got an idea into his head, however, he was like a terrier and never gave up, continually coming back to the attack with fresh arguments. I continued to express many points of concern, the chief of which was that I did not believe that I could cope. 'Nonsense, Victor!' he would reply. 'At least make an attempt.'

Finally, against my better judgement, I submitted an application to Cornell and was highly delighted and amused to be able to show Dr Pickard the letter in reply. This stated that as I did not possess a first degree, I could not be considered for a Masters degree. Dr Pickard's response was to give a characteristic grunt and say, 'Then you had better try Michigan State University!'

This I proceeded to do quite cheerfully, fully believing that I would receive a similar reply. Instead, the answering letter offered me a place on an MBA course commencing September 1968. Michigan were prepared to accept my experience as equivalent to a first degree. This was followed a few weeks later by a request to teach a course on quantity food production two mornings a week for the Bachelors degree programme.

Letty and I went to the boys' school for a chat with the headmaster who gave his permission for a year's absence, adding that he thought a year in school in the States would be a good educational experience for them. Furthermore, he said they would probably find that they were ahead in study compared to similar age groups over there. It was an assessment that was later shown to be correct.

Paul White readily agreed to take over the school during my absence. We put up the house for a year's let, and were fortunate to find four young male student teachers from Borough Road Teacher Training College to take it on for the twelve months. It was only by a chance remark from a neighbour on our return that we learned that six, not four, young men had taken up residence!

I wrote to Henry Barbour, head of the hotel school at Michigan, asking for more detail about the food course I had been asked to teach before accepting the offer. By return I received a detailed set of lesson notes and an accompanying textbook entitled *Quantity Food Production*, by Lendal Kotschevar. There was also a large number of slides to accompany the lectures. Kotschevar, probably the most prolific writer on catering education (known as 'hospitality' education in the States), had also prepared and taught the course, but he was leaving Michigan State in the summer and the course was required to be taught for one more year, hence my invitation. After studying the course material I mentally decided to use about two-thirds, and to inject some European thinking for the balance, and wrote back to accept the offer.

In the spring of 1968 I came home one day to hear Letty's account of a talk given on television by someone inviting ordinary men and women from all walks of life to apply for appointments as magistrates. Initially, I veered against the idea because of the time I thought it would take, being already fairly heavily involved with committee work outside of college, such as the HCI council and education committee and City and Guilds advisory and syllabus sub-committees. I then began to think of the Juvenile bench, that I might be able to help, and with that in mind submitted an application. Subsequently, I was called for a fairly stringent interview, and then awaited the result. The American trip intervened and I wrote to the committee who requested me to submit a fresh application on return from the United States.

Summer term 1968 ended, I handed over to Paul, and we then set about preparations for the trip. Visits to the American Embassy in Grosvenor Square were undertaken to obtain visas which allowed us to remain in America for 365 days only. I obtained an international drivers licence, and we bought two large luggage bags as the advice we had received on what temperatures to expect was extreme humid heat in summer and extreme cold in winter.

We'd booked our holiday on the Isle of Wight in August 1967, and decided to continue with the plans. It turned out to be a good summer, an enjoyable, happy, relaxed vacation, and I returned home feeling very fit, well and in AI condition. We completed final arrangements for the trip, and with considerable difficulty, squeezed our clothes into the travel bags and six cases.

At last we were ready. The house was handed over, and our parish priest, Father Moore, came along with the church minibus to drive us to Heathrow and give us his blessing for a successful visit.

We finally climbed aboard the BOAC Super VC10 which was only part full for the flight. John and Michael were jumping around in great excitement, and could not believe their luck when they were allowed on the flight deck. *Au revoir* England until September 1969!

CHAPTER 9

1968–1969

East Lansing, Michigan, USA

After an uneventful flight we landed at Boston for health check clearance, and flew on to Detroit, where we changed planes for the final leg of the journey to Lansing, the capital of the state of Michigan. The departure gates at Detroit were laid out in a huge circle, and as we emerged into the main concourse laden with hand luggage, we uncomfortably realised our clothes were too thick and heavy for the temperature and humidity.

We checked on the flight gate number, and set off around the circle with about ten minutes in which to catch the local plane. After walking for five minutes or so, it appeared that we had set off the wrong way around the circle, and whether we continued on, or went back, the distance to go was about the same. With only five minutes to flight departure we started hurrying, finally arriving at the check-in desk two minutes late, feeling very hot and bothered. Fortunately, the plane had been held, and as we emerged from the departure gate, twenty yards away we saw an ancient-looking, four-engined propellor-driven plane. Michael took one look at it and piped up in a loud voice, 'We're not flying in that, are we?' The engines were revving up and the plane appeared to be shaking and creaking – it was a marked contrast to the Super VC10 and his remark, although embarrassing, was understandable. Hurriedly, we scrambled on board feeling self-conscious at all the curious stares that were being cast our way, and flopped into four vacant seats.

John and Michael sat the opposite side of the aisle with seats facing two American gentlemen. In no time at all, they were chatting away to the boys, showing considerable interest in the trip and in England in general. It was a short flight, only 100 miles, and as we neared our destination one of the Americans said to Michael, 'My son has a bike that is too small for him, would you like it?' Michael beamed and said that he would. 'I will bring it round for you in the next day or so,' was the reply.

He was as good as his word, calling the next afternoon with a bike in very good condition that Michael made full use of during our stay. That was the first of many kindnesses shown to us over the next twelve months.

Lew Minor was at the airport and had arranged to take us to his home to meet Ruth, his wife, some members of the family, and one or two friends. Feeling somewhat travel-weary we would sooner have gone to our apartment but couldn't possibly refuse his kind hospitality. Lew's home was at one time the farmhouse of Ruth's parents, a large, rambling, comfortable property set in spacious grounds. Everyone was very hospitable. We chatted for ages and finally sat down to a splendid dinner that Ruth had prepared. By this time we were all famished because it was now the equivalent of 3 a.m. English time. Home-grown corn on the cob appeared and we tucked in, Michael demolishing four, much to the amusement and pleasure of Ruth Minor. This was followed by a tasty dish of braised beef with a good selection of vegetables, and dessert. Finally, at about 4.30 a.m. UK time, Lew said, 'I'll drive you to your apartment,' which was one of a block of twelve, married-student apartments on the edge of the university campus in Cherry Lane.

It was a short drive, and Lew helped us with the baggage up to our accommodation on the first floor. Everywhere was in pitch darkness, and none of the lights worked; with the aid of a torch we found that all the light sockets were without bulbs. Further investigation showed there was no bed linen, pillows, crockery or cutlery. The flat contained three beds and mattresses, a dining-room table with four chairs, a couch with two easy chairs, and an electric stove. Lew rang Ruth who immediately gathered together a car full of the necessary items to start us off, and drove over.

We soon settled down after that, and Lew and Ruth left saying that they would be around first thing in the morning to take me to a second-hand car dealer, as a car was essential. With that, we went to bed and slept like logs.

The flat was fairly spartan, but adequate, consisting of two bedrooms, kitchen-diner, toilet and shower. Letty and I knew that money was going to be tight and had decided to take the cheapest accommodation possible so that if there was any spare money we could use it to explore the country. We took this view as this was our first trip to the United States, and might well be the last!

The next morning, Lew and a friend drove me to the second-hand car lot where I wandered up and down looking for the smallest car I could find amongst a large variety of huge American models. In 1968 most Americans were still driving large cars, but I finally settled on the smallest car in the lot, a six-cylinder Plymouth Valiant with automatic transmission and power-assisted steering.

I returned to the apartment to collect Letty and the boys, and we drove over to the supermarket about a quarter of a mile away where we shopped and stocked up the larder. It was a smallish, private store with about six check-outs, owned by Bob and Evelyn Scheffel. At each check-out was a young lad who bagged the groceries, took them out to your car, and deposited them either in the 'trunk' or inside the car.

We then learned that there was a central store on campus run by volunteers in which was collected all unwanted household effects acquired as students moved out on completion of their studies. We made a most profitable trip to this store, and again, we found everyone very interested that we came from England and very helpful. By lunch-time we had everything we needed to make ourselves comfortable, including curtain material Letty had bought, made up and hung at the window.

Paint, rollers and brushes were available free of charge for those wishing to redecorate, and we decided to take advantage of this. In a temperature of 100 °F, clad only in a pair of shorts, I redecorated the apartment using a roller, while Letty filled in with a brush. The apartment began to feel like home. For the finishing touch, Letty placed a vase of gladioli in the window.

Behind the apartment block was a launderette and a fresh milk dispensing machine. In between was a stretch of grass, trees and shrubs, out of which chipmunks frequently popped. We would sometimes find Michael, quiet as a mouse, flat on his stomach a yard or so away from a hole, waiting patiently with his camera for the fascinating little creatures to pop out.

Our eleven sets of neighbours in the block included students from Canada, Germany, Italy and Argentina, and in almost every case they were studying for a Ph.D. Their children were very young (all under school age), and their homes, without exception, all had a barbecue outside on which most of the cooking was done during the hot evenings.

As classes didn't begin for a few days we took time to explore the campus, and were most impressed with what we found. Michigan State University started out life as an agricultural college, expanding steadily over the years. By 1968 it occupied a huge spacious site housing 40 000 students and approximately 10 000 teaching, administrative and support staff. All the university buildings were on one campus, which was well landscaped with large areas of grass, shrubs and trees, making it a most pleasant area to work in and stroll around. The Red Cedar river ran through the campus and the whole area was in East Lansing, a suburb of Lansing, the capital city of Michigan. The state of Michigan is larger in area than Great Britain, but its population is smaller than that of London.

Walking around the campus you could not help but envy the amount of space everywhere. During our year, ample space was available for a massive new building to house the main administration of the whole university in the centre of the campus, which was started and completed, with sweeping lawns, trees and shrubs, before we left.

The sports facilities were impressive, and because the usual severe winter, with temperatures well below freezing, could last for four to five months, ample provision was made for both indoor and outdoor pursuits.

The football stadium had a capacity of 76 000, all seated, and was only used for five matches per season. The playing surface was of immaculate Kentucky blue grass, and no one was ever allowed on it outside the annual five-match schedule. After the 1968–69 season the turf was removed and replaced with an all-weather surface. The outdoor athletics track was used from April to June, and the indoor, known as Jenison Field House, from January to March. There were baseball and soft-ball fields; rows of outdoor tennis courts (as well as numerous indoor courts); an Olympic-sized outdoor pool and three indoor pools; soccer, rugby, hockey and lacrosse pitches; halls for basketball, squash, badminton and other racquet games; an ice-hockey stadium and a general skating rink. In fact, I cannot think of a single sport that was not catered for, and each had excellent provision, as the American takes his sport seriously.

The students' union building also had a large hall, with twelve pool tables, four full-sized tables for billiards or snooker, and one continental-type table without pockets.

It was now time to consider schools for the boys. Lansing High School was about three miles away, and students were bussed in by a fleet of yellow school coaches. Lew had warned us that incidences of drug taking had been reported, but we arranged for an interview between the school admissions tutor and John.

We were cordially received, had a satisfactory interview, and decided that John should attend. The decision was made that he would start in a class of his own age group, but it was soon established that he was way ahead of them in his studies. This resulted in his being moved up two classes and put with pupils two years older, and he fitted in quite well at this level.

Michael, we felt, was rather young for this environment, and it was arranged for him to attend Red Cedar School on campus, which was within walking or cycling distance. There were forty-two different nationalities of pupil, and he was in the top class, but so far ahead of the rest of the class that he really had an easy time for his year. Bearing in mind his age and what the headmaster at Latymer had said, we weren't too worried.

Two amusing incidents occurred at Michael's school. On the first occasion, he came home one day to announce that the history of the American War of Independence was considerably different to what he had learned at Hammersmith. Furthermore, he had told his teacher this. The good lady came home to see us, we had a pleasant meeting, and as a result, sent home for a copy of the history book used at Latymer in order to acquaint her with the British version of the facts.

On the second occasion, local television were filming a programme at the school and the interviewer introduced 'young Mike from England' and then proceeded to ask him question.

'What do you think of the soccer played here in America?'

'Not much,' came the reply. 'You don't understand the rules!'

Once again, we sent home for a book, this time on the rules of Association Football.

We were settling in quite well by now, and were impressed by the degree of fondness that so many Americans had for England and the English way of life. Many strangers, hearing our accent, would come up with smiles, introduce themselves and chat away in a most friendly fashion.

The weather was hot and humid, and everyone dressed in light, casual clothes at almost all times. During our next visit to the supermarket John asked Bob Scheffel whether he could have a job as a 'bagger'. Bob said that he was too young and would have to wait until his birthday in February.

Just along from the supermarket were two very busy food take-away and delivery stores; one sold huge pizzas of about twelve inches in diameter with a large variety of toppings, and the other, French bread sandwiches known as 'torpedoes'. These ranged in size from six to eighteen inches, and were usually packed with a large quantity of assorted fillings. By now we were beginning to realise that many things in America were big!

The main street in East Lansing ran along one side of the campus for about a mile and consisted chiefly of shops, offices and banks. When we walked into the ice-cream parlour and saw the long list of mouthwatering flavours on the board, the boys' eyes popped out. With such a warm, humid atmosphere Americans consume large quantities of ice cream, and we were all most impressed by the quality of the product. The American ice-cream parlour had not yet made the inroad into Britain, so this was an eye-opener to us.

The drug store sold medicines and a wide variety of other goods, and we often saw a preview of patterns which would emerge in England years later. We were not impressed with American 'candy', or sweets, and noticed that the few items of British confectionery were popular and quickly sold out. The bank was most efficient, open from nine to five daily and Saturday mornings, a practice we envied when comparing it with the home counterpart. The cinema had the indispensable popcorn machine in the foyer which worked flat out before performances. Americans love popcorn and expect it to be freshly popped to order, and many eat it unsweetened with melted butter. On one visit to the cinema I stood watching this machine for a few moments, quite fascinated. A patient queue waited at the counter, hot popcorn was scooped into large bags, topped with a generous ladle of warm, melted butter and handed to the customer who would help himself to a serviette from the counter and proceed into the darkness of the cinema. I couldn't help but think of the effect of all those greasy fingers!

Letty and I had invitations to two evening receptions, one given by the President of the University and Board of Trustees for incoming members of the faculty, and the other given by the Dean of the College of Business. These were two pleasant, interesting evenings at which we were surprised to find only non-alcoholic drinks being served. We later learned that East Lansing and the university campus was a 'dry' area. Alcohol could, however, be purchased in down-town Lansing.

All Christian denominations were amply provided for on the campus, and we became regular attenders at the nine forty-five mass at St John's student parish church on Sundays. The church was large, with an equally large basement into which the service would be relayed if the church was full. Seven masses were held on Sundays, four on weekdays and three on Saturdays. The church and basement were always packed at nine forty-five, which was a sung mass with guitar accompaniment, and all the hymns enthusiastically sung by the congregation were of the modern swinging idiom. Although the service faithfully followed the ritual of the mass, the priest often spoke informally during his sermon, involving the congregation where appropriate, and it was not unusual to hear peals of laughter ringing out. We all enjoyed the service and were impressed by the degree of student participation and their attitude as a whole.

Immediately after mass we would dash for the car and make the short drive to have breakfast at the Kellogg Centre where orders were taken up to 11 a.m., usually making it with five minutes to spare. The Kellogg Centre for Continuing Education had been designed as a large teaching block, combined with hotel accommodation and a restaurant, for use by students of the School of Hotel, Restaurant and Institutional Management (HRIM). Here we received our first introduction to the American breakfast, with pancakes or waffles served with whipped butter and maple syrup, streaky bacon so crisp that if you put a knife to it, it would shatter into pieces, French toast and sweet rolls. The coffee was always good. We would make a hearty breakfast and then usually ate only one other meal during the day at about 5.30 to 6 p.m.

I had by now found my way to the School of HRIM, met Henry Barbour, the head of department, been allocated an office and received full instruction regarding both the teaching of the quantity foods course and my degree requirements.

I was very happy with the arrangements and information for the course I was to teach, particularly as I had a graduate assistant to help. The university course information was contained in a large, thick book which listed every course offered, together with the various degree requirements. I found the sheer size and volume of information quite fascinating. A four-term year operated, but not every course operated in each term. High demand courses would be offered three or four times a week, each given by a different professor. Each student made up his own timetable and had access to a student counsellor for advice and guidance. Every course carried a number of credits which the student could only carry forward if, on completion of that course, a sufficiently high grade had been given by the professor.

The numerical requirements for an MBA consisted of a certain number of credits which, in total, also had to have an average above a minimum grade-point level, the grading scale being from 0–5. The course requirements for the MBA consisted mainly of courses which were mandatory, plus a smaller number of courses which could be chosen from any course offered in any school of the university.

I had a useful session with my counsellor who indicated the varying degrees of difficulty of each course, making a special point of saying, 'Leave QBA [quantitative business analysis] to the last term. That one's a killer!'

Lew Minor popped his head into my room to ask how I was getting on and when he realised what I was doing he sat down and said, 'Victor, if I was you, I would consider just sitting-in on the various classes. Don't put yourself under the pressures that attempting to achieve grade points will give.' I thanked him for his kind, well-meaning advice and thought long and hard about it.

At this time I was feeling very fit, thoroughly enjoying the American experience, and fully realised what a world of opportunity, experience and knowledge was available to me over the next few months. I could not see myself being sufficiently motivated to merely sit-in and take notes on such a large number of classes, and didn't consider it fair to my employing authority at Ealing, or my colleagues at home. So I decided 'in for a penny in for a pound', and prepared for student enrolment.

Student enrolment took place over five full days in a number of buildings and halls. We were required to attend alphabetically on a special day, and it took several hours to pass through the various stages of administration, for which a small army of people were recruited. On the advice of my counsellor, I had prepared an outline timetable of preferred courses, days and times, and was curious to see how the massive jigsaw fitted together. To my surprise, almost all my preferences fitted in first time. Two needed an alteration in times and days, but this was easily dealt with. I chose courses in the College of Education for my free choice.

All foreign students were required to attend an interview to test their understanding and use of the English language. I duly presented myself in front of a young man who spoke with a slight accent. After talking for two minutes he smiled and said, 'We are in the wrong seats. You should be here instead of me!'

In and out of halls and buildings I went, receiving various identity cards and related information and, at long last, feeling decidedly hot and weary, came to the final bay which was the taking of a 'mug shot' for the student identification card. The picture showed more clearly than any words how I was feeling by that time – hot, harassed and weary. So, all was set for the start of the term.

On the last Saturday before classes began, the first football match of the season was played – Michigan State Spartans versus Syracuse Orangemen – and acting on advice from Lew I had booked seats early. In accordance with tradition, this was also Band Day, which meant that in addition to MSU's 180-strong marching band, marching bands from thirty-six Michigan high schools, 3 600 young musicians in all, would be marching on and off the pitch. This was a most impressive spectacle which began at 11.30 a.m., each band marching on individually for a two-minute performance. It was interesting to note that one band came from Chelsea, Michigan. After listening on numerous occasions back home to the jeers, hoots and catcalls given to the playing of our national anthem, the contrast when, at half-time, the combined bands played 'March America', 'America the Beautiful' and 'Battle Hymn of the Republic' was noticeable. The whole audience of 76 000 rose and sang along with the bands.

I had been told that this was a family day out, and, indeed, it was. Popcorn stands were furiously popping corn non-stop, and hotdogs, hamburgers and torpedoes were consumed in quantities, flushed down with coke or root-beer (a drink that John Beavis of the Scottish Hotel School once described as something that tasted as though it had been dispensed in error at a chemist). Everyone was intent on having a thoroughly enjoyable day out. The weather was perfect, warm and sunny, and we never saw a semblance of an incident of bad behaviour by any spectator from start to finish.

The kick-off was at 2 p.m., and from 1.30 p.m. we watched the preliminaries of each team's ninety-man squad going through their warm-up, followed by the individual introduction of each player as he ran onto the field. Alongside each touch-line the respective groups of attractive young cheer-leaders were athletically encouraging everyone with the respective team's fighting songs and chants.

After what to us first-time viewers had been quite a spectacle, although it appeared to go on interminably, a ball was placed on the centre spot for the kick-off. The MSU band broke out into the Spartan fighting song, the volume of sound increasing as the player ran up to kick-off. Just before he actually kicked the ball, the whole crowd rose to their feet as one, cheering furiously. We were left sitting, our view blocked, wondering what all the fuss was about, particularly when the crowd resumed their seats and we saw that the game had stopped and the kick-off player and several others had trotted off the field to be replaced by a fresh bunch.

The game was televised live, which meant there were numerous breaks for commercials which were shown during the time-out periods frequently called by either side. The playing time of the match is calculated on the time the ball is in play only. Consequently, with what to us seemed an incredible number of stoppages, the final whistle was not blown until almost five o'clock. The crowd dispersed in good humour, and we strolled back to our apartment, slightly sunburnt, realising that any relationship between American football and our soccer or rugby was completely accidental.

On Monday morning I was back to being a student, and was interested to find that academic activity started at 8 a.m. on the dot. The first week passed quickly, as there was so much of interest in all that was happening. The smallest class was eighteen in number, and the largest was 120. In almost every case, the required course book had been written by the professor teaching the class, and it was absolutely essential to have a copy because the pace of course work and the assessments, projects, tests and homework were demanding and without the course book for constant reference there was scant hope of a successful grade.

Where a course in heavy demand might be offered on four days of the week, taught by four different professors, the situation could be that a different course book was required in each case. I found this out the hard way when studying required book lists which were available in the very busy second-hand bookshop on campus. Referring to the list for a course I was scheduled to take the following term, I purchased the required book in order to be able to do some advance reading during the vacation. At the end of term, however, the list was revised – the course was to be taught by a different professor who required the book he had written!

Professors with large classes were given the assistance of one or two graduate assistants who, under his direction, would take an active part in class sessions, particularly during questions or discussions. On meeting the class I was to teach for the first time (they were twenty-four in number), I found that they were mature students in their twenties, who greeted me with considerable respect. I was embarrassed when they initially called me Doctor (the large majority of professors hold Ph.D. degrees) but after clearing that point, I was always referred to as professor, which I also found embarrassing. However, as it was the norm in the United States to use this term, I became used to it.

They were an attentive, enjoyable group which gave me the confidence necessary for a satisfactory two-way communication in the classroom. I had already mentioned that, although we all spoke the English language, there were different understandings of certain words and terms on either side of the Atlantic. If I ever used a word they did not understand I asked them to let me know immediately.

The need for clarification never arose, but there was one situation which gave us all a smile. At the end of each class I would invite questions. On one occasion I said, 'That's it for today, are there any queries?' and immediately a grin broke out on each member's face. On asking the reason, they informed me that in the United States a query does not refer to a question, but to a man with homosexual tendencies!

Some people expressed the opinion that I was taking on too much in teaching class as well as grappling with a demanding course of study, but I found the classes I taught relaxing, and they had the effect of switching off my mind from the MBA studies for brief periods, which was no bad thing. I was also fortunate to have helping me an experienced graduate assistant, Bill Stafford, who had worked with Lendal Kotschevar. He knew and understood the course and the system, and proved to be a tower of strength.

A situation that gave several of my students a problem initially was that, in addition to sitting facing me in our food class, some also found me amongst them in MBA courses. They were obviously embarrassed, but I told them, 'In these situations, call me Vic!' After that they accepted the position readily, and me as a fellow student, for which I often had cause to be grateful as on many occasions when I needed help or advice it was always willingly offered.

Amongst the MBA group were two ex-Scottish Hotel School students, Graeme Laird and Ian Christie, who were also working as graduate assistants. They were pleasant young men who fitted in well and gained credit not only for themselves, but also for their school. Graeme kindly invited Letty and me to dinner at his apartment one evening, where we enjoyed a pleasant relaxing meal in his company.

Letty was coping quite well with daily shopping at the supermarket and often had a chat with Bob and Evelyn Scheffel. The electric cooker was causing problems which, because of a temperamental thermostat, had a tendency to be on the fierce side, but all in all she was managing well. At home we are fond of roast lamb occasionally, but as there was never any sign of lamb in the butchery department Letty asked Fred Scheffel (Bob's brother who ran the department) if he ever sold it. Fred went into his cold store and reappeared with a leg of 'lamb' weighing 8½ lb.

'That's not lamb, it's an old sheep,' said Letty.

'It's an American lamb,' said Fred.

'The legs of lamb we cook back home are about 4–5 lb,' she replied. 'Can't you get some that size?'

'I'll try for you.' Fred was true to his word and a few days later proudly produced a 4½ lb leg.

Two of our neighbours were nearby and showed interest at the purchase. 'You haven't got a pan big enough to pot-roast that,' said one.

'I shan't pot-roast it, I'll just roast it,' said Letty, whereupon she gave a brief résumé of the traditional British roast, which most intrigued them. After all that we were somewhat disappointed at the flavour and eating quality of the meat, and did not bother to repeat the order.

Having explored the immediate vicinity of Lansing, we now decided on longer Saturday trips around the state. We spent a weekend at Traverse City in NW Michigan, and on the way we found ourselves on a long, straight road that went for miles through sparsely populated areas with hardly any traffic. The speed limit was 50 m.p.h. which, in a powerful car, seems like a crawl. John and Michael started saying, 'Go on dad, open her up. See what she can do, there's no one around.' Letty was saying, 'Don't you dare!' Gradually the speed increased and I was doing about sixty-five, when a long wailing noise started. Looking in the rear view mirror, there was a speed cop on a Harley Davidson motor cycle signalling me to stop. Pulling over, I immediately got out of the car. The policeman, who had parked some ten yards away, got off his bike, adjusted his revolver holster looking at the back of my car (on which I had put a GB sticker) and walked over.

'I'm sorry, officer,' I said. 'We're strangers in your country, and with a powerful car and no traffic on the road, I overlooked my speed.'

'Oh, you're from England,' he replied.

'Yes, that's right.'

'I've got an aunt who lives in England, she lives in Bury – I wonder if you might know her?' With that he proceeded to tell me her name and address.

'I'm afraid that I don't', I replied, 'but Bury is in Lancashire, and that's where they make the best black puddings in Britain!'

We chatted for a further minute or two and he then said, 'Well get on your way now. You won't exceed the speed limit again, will you?'

'No, I won't officer, and thank you very much,' I replied.

Much relieved, we continued with our journey. I did receive two tickets for motoring offences during the year, but they were for parking misdemeanours!

By now we were into autumn, and the natural beauty of the trees and shrubs was delightful. In addition to the normal shades of yellow and brown, there are large numbers of maple trees with vivid red leaves which blend into, and contrast with, the yellows and browns, giving them a further dimension which, when seen in large stretches along highways, is truly memorable.

Lew and Ruth Minor invited us to spend a weekend with them and their two youngest daughters, Mary and Rosalie, taking a 400-mile drive to the upper peninsular, which is joined to the mainland of the state by a long bridge called the Mackinac Bridge. Lew suggested that we spent Friday night with them at the farm, ready to be on the road at 4 a.m. on Saturday. We went to bed early and were called at 3.30 a.m. Struggling out of bed we wondered what there would be to drink before setting out. We were dumbfounded to find that at 4 a.m. sharp, we all piled into Lew's camper and set off in pitch darkness with not a drink in sight. There were murmurings and stifled grumbles from the English contingent who were not accustomed to this routine, but Lew drove at a steady 50 m.p.h. non-stop until 11 a.m. when we pulled into the parking lot of a pancake house this side of the Mackinac Bridge.

By nine o'clock, listening to the protestations of hunger coming from John and Michael, I had thought that I was going to have a mutiny on my hands but their faces soon perked up when we sat at a table and were introduced to pancakes about two inches in diameter, known as dollar pancakes. Also on the table was a round swivel-stand containing five different flavours of syrup, in addition to the usual maple. A good sized stack of pancakes was served, well laced with whipped butter and syrup, and the boys enjoyed them so much that they demolished a second pile. Letty and I agreed we couldn't remember enjoying a cup of coffee more. I explained to the family afterwards that the reason we were able to keep motoring non-stop for so long was because we hadn't any excess fluid in our bodies to dispose of, but I don't think that cut much ice. Lew and Ruth were good hosts, and we spent a most enjoyable weekend passing show after show of breathtaking autumn colours.

We often visited Lew at the farmhouse where, in the basement, was his playroom with a pool table. Lew explained the rules, and we had many an enjoyable game but try as I may, I could never beat him. If I ever applied 'side' to the cue ball to help my positional play, he would refer to that as 'putting on the English'. The great majority of houses had cellars or basements for shelter as Michigan is in the hurricane belt.

The MBA classes were progressing steadily, and I soon found my way

122

into the huge university library. Computer facilities were available to students seven days a week, twelve hours a day, and student facilities for study were impressive. Some of our courses were taught by visiting lecturers, high-powered successful businessmen who packed a great deal into their classes, teaching with drive and enthusiasm. They were also demanding in their requirements from students.

I was interested to find that a great number of students were working part-time – in some cases up to twenty or thirty hours a week – in order to pay their way through college. This, it appeared, was what motivated the students who, on the whole, were desperately keen to learn and gain maximum benefit from their time at college. I was able to judge this even more closely as several professors formed their class into small syndicates of three or four, and set projects to be researched, written up and presented before a panel. Many of these tasks were extremely time consuming, but the students gave top priority to the work and no short cuts were ever taken. It was a most interesting experience for me to be so actively involved.

We were all thoroughly at home by now. The ice rink was only ten minutes' walk from our flat and the boys learned to skate, soon becoming proficient and scorning the idea of taking lessons. It was always interesting walking round the campus as there was plenty of activity, and some attractive, well-cared for gardens for quiet strolling. Skiing lessons were to be offered later in the year when the snow came, and both the boys decided to enrol. The university auditorium had a varied programme of shows and concerts to offer. The way of life was free, easy and relaxed. No one stood on ceremony and, to complete the picture, the weather was most pleasant and had been almost continually since our arrival. I was working hard, but still feeling fit and well.

In October, three visitors from the catering education sector in Ireland visited the school for a few days. At the conclusion of their visit they were travelling to Detroit, and I had volunteered to drive them. Early on the morning we were due to depart, we were all breakfasting in the Kellogg Centre when suddenly I began to feel giddy, and fainted. I was taken to the Olin Memorial Hospital on campus where Dr Johnson, from the University Medical School, attended to me. I was confined to bed for a few days at Dr Johnson's orders while tests were carried out. These indicated that the left arm, blood pressure and pulse were weak. On discharging me Dr Johnson indicated that I should have further exploratory tests at a nearby hospital in January. With that, I resumed studies, fellow students helping me to catch up on the classes I had missed. Bill Stafford had dealt with the foods course, so all was well and life continued as before.

By now, autumn was retreating fast. In late November heavy falls of snow arrived with temperatures below zero, which were to be with us for about the next four months according to the locals. The *East Lansing Gazette* announced the opening of the ski school which John and Michael started, quickly picking up the basic techniques. They were thoroughly enjoying themselves until Michael had an unfortunate accident which prevented him from skiing for some time, after which he did not wish to continue. John kept going and achieved a reasonable degree of proficiency by the end of winter.

One Sunday afternoon after lunch, with the temperature by now remaining steady at well below freezing, I decided to go for a walk for some exercise. Putting on all my warmest clothes, I set out at a brisk pace for about a quarter of a mile, then turned a corner to find a bitterly cold semi-gale blowing into my face. The sudden shock took my breath away, but I plodded on getting colder and colder until I felt my senses beginning to reel. It was a rather frightening experience, so I about-turned and hastened back to the apartment at all possible speed. Bursting in, I gasped, 'I have never been so cold in all my life. I'm not going to shave until the Spring!'

With the arrival of winter all the indoor facilities of the university were fully utilised. We saw the respective university teams play matches at basketball, ice-hockey and indoor athletics. The ice stadium had a *Talents on Ice* show featuring international skaters. Productions in the auditorium featured *Fiddler on the Roof*, *Cactus Flower*, Gina Bachauer (pianist), the Royal Winnipeg Ballet, the Hague Philharmonic Orchestra, the Stuttgart Ballet, the Prague Symphony Orchestra, the Chicago Symphony Orchestra, the African Dance Company of Ghana, Mantovani and his Orchestra, the Royal Choral Society from London, the Moscow State Symphony Orchestra, the NHK Symphony Orchestra from Tokyo and *Don Giovanni* and the *Tales of Hoffman* by the St Louis Opera Theatre.

The end of term was in sight. Tests, examinations, projects and assignments were dealt with, and the main topic among the students was grade points. In the large classes, tests were designed so that the results could be speedily processed by computer. Grade-point lists for all classes were pinned to the appropriate notice board so all students were aware of how the whole class fared. If any student violently disagreed with the allocated grade point he could make an appointment to discuss the matter with the course professor. If he had a convincing argument, the grade point might be changed. I just scraped through with minimum grades, thanks to a considerable amount of help from fellow students, and ended term feeling reasonably satisfied with my progress.

Rummaging in the school office one day, I found some papers that interested me, known as teacher rating forms. These listed about twenty comprehensive questions concerning the ability of the teacher and how he put his subject across. A choice of five answers was given for each question, and the form was designed to be marked by computer. Students had the option of signing the forms or leaving them blank, and the forms were available for use by any professor. There was no requirement for them to be used, and when processed the professor could destroy them. I considered them a good idea, put them into effect at the end of the spring and summer terms, and found the answers revealing and helpful. I brought back samples and enthusiastically introduced them to the Ealing staff at our first meeting on my return, but they emphatically turned the idea down. Persuasive argument got me nowhere at all, I couldn't ever recall the staff being so mutinous, so I dropped the idea.

We prepared for Christmas, decorating the apartment and a small tree, but were surprised to learn that only one day was given over to festivities. Boxing Day is an unknown term in the US, and Americans were intrigued to hear of our second day of celebration and the origin of the term Boxing Day.

Shortly after Christmas, a large conference of catering educationalists was being held in New Orleans. Three staff from the school were attending, and Henry Barbour arranged for me to join them. The conference was interesting, particularly as almost all the problems raised were similar to those we experienced in Britain. In fact, at times, it sounded like an amalgamated meeting of the Catering Teachers Association, City and Guilds and the Hotel and Catering Institute Education Committee! I also gained a brief snapshot impression of New Orleans outside conference hours, seeing the historic parts of the city and the above-ground cemetery.

A jazz session was to be held at Preservation Hall in the evening, and the four of us decided to attend. Luckily we had been warned that it would be popular so we went early, and were able to gain seats on one of the six, hard, wooden trestle benches. The hall was not over-large and looked fairly tatty, but we sat facing an old upright piano, a set of drums, double-bass and six chairs about an hour before the session was due to start. The few remaining bench seats were quickly taken, after which people either stood around the room or sat on the floor. Eight o'clock was the starting time, and just after seven-thirty an elderly Negro languidly shuffled in, took off his hat and coat, sat at the piano and started tinkering. He was followed at intervals by five other characters, some of whom looked so old and weary that we began to wonder what we were in for. Music cases were undone, and out came a saxophone, clarinet, trombone and a trumpet. After this activity they sat, had a rest, and chatted amongst themselves for ten minutes or so.

By five minutes to eight the hall was packed solid with spectators talking excitedly, and creating a torrent of sound, while the performers seemed oblivious to it all. At two minutes to eight, with their instruments at the ready, they indulged in a semblance of a tune-up, and at eight sharp began playing a well-known jazz number in the traditional way. All the players were obviously talented jazz musicians and their renderings, particularly the solos, drew a tremendous applause which, as the evening progressed, became even more rapturous. This seemed to affect the musicians by motivating them to even greater efforts, and their years appeared to shrink away as they reacted to the generous appreciation of the audience. It was a memorable evening.

In January, I went to Ingham Medical Hospital for an aortogram, cine-arteriogram and cardiac catheterisation, which produced a diagnosis of a subclavian steal syndrome (blockage in a main artery near the heart) probably caused by arteriosclerosis. After discussion with the doctor, he gave the opinion that a heart bypass operation would be advisable which could be carried out in the US, or could wait until I returned to England and got a medical opinion back home.

Letty and I talked the situation over. I didn't relish the idea of waiting nine months for something to be done, and it was agreed that I would have surgery at Ingham Medical. I asked the surgeon whether I could be admitted at the end of the spring term, in March, and he readily agreed. Fortunately I possess a philosophical nature, and was able to put the matter out of my mind for the time being.

During the break before the start of the spring term I was able to do a fair amount of preparatory reading for the next set of courses as I had purchased almost all the required textbooks at the end of the autumn term, which was most helpful.

Occasionally we would eat out, but modestly. John and Michael liked going to Howard Johnson's in Lansing where one night a week you could eat as much as you wanted of one selected dish, usually fish or chicken. One particular evening the boys chose fried chicken, and were having great fun with a pleasant young waitress who was encouraging them to refill their plates – they readily accepted the invitation. Sitting at the next table were four, hefty, young students who were fascinating us by the amount of chicken they were eating. Their waitress, also a student working part-time, was entering into the spirit of the occasion, but we could hardly believe our eyes as pile after pile of chicken was brought to the table and demolished. Michael was keeping count, and he calculated that they ate about forty pieces each!

Following his birthday in February, John went to see Bob Scheffel at the supermarket about a job as a bag-boy, and Bob started him at a few hours a week which he was able to increase later. At this time John, in common with many English boys, wore his hair long. One day, when Letty and I went to do some shopping, we observed that four check-out lanes were operating, all complete with bag-boys, but one had far more customers than the others in the queue. We then noticed that this was John's lane and as we passed along to get our trolley, we overheard two young American ladies at the rear of the queue chatting.

'Why don't you go into one of the shorter queues?' said one.

'I like to wait for the English boy with the long hair. He's cute and I love the way he talks!' As John bagged their groceries and carried them out to the cars they would engage him in conversation, and he seemed to do very well for tips!

One day, Michael was going ice-skating with some of his pals and, as they went running into the hall to see who could be first in, he was in the lead. He turned his head to laugh at the others and instead of pushing the door frame to open it, he put his hand through the glass panel as the person in front of him swung the door back. Letty was at home on her own and saw the spectacle of a campus police car pulling up outside to deliver Michael spattered all over with blood. The policemen were kind and helpful, and hearing that I was in class, they drove Letty and Michael to a hospital in Lansing where the doctor removed numerous glass splinters from Michael's hand and arm. Letty rang me at school and I went to collect them and take them home. Luckily, Michael's injury was not serious and he was soon back to full mobility.

The spring term passed fairly uneventfully. Henry Barbour, head of the school, had resigned at the end of the autumn term and I was intrigued to watch the process of obtaining his successor. The first thing that happened was that at a staff meeting at 8 a.m. nominations for the post were invited from all members. Eventually, a caretaker head was appointed until Dr Blomstrom (on a year's secondment overseas) returned and took over the position.

I was taking one of my preferred courses in education this term which I found very interesting. The professor, who I got on with extremely well, introduced the class to educational research and for our end of term test assignment we were required to carry out a lengthy project which I found enjoyable. My delight increased on gaining a 4-point grade mark which was considered excellent. That was just as well, as it helped to counterbalance lower grades in other courses!

On 8 March I entered Ingham Medical Hospital for surgery to deal with what was by now a complete blockage of the left subclavian artery. A bypass graft was inserted between the aorta and the artery, and with a drainage tube inserted, I went back to a private room. When I recovered consciousness Letty was at the bedside, and she was able to visit as often as she wished, with friends and fellow students acting as chauffeur. I had completely lost the use of my left shoulder as a result of the surgery, but with the help of an excellent physiotherapist and strenuous daily work-outs, fully recovered the use before leaving hospital.

The food and service was good during my stay in hospital, with a reasonable choice of menu always on offer. The nurses were efficient and friendly, and everything was done to make the stay as comfortable as possible.

By a stroke of luck a set of proofs for the second edition of *Theory of Catering* arrived from England for checking, which was a blessing for they couldn't have come at a better time. I was able to keep them at my bedside and correct a few pages at a time whenever I felt like it. When the doctors came around for the daily check-up they were always interested to know what particular topic I was dealing with at the time. By now the beard had grown to respectable proportions. All the hospital staff were extremely kind, and I was generally referred to by all and sundry as the English professor with the beard.

On 23 March I was discharged, and presented with a bill for $3220.75 which rocked me back on my heels. We had taken out full comprehensive medical insurance for the family, and in my inexperience I had assumed that this would cover all medical expenses. The insurance did cover part of the medical expenses – $1556.70 – but did not include the cost of surgery. The bill was for pre-surgical tests, the operation and post surgical procedures. After paying the bill, Letty and I were thankful we had made the decision to live in modest-priced student accommodation for the year!

I missed the first few days of the term but managed to catch up, and prepared to knuckle down for what was almost the last leg of the course (there would be only two courses to finish in summer school). At the first class of the notorious QBA course I sat through a painful hour, realising that I might just as well be in a non-English speaking country for all the sense that I could make of it. The professor was an exceedingly pleasant man who lectured clearly and appeared to have a helpful disposition. I spoke to him after class and said, 'I found this topic difficult to follow. Is the remainder of the course likely to be as bad?'

'It will become much more difficult,' he replied.

'In that case I'm finished. I shall never be able to cope,' I said. With that my heart sank, as I thought that must surely be the end of my attempt to gain a degree.

'Go and see the Dean of the Business School and explain your problem,' said the professor.

I thanked him, said goodbye, and went to make an appointment to see the academic dean of the college of business. I saw him later the same day and explained the problem, and he asked questions about my age, background and job in England. I gave him a rapid potted life history since entering teacher training college, to which he listened attentively.

When I had finished, he thought for a moment or two then said, 'It seems quite clear that your business is education.'

'Yes, and it will be for the remainder of my working life,' I replied.

'I gain far too much satisfaction from it to ever want to change.'

He paused, then said, 'Well, in that case I consider it quite proper to allow you to omit the QBA course from your degree requirement, as it is severely geared to the needs of commercial business. In its place I shall require you to take two education courses totalling one credit more than the QBA course.'

I thanked him for his time, courtesy and consideration and left, full of admiration for a system encompassing 40 000 students that had the in-built flexibility to deal so sensibly with one individual's problems. My education professor was delighted to see me back, I told him the story and with his guidance signed on for two appropriate classes, one of which was educational research.

The weather was good with long, warm, sunny days, I was feeling well and all classes were progressing satisfactorily. During this term we saw our first baseball match, as well as soft-ball matches, a major athletics meeting and a swimming gala. Letty learned to drive on the learner-driver track within campus, subsequently took the driving test and was given a driving licence.

Lew and Ruth Minor invited us around one Sunday afternoon for a barbeque, where Lew was to show me how to make a genuine hamburger. On arrival at the farm, John and Michael went off to play with Rosalie and Mary, Letty was chatting to Ruth and Lew said, 'Come on; Victor, let's pitch some horseshoes.' He then took me to his 'pitching range' and initiated me into the sport which, I must say, I found extremely difficult, but good fun.

The barbeque had been lit, had stopped smoking, and was now glowing red ready for cooking on. Ruth produced a 6 lb bowl of freshly ground chuck rib and thick flank of beef, and proceeded to mould it into eight-ounce burgers which Lew placed on the fire. The buns were set to warm and a tray of seasonings and relishes prepared. 'Never prod the burgers with a fork', said Lew, 'otherwise you release the natural juices which run out, taking with them the flavour which is lost. Always turn and handle the burgers with a pair of tongs.' Hot dogs were also cooked, and at that moment Lew's brother and family of four arrived unexpectedly, declaring, 'It looks as though we're just in time,' and proceeded to tuck-in. This reduced the rations somewhat, but we all enjoyed a good party.

Michael had been given a baseball catcher's glove (mitt) for a Christmas present and a frisbee, and spent many hours outdoors playing with his American friends. John used to spend time in the late evenings outside the apartments where many of the residents (our neighbours) would congregate to sit and chat, or strum a guitar.

Letty and I started to plan a trip at the end of the summer term before summer school began. Term ended, I managed once again to scrape by with grade points just off the minimum, and we set off on our trip. We had four visitors while we were away. Ron Kinton, Fred Sharman, Les Miller and Ian Nutbourne took a study tour of the United States, and as their schedule passed nearby, they stayed for a night or two in our apartment. We were sorry to miss them but it helped them along the way. During the year other visitors from the UK included Rik Medlik and John Beavis from the University of Surrey, and Miss F. Morkam of the Surrey Schools Meals Service who was for a number of years my co-chief examiner for the City and Guilds 147 examinations.

Detroit was the first stop, where we stayed at the Dearborn Inn alongside the fourteen-acre Henry Ford Museum which contains vast collections of Americana, and is divided into three main sections: decorative arts galleries, a street of twenty-two early American shops and a mechanical arts hall which housed a collection of 200 automobiles. Alongside the museum is Greenfield Village which portrays three centuries of American life by means of nearly 100 life-sized historic buildings on a 260-acre site. We were intrigued to find an authentic Cotswold stone cottage among the collection.

We then motored on to Canada and stayed overnight at Niagara Falls, a magnificent spectacle. We were surprised to find how close we were able to get to the water before the drop. A stone wall runs alongside the Niagara river and the boys found an empty space about five yards before the fall where, by leaning over, John was almost able to touch the water, leaving his mother's heart in her mouth. Because of Niagara's tremendous popularity as a tourist spot the nearby town, with the Skylon (the world's tallest reinforced concrete structure complete with tower tapering to a height of 520 feet) is like Blackpool on a bank-holiday. The Skylon contains a modern exhibition building, and the tower features a revolving dining-room and indoor and outdoor observatories, which give unsurpassed views of the Falls. We stayed overnight at a nearby motel and, after we had eaten, John persuaded us to let him spend two to three hours in the town. I took him down in the car, set a time for collection two-and-a-half hours later, and he was there on the dot looking very pleased with himself, having spent a 'fun evening'.

Our next stop was Ithaca, New York State, to visit Cornell and here we stayed at the Statler Inn. Having heard of the world-wide reputation of this famous school it was interesting to see their facilities and accommodation, and to meet members of the faculty. As at MSU one of the features that struck me was the generous support of school graduates who made successful careers in the industry. This support was evident in a number of ways, including the donation of buildings, rooms, interiors, equipment, fellowships and scholarships. This left me with the impression that although most American students make far greater financial sacrifices to be able to study at college than their British counterparts, they are more grateful for what they have received, and show this by the generous way they contribute to their colleges, growth, development and well-being.

We visited Matthew and Helen Bernatsky at their home, and were fascinated by the collection of china collected from all parts of the world. Matthew, in common with most other faculty members from Cornell, received requests for consultancy from many countries and the university as a matter of policy encouraged this.

Leaving Ithaca, we motored through the pleasant countryside of New York State to New York City, where we had booked in for two nights in the heart of the city. It was a hot day, the temperature and humidity continually rising, and as we entered the city the traffic was very heavy. Realising the jungle of roads with numerous combinations of ups and downs, turn-offs and flyovers could present difficulties, I was praying that I would hit the right turn-off first time, and thankfully my prayers were answered! Leaving the main highway, we found the hotel almost at once. By now it was mid-afternoon and the temperature was in the high nineties. We checked in, were delighted to learn that the hotel had a pool on the roof, and within the next twenty minutes we were thankfully cooling ourselves off.

In the evening when the temperature had subsided, we went for a stroll, passing through Times Square and 42nd Street, and wandering for about an hour before returning to the hotel. On our return to Lansing when we told Lew Minor where we had walked he was horrified, and said that we were lucky not to have been mugged!

The following day we explored the city a little further and went up the Empire State Building. However, it became too hot for comfort, so we took a tourist trip around the city on a boat with a sun canopy, and then drove off for our next destination, Amherst and the University of Massachusetts. Here we stayed for two nights at the home of Donald Lundberg and his wife. Donald was in charge of the hotel school at the university, which was modest compared to the size of Cornell, but interesting none the less.

We finally set off for home with a lengthy drive across the state of Pennsylvania, where we experienced toll highways for the first time. The whole trip had taken seven days. Petrol at that time was very cheap compared to England, modest-priced eating houses were plentiful, and we were pleasantly surprised to find how reasonable the total cost had been.

On our return we started to calculate how much time I was likely to be studying, and how long that would leave us before we returned to England. It seemed that a good six-week period would remain, so we discussed how best to utilise this time to the full. We decided to head west on one last long trip, possibly reaching the coast at San Francisco, and had great fun planning our route. We were given sound advice that the temperatures would be very hot, in some places reaching up to 100 °F and as schools were closed for summer holidays, accommodation might be difficult at the more popular resorts.

With that information, we went to the second-hand car lot to look for a larger car with air-conditioning. We made a good part-exchange deal for a large eight-cylinder Story Oldsmobile brake with ample space for us all to sleep in if necessary, and were able to get a reconditioned air-conditioning unit installed at reasonable cost.

Summer school commenced, I had a relatively light schedule in the final term of the MBA, and as the quantity foods course was not being offered this term, no teaching commitment. It was very hot and humid by this time and we were warned that this could be the season for hurricanes. I would go off to class dressed only in a light short-sleeved open-necked shirt, Bermuda shorts, a pair of sandals, carrying a brief case.

One morning towards the end of June I was shaving (I had shaved off the beard as soon as the weather warmed up, as I found it irritating) when I became giddy, and had to be taken to hospital. An aortogram was taken which revealed that the previous blockage had re-occurred, and that the surgery would have to be repeated. It appeared that I should have been kept on a daily dosage of anti-coagulant, but this had not been prescribed.

On 24 July I had surgery, which went more quickly than on the first occasion. The blockage was removed, a fresh bypass inserted, I made a good and speedy recovery, and was discharged on 5 August, feeling comparatively well. That is until, once again, I was presented with a bill for $3034.27 of which the insurance this time only paid $836.98. I returned to college the following day, and within a few days had completed the MBA course, ending by the tightest of margins with an average grade point sufficient to be awarded the degree.

All our carefully made plans for the trip out west had long since been cancelled, and on making enquiries for somewhere quiet and pleasant for a two-week holiday, we were recommended Portage Point Inn, Onekama, near Manistee, on the shores of Portage Lake, with Lake Michigan 300 yards in the background.

Bob Macintosh, Professor of Tourism at MSU, occupied an office adjacent to mine and usually popped his head in when he passed to give a cheery smile and enquire how things were going. When he heard about the Portage trip he said, 'We have our summer cottage the other side of Lake Portage. We'll come over and see you when you arrive.'

The journey was 150 miles and I was glad to have such a large easy car to drive, for with automatic transmission, power-assisted steering and power-assisted brakes, all the effort is taken out of driving. This is why many Americans think nothing of driving hundreds of miles at a stretch in their vast country.

We couldn't have selected a more idyllic spot. The sun shone non-stop daily from early morning until dusk, and the accommodation was comfortable. Meals were waitress-served in a restaurant which, four nights a week after dinner, offered dancing to a four-piece band. There was plenty to occupy the boys. John learned to water-ski, and Letty and I made friends with three American couples and often played shuffleboard with them. I was able to relax completely and do nothing but enjoy the peace and calm of the resort, which made a perfect convalescence and finale to the American year.

Bob Macintosh drove over in his motor-boat and took us for a spin around the lake, into Lake Michigan, and back home to his cottage to meet his wife, Ruth. In common with most American summer cottages, Bob raised the Stars and Stripes when in residence.

Michael was so intrigued with the motor-boat that Bob said to him, 'Would you like to take it out for a spin?'

'Yes please!' Michael replied, thinking that Bob would at least go with him.

Instead, Bob gave him the brief instructions needed to control the boat, helped him into the driving seat and said, 'Off you go then. Don't go too far away.'

Michael couldn't believe his ears, and we were also surprised, but he didn't need telling twice. He drove off with a grin from ear to ear, kept well within sight, and came back slowly and carefully alongside the landing stage twenty minutes later. He climbed out and received a pat on the head from Bob, together with a 'well done,' which made his day.

The holiday passed happily, and on 28 August we bade farewell to our new-found friends and returned to Cherry Lane to pack for the return home to England two days later. We put a 'house contents for sale' card in the launderette, giving a time the following day when the sale would commence, and our household goods disappeared in a flash.

The last job was to sell the car, for which we got a fair price. Lew and Ruth Minor collected us and our luggage to take us to the airport, and, as I said my last goodbye to Lew, I realised what a great help he had been over the past year. Without his unfailing support, advice and friendship the year would not have been possible, and would not have reached its successful conclusion.

So ended a momentous twelve months which had considerably widened my experience and horizons, left me with many memories and made me a much more open and broadminded person. Before going to America, when asked by potential management students for advice on leaving college, I had frequently said, 'Invest two years in working overseas. Spend eighteen months in Europe, in three countries if possible, and then six months in the United States. After this the world should be your oyster. You may have to work harder than you have ever done in your life, but at your age you should be able to take it.' The year in the USA did nothing to change this advice.

CHAPTER 10
1969–1980

The Ealing
Years – Part II

Before leaving for America I had sold the car and arranged for a new one to be at Heathrow to meet us on arrival. After an uneventful flight, we landed on schedule to find the car waiting, piled our luggage on board and drove home. We'd bought a large trunk in the States, packed it with heavy clothing, and sent it on by sea to lighten our load.

Inevitably we began to wonder in what condition we would find the house after four young men had occupied it for twelve months. Around Heathrow, houses are frequently let fully furnished for varying periods of time, and we had heard many examples of property abuse and damage. To our pleasant surprise we found the home virtually as we had left it, and on learning subsequently that the number of tenants had been increased (without our permission) from four to six, we were initially indignant, but subsequently gave them full marks for cheek! The lawnmower had one broken part which cost five pounds to replace. I sent the bill to the previous tenants and a cheque was returned with a letter of apology by return of post.

Letty and I weighed ourselves. I had lost a stone, but much to Letty's consternation, she had put on two stone!

I reported the events of the past year to my GP, Dr Walsh. He gave me an examination, made an appointment for me to see a consultant at

Ashford Hospital, and finally said, 'Now, reduce your weight by two-and-a-half stone!'

'I've already lost a stone in the past year,' I told him.

'Good!' he said. 'You only have two-and-a-half more to go!'

'You're a fine one to talk,' I replied. 'You're the same size as me!'

'Yes, but I'm the doctor and you are the patient,' he answered with a grin. With a twinkle in his eye he then offered me a diet sheet.

'No thank you, I'm supposed to know something about food. I'll work that one out for myself.'

I cut out cooked breakfast, eating a little cereal and fruit, except when on holiday. If I wasn't hosting visitors in the Mary King Room, or out to lunch, I would have two Ryvitas or a thick slice of granary bread with a small piece of cheese and an apple for lunch, locking the office and eating out of my desk drawer. I reduced starch intake by half, drank tea and coffee without milk and sugar, and only ate dessert when in company. Every morning after showering I stood on the scales. It took me two years, but I finally reduced my weight to ten stones, and have maintained that weight ever since by eating sensibly and weighing myself daily. Initially I often felt famished by mid-afternoon, and on more than one occasion went out surreptitiously to buy myself a Mars bar which I would consume furtively. Judging from my experience, I would say that taking off weight requires three factors: a little knowledge, common sense, and a great deal of self-discipline. I was determined not to become a martyr to a diet, and still am. Food is too important in my life for that, which is why, whenever I eat out, I do so with enjoyment and pleasure. I was also helped in losing weight by the anti-coagulant which restricts my consumption of alcohol to no more than the equivalent of one pint of beer daily.

The consultant at Ashford Hospital, Dr Royds, was extremely interested in the treatment I had received in America, and asked questions on various aspects of my time in hospital. After a number of tests had been processed, he prescribed a daily dose of Warfarin, an anti-coagulant, and told me to make arrangements for a blood test every six weeks, and to see him every six months. I asked him how long I would need to take Warfarin, and he replied, 'Permanently.'

John had come back with a wad of dollars from his part-time job in the supermarket which, when changed, gave him a sum of over £400. I offered some fatherly advice about saving some of the money, but he 'pooh-poohed' that idea and replied, 'I worked hard for this money. It's the first time in my life I have ever had such a sum and I am going to treat myself with it!' He then declared that he wanted a good bicycle. 'Ah! I know just the place for you – Savilles of Battersea Rise, near Clapham Junction,' I replied. This was a famous cycle shop in south-west London where, as a teenager, I had seen the bike of my dreams, one that I could never afford – the Claud Butler.

On reaching the shop, there, suspended in the centre of the window, was a sparkling Claud Butler. My eyes gleamed. I turned to John and said, 'How about that for a bike?'

He took one look at it and said, 'I don't want an old thing like that!'

Feeling very deflated, I kept quiet while we went into the shop and John purchased a second-hand, hand-built Gillott frame which, by the time he had bought all the necessary additions, came to about £100. This was almost twice the price of the Claud Butler, but he sold it at a profit two or three years later. He also bought a guitar, and put the remainder into his savings account.

Michael now declared that he would like a pet, and to Letty's horror he mentioned a snake. Luckily, in a pet shop opposite his school, he spied a pair of wire-haired terrier puppies and took us in to see them. He was in a dilemma regarding which one to choose as like most puppies they looked irresistible, but he finally settled on a bitch that we called Sharon. In the car on the way home she asserted herself at once in the family by leaving a puddle on John's lap!

I returned to college for a meeting with Paul White and heard his account of how the year had gone. According to Paul it had gone smoothly because everything had been left in good order, but on learning that he'd had problems with a member of staff who had begun to prove difficult before I had left, I realised that he had understated the situation and had experienced a more turbulent year than he cared to mention. That appeared to be the only fly in the ointment and Paul, in his typical way, made light of it. The school was in good shape and I was happy to be back.

Dr Pickard had said we should develop a course in tourism as this was going to be an important part of Britain's economy in the future. As a result, I asked a particular hard-working enthusiastic member of staff who had been with us a relatively short time to prepare an outline scheme at Higher National Diploma level. He was Armand Borisewitz (Boris), later Head of the Robert Gordon School, Aberdeen, an earnest young man who, in typical manner, leapt at the opportunity with his usual enthusiasm and drive. He produced a scheme which he steered through the various internal and external committee stages in little over six months, an unusually short time for an academic project at this level. Because of the success of including periods of industrial release within our catering courses, a similar feature was included in this course which, under Armand's guidance, went from strength to strength.

The late 1960s and early 1970s were a period when the reputation of the school grew both nationally and internationally, and the high quality of the majority of the teaching and support staff was undoubtedly a major factor. Bob Kidner, an ex-student at Acton in 1948, had been the senior lecturer in food and beverage service for several years and led his team by example. Outstanding personalities in this group of teachers over the years included Alfie Liebold (later Head of Department, Wolverhampton), the late Jimmy Greer (later Head of Department, Hastings), Dennis Lillicrap, Vic Dewhurst and Andy Durkan. Bob in particular was a gifted teacher and popular with students and colleagues. He was seconded from 1966 to 1968 as Director of the Barbados Hotel School, during which time he was re-seconded to Guyana to do on-the-job training for Guyana Tourist Corporation.

By 1968 our cherished four-year sandwich course had to be withdrawn in order to make way for the incoming Higher National Diploma. We fought hard to keep the four-year course because it had stood the test of time and industry approved of its practical format. We fought a losing battle, as the Department of Education and Science withdrew its approval which meant that student grants would not be available, thus forcing us into producing an HND scheme.

This was in 1968, and with Bob Kidner due back, I had him in mind to take over as course director to get the HND off the ground. When Bob returned he said that he would prefer a change from the food and beverage service section so we were mutually satisfied. Bob did a splendid job getting the HND started, and being a committed Ealing man, he was able to give the course the 'Ealing flavour'. It was a just reward for his ability as a teacher and organiser and the contribution he had made to the success of our school that he was appointed Head of Department of Hotel Administration at Westminster College in 1972, where he remained until taking early retirement in 1986.

Brian Price led the team of chef teachers, which included a well-known Ealing stalwart in Freddie Sharman. Brian was a craftsman of the highest order and he won the coveted title of 'Chef of the Year' during his time with us.

Vic Regnaud, who was responsible for the larder, was a brilliant cold-work man. Under his eagle eye and dedicated coaching, students gained numerous awards at Hotelympia, one of the highlights being the five dish team entry for which, on three occasions, we were awarded the gold medal and challenge trophy. The team would begin its final preparations for this prestigious event in the late afternoon and work all through the night, leaving the final finishing of their dishes until the early hours of the morning in order that they appeared before the judges at 9 a.m. in the freshest possible condition. To achieve gold medal success in major competitions this is the way that entrants have to be prepared to work. The winning of a major award quickly removes the weariness of a sleepless night, and the memory of the victorious occasion remains for a long time.

Vic Regnaud, younger brother of Stan Regnaud, had two other brothers, both of whom were chefs and who lived in Radnor Street, Chelsea, in the 1930s several doors away from us. Stan Regnaud taught cookery at Ealing for several years, and left to take up the post of senior lecturer at Slough College.

Ella Ramsay, teacher of shorthand and typewriting, and Jan Scorgie, an ex-student of the school, taught hotel bookkeeper reception. They were two hard-working members of staff who, together with Stan Hopkinson, followed by Tony Thornfield (teachers of accounting), provided the continuity and backing for a Students Association.

The major activity of the Students Association was to organise a going-down dinner-dance and reunion annually at the end of the summer term. Over the years this happy occasion was successfully held at one of the big hotels where there was usually an ex-student in management, such as the Savoy, Dorchester, Royal Lancaster, Royal Garden, Europa, Inn on the Park, Hilton and Connaught Rooms. The first was held at Quaglino's, and I still have the empty magnum of champagne in my room which, so the story goes, I was brandishing at 1 a.m. sitting on the bonnet of my car outside the hotel!

I received a phone call one day from Louis Darsonval, ex-senior lecturer in larder work at Westminster College. The Head of School, Jean Vincent, had retired several years earlier and was acting as a consultant to Birds Eye frozen foods. His successor had been George Hambidge, who was about to retire, and Westminster was headhunting for his successor. Louis wanted an opinion from me on the capabilities of Stan Regnaud. I replied by suggesting that he spent a day at Slough College, met Stan personally, and assessed the quality of the job he was doing. As a result Stan Regnaud was appointed Head of Department of Professional Cookery at Westminster College. We pulled our colleagues' legs at Westminster unmercifully after that saying that with ex-Ealing members of staff as heads of their two schools, we had achieved a take-over.

Eddie Jonckheere, ex-RAF civilian instructor and a chef lecturer at Acton, had left to take up the post of head of department at Birkenhead, and other Ealing colleagues who gained headships elsewhere over the years included Nancy Brien, at Guildford; Mary Martin, at Ipswich; David Wilks, at Hendon; Geoff Cowell (lecturer in chemistry on the Dietetics Diploma Course), at Blackpool; Eric Beckley (now training officer in the Savoy Hotel Group, London), in Fiji; Dennis Searle, at Northampton; Neil Hansford-Smith, in Bermuda; Gerry Hudswell, in Antigua; Fidelio Etim, at Kaduna Polytechnic, Nigeria; Bob Henchoz – Illingworth, at Liverpool; Richard Gunter, at Middlesex Polytechnic; Jimmy Greer, at Hastings; Bob Leighton, at Swindon; Paul Lock, at Middlesex Polytechnic; Eddie McIntyre, who became Principal at Birmingham College of Food; Linda Formesyn, at Hounslow; and George Bennett, at Worthing. A grand total of twenty-three in all, which justly symbolises the quality of the Ealing teaching staff.

I had served for several years as chairman of the Junior Salon Culinaire, Hotelympia, with the benefits of an excellent vice-chairman in Chris Read of St Thomas's Hospital, and a comparatively small but hard-working committee. Since my return from America, however, I had noticed a decrease in my stamina, and decided to cut back on outside committee work. I resigned from the Junior Salon, and was delighted to hand over to such an able chairman as Chris Read who held the post until the senior and junior committees were amalgamated in the 1980s. Having previously declined the nomination for chairman of the HCI (now the HCIMA) education committee, I now also resigned from the council.

It was with regret that I carried out these and other resignations, as I had always enjoyed the work, and the opportunity to meet with practising industrialists is something that no head of a catering school should ever miss. However, the school was, by now, so well respected by all sides of industry that we had few problems gaining information and co-operation on any topic when required.

Full credit must be given to Dr Pickard who was a stalwart supporter and constructive critic of us and our work. On more than one occasion when we had appointed a new member of teaching staff, it would transpire that he was an ex-Ealing student. Dr Pickard would say, 'Victor, this in-breeding is a bad policy!' to which I would reply, 'Well, I cannot be blamed if our man happens to be the best qualified on the short list!'

I had now re-applied and been interviewed for consideration as a magistrate, and in April 1970 at the Middlesex Guildhall I was sworn in with about twelve others. We undertook evening training classes given by the Chief Clerk to the Justices of our bench (Brentford) which had two courthouses, the other being in Ealing.

While we were under training we were only allowed in the well of the court on general observation. Subsequently, we sat on the bench, but always with two experienced magistrates. I had only contracted to sit one half-day a week, on Friday. The Brentford courthouse was over a mile and a half from the college which meant that I left the office at ten. The bench sat at 10.30 a.m. and normally rose by 12.30 to 1 p.m., which meant I was back in the office just after one o'clock. Offering my services I was told that there was an upper age limit of fifty years for appointment as a Juvenile Bench magistrate and I was now fifty-one. It was disappointing, but I had no alternative other than to accept the rule.

The cases on the whole were interesting, although inevitably some were petty and tedious, often depending on the quality of advocacy involved. In common with many members of the public, I had not realised that well over 90 per cent of criminal matters in England and Wales are dealt with in magistrates courts, thus making them an essential part of the country's judicial system. The old-fashioned concept of only local dignitaries being appointed as magistrates has long since passed, and the Lord Chancellor now strongly urges all local benches to recruit a membership that maintains a sensible balance between the sexes, political persuasion, religious creed, colour and occupation.

Occasionally, magistrates are encouraged to sit for a day at the Crown Court alongside professional judges, and can take lunch with them in their private dining-room. I would normally fit in a day during school holidays, and found the experience most interesting.

The Brentford bench had an active social committee who organised various events three of four times a year. The major function was a dinner-dance held at a nearby hotel at which the average attendance was about 250. After attending for a number of years, we habitually made up a table with ten good friends.

One year we met at a large, modern hotel near Heathrow. After a tasty first course, followed by a pleasant fish course, we sat back awaiting the main course which was to be chicken suprême princesse. A waitress arrived with a large, oval, flat, silver dish containing ten egg-and-crumbed fried portions of chicken. As she started to serve on the opposite side of the table, I saw at a glance that two or three portions had a dark tell-tale ring around the outside. As the waitress approached, it was clear that the three portions were to be served to Letty, myself and a colleague on Letty's other side.

The waitress deftly spooned and forked a portion onto my plate and I immediately picked up the knife and fork and turned it over. By this time the remaining two portions had been served.

The waitress, seeing what I had done, came back, and we both looked at a badly over-fried piece of chicken. Without saying a word I looked at her. She looked at the chicken, then at me and said 'You can't eat that sir, can you?'

'No,' I replied. 'I like my chicken well browned, but this has gone too far.'

By this time, the conversation around the table had stopped and a cloud of embarrassed silence hung over the proceedings. 'I'll take it back for you, sir,' said the waitress.

Letty had found her chicken to be the same, so the waitress removed it and enquired of my colleague, 'Shall I remove yours, sir?'

He had been to embarrassed to even turn his chicken over, and hastily said, 'No, no, that's all right!' I urged him to have it removed but he declined.

The vegetables had now been served, so I suggested my friends got on with their meal and reluctantly they complied. Our waitress came beetling back and apologised for the incident, for which I thanked her, and assured her that as she had not cooked the food it was not her fault.

Then the head waitress came, followed a few seconds later by the banqueting manager, both of whom made genuine polite apologies.

The only sound at our table was of knives and forks, when a colleague said, 'What will happen now, Vic?'

'One of three things,' I replied. 'If they have any more suitable chicken cooked, then it won't be long before we are served. Or they may have some prepared chicken to cook, in which case it will take a little longer. Or they may not have any more chicken, in which case your guess will be as good as mine!'

Our fellow guests had three-quarters consumed their meal when the service door burst open (I had been keeping one eye on it), and out came our waitress bearing two plates which she triumphantly placed in front of Letty and me with a smile and a further genuine apology. Around the table ten pairs of eyes rivetted as one on the plates on which were tastefully presented a beautifully cooked fillet steak, grilled mushrooms, tomato, a green vegetable and golden-brown potatoes garnished with a fresh sprig of watercress. It was a mouthwatering sight!

As we started to eat our friend on Letty's left said, 'I wish that I had sent mine back now!'

I frequently received telephone calls or letters asking whether any students would be interested in catering for a small party in a private house. If I considered that the experience would be useful, we looked for suitable students who might be interested. One such call came from a Mr Lowenthal, who was arranging a celebration party for a small number of guests. We offered the job to a pair of outstanding students, who carried out the evening's work so satisfactorily that the occasion provided the whole column for Sam and Mary Cobb, who wrote regularly in the *London Evening News*, for Mr Lowenthal was Sam Cobb, and the school received a good plug!

As frequently as possible, I encouraged members from all sections of industry to visit the school when either a member of staff or myself would welcome them with coffee at ten o'clock and give them an outline of the work we did. This would be followed by a look around the facilities, questioning staff and students where convenient about what they were doing and why they were doing it, and ended with lunch in the Mary King Room and the opportunity to deal with questions the visitor wished to raise. In almost every case an invitation would be given to return the visit, thus making yet another useful bridge between industry and college.

Early each year we would arrange a careers convention for students leaving that summer, and always invited a good wide spread of industrial representation. The Mary King Room would be closed to the public and a special lunch offered for the delegates. The convention would run from 2.30 to 4.30 p.m. with each delegate being given a table and chairs. There were no speeches – students circulated freely, talked to delegates and gathered information for the future. Here again, when the students had finished, there was an opportunity for staff to talk to members of industry.

In the spring term we held our Presentation of Awards evening, when a guest of honour would make the presentation which would be followed by a brief address. With the exception of those receiving awards, their parents and some members of staff, all remaining guests were from industry, chosen from those who took students on industrial release. We regarded this as a small thank you for the help given. An attractive supper would be offered and a useful pleasant evening followed.

Among guests of honour over the years were Sir Lindsay Ring and Sir Maxwell Joseph, who began his few words by expressing the hope that we could learn how to serve a decent cup of coffee! Sir Hugh Wontner was accompanied by Lady Wontner who so enjoyed the evening that she remarked at the end, 'You should invite the Duke of Edinburgh one year.'

I looked at her with surprise, and replied, 'He wouldn't come, would he?'

'Take my advice and write,' she said.

The idea sounded most attractive, and as I thought it would be a major PR coup for the school if he accepted, I mentioned it to the principal, Mr Tyler. Dr Pickard, who did not condone award ceremonies and never attended, had left the college to be followed by Geoff Tyler, and he regularly attended. 'I must mention it to the town clerk,' he said. The next I heard was that a long list of local dignitaries would have to be invited to satisfy protocol. When I saw the size of the list I protested that there would be no room for our industrial friends, but I couldn't beat protocol, and with that, my enthusiasm for the idea waned and I proceeded no further.

When Sir Charles Forte came he was alone. We had delegated one of our receptionist students to greet him on arrival by presenting him with a flower for his buttonhole. He obviously enjoyed the relaxed, friendly atmosphere, and after the presentations when he rose to speak he took out his notes, looked at them, threw them away and gave a brief stirring address off the cuff.

His words were generously received by the company, following which he turned to me and said, 'Mr Ceserani, what can I do for the school? Can I offer an annual scholarship of say, £500?'

I beamed and replied, 'Yes please!' My first task the next morning was to send a letter thanking him for his attendance and generous offer!

The majority of school staff were enthusiastic and willing to put in free time for extra-curricular activities. For a number of years a small group would encourage a party of students to save and embark on a wine study trip during the Easter holidays. Two or three members of staff would accompany them, and in order to economise they slept under canvas. The hospitality of the French wine houses was generous, but in all the years I never heard of one instance of that hospitality being abused. Glowing reports usually came back about the attitude and behaviour of the Ealing students. Another group of staff would coach a small team of students for competitions in Eastern Europe, where they would travel by mini bus. On two or three occasions groups travelled to Hungary. For weeks prior to Hotelympia and other national cookery competitions, it was usual to observe students being coached and advised by staff after hours, and for many years various students enjoyed considerable success. This type of enthusiastic input by teaching staff rubs off onto students and is reflected in their attitude, which they carry with them on entering industry.

The author sampling the results of a class in a training kitchen at Ealing College in the 1970s

Frequently industrialists would say to me, 'Victor, why is the attitude of Ealing students so sensible, practical and down-to-earth in comparison with students from some other colleges?'

I could only reply by saying, 'We do our job in preparing students for careers in the industry the way we believe to be right, but it is encouraging to hear your endorsement, thank you.'

Over the years, I have read in the trade press and heard at various meetings, time and time again, of dissatisfaction at relations between colleges and industry, and whose responsibility it should be to bridge the gap. In my opinion, it should be a two-way exercise, but the colleges should always be prepared to take the initiative.

In the early 1960s during the summer recess, the heads of a handful of hotel schools in Switzerland met informally to discuss their work and its problems. The meeting was so successful that they decided to repeat it the following year. The heads of two German schools heard of the idea and asked if they could join. This was agreed, and in succeeding years the meetings developed, and grew into a European Association of Hotel School Directors who held a three-day congress annually.

The first year I attended the congress was in Strasbourg, followed by Toulouse, Florence then Brussels. By this time the number of delegates was about 100, and the meetings were held at the local hotel school who also supplied most of the lunches and dinners. There was intense rivalry to gain the prestige of holding the congress the following year, and I always remember the Belgian delegates saying, after we had visited France twice, 'Come to Brussels next year, and we will show you what good cooking really is!' It was no idle boast, for the Brussels Hotel School was a splendid building, and with a national educational system whereby twelve-year-olds could take vocational education, this meant that by the time they reached their middle and late teens they were fairly competent. The last night of each congress was traditionally a gala dinner, and when we entered the Brussels School we were greeted by a truly magnificent sight of staff and students impeccably attired in smart uniforms, formed into lines to greet us on arrival at the school entrance. We walked around the large hall and up a sweeping staircase to the rooms where reception canapés were offered, and then into the dining-room for a memorable dinner and evening.

Every four years the congress was offered internationally and a contingent from American colleges would usually attend. Oxford hosted one international meeting where, if my memory is correct, the gala dinner was held in a university college hall. Another was held at the University of Lancaster, where it was a pleasant surprise to see Bob and Ruth Macintosh from Michigan attending. Bob read a paper on 'International Tourism'.

At Strasbourg, in the early days, when the numbers attending were about sixty to seventy, the restaurant of a village an hour's coach ride from the hotel had been taken over for the gala dinner. As the coach pulled up in the village square the local brass band struck up a rousing tune and we were formally welcomed by local dignitaries who joined us for dinner. We enjoyed a truly festive evening, and by the time we clambered onto the coach for the journey home everyone was in a merry mood. Our courier was a delightful young French girl who led the party alternately in singing and telling saucy tales!

On the first evening in Strasbourg we were hosted by the local Confrérie des Tastevins, and given an introduction to six wines of Alsace: Riesling, Sylvaner, Gewurztraminer, Pinot Blanc, Muscat and Pinot Noir. The whole company were assembled in a huge wine cellar, sitting at benches and tables. The members of the Confrérie, dressed in traditional costume, entered singing one of their traditional songs and in slow procession mounted a platform at one end of the cellar. A brief address of welcome was followed by a producer of each of the six wines in turn rising to his feet and delivering a brief eulogy extolling the virtues of his wine. The company then had their glasses filled with his wine and we tasted to the accompaniment of a drinking song with a rousing chorus. By the time this had been repeated for each of the six wines, the chorus had risen to a crescendo. It was a memorable evening.

From Toulouse we were taken to see how Armagnac was produced, an interesting visit which ended in a cellar for a glass and a snack. Down the centre of the cellar were a line of barrels which served as tables, on each of which were half bottles of Armagnac for us to take home. On the labels had been printed our names. It was a pleasant souvenir of the visit.

In reducing some of my outside commitments I had resigned from most City and Guilds meetings, leaving only the moderating committee for the Advanced Cookery for Hotels and Restaurants 152 course, now renumbered as 706/3. I was, however, asked to take on a light task which was too interesting to refuse. This was to act as services assessor, which involved an annual visit to each of the training schools: the Royal Navy, at Chatham; the Army, at Aldershot; and the Royal Air Force, at Hereford.

The services' schools applied to have their courses equated to, and certified by, the City and Guilds. When men and women left the service they then possessed a national qualification which would be recognised by industry. It was a sound idea, and my function was to spend a day assessing the syllabuses, schemes and records of work, and to observe training and testing methods.

A services liaison officer from the permanent City and Guilds staff usually accompanied me. We would visit Chatham and Aldershot, getting there and back within a day, but Hereford required an overnight stay. Meeting at Paddington, we would take a late-afternoon train, dining on the way. Sharing a bottle of wine this made a pleasant way to travel, and the journey soon passed.

Then, one year, British Rail Catering decided to stop serving the dinner menu, which had always included a modest choice of dishes, and replaced it with what they called an 'all day menu'. On studying what was on offer, we had the choice of a salad or a fry-up, and we both ordered the fry-up. A waiter then appeared with what seemed to be the identical wine list that had been used previously. We looked at each other, smiled, and agreed that we couldn't think of a wine that could accompany our chosen meal and settled for coffee!

John was now a sixth-former back at Latymer, having passed a handful of O levels, and was studying for A levels. The annual school reports were much as before, and when we enquired of John's form master his chances of success in A levels and a university place, he smiled gently and indicated there would be little hope of either. Shortly afterwards arrangements were made for a small party of sixth-formers, including John, to go to UMIST (University of Manchester Institute of Science and Technology) for a weekend business game. John came back enthusiastic about everything he had seen and done to declare, 'That's where I'm going when I leave Latymer!' This he eventually did, and gained an honours degree in management sciences, leaving with the additional bonus of also having met his wife-to-be, Tricia.

Michael followed John into the sixth form, gained A-level passes in English, French and mathematics, but refused to consider university because he did not know what he wanted to do. After a year in Australia, two years working in the education offices of the local authority, and a further year in Australia, he returned home to take a TOPS course in computer planning, in which field he has worked ever since.

I now began to experience attacks of vertigo from time to time. Some were mild and wore off after resting quietly, but others were more severe and sent me to bed for a day. If out walking, the effect would be to cause me to veer to the left, and try as I might, there was nothing I could do about it. On one occasion I had been to an industrial liaison meeting in the City at which Bob Kidner was also present. Leaving the building I felt a mild attack coming on, and with apologies I hung onto Bob's arm all the way to the station.

Several months later I attended a meeting with the BBC catering department, followed by lunch. On the way back I felt pains in the stomach, and by the time I reached college, I was doubled up in agony. A colleague immediately took me home where I went straight to bed. Letty rang for the doctor, but Dr Walsh was away and a new young doctor was called in from his day off. When he arrived Letty told him I had been out to lunch, and he came into the bedroom grumbling about patients who over-indulged at lunch, dragging him away from his day off. Letty showed him my American hospital records which he scanned, and his demeanour completely changed. He examined me, I attended the surgery the following day, and then went into Ashford Hospital for a couple of days for further tests. This was late summer, and the ward I was in had virtually been closed for several weeks to assist in giving staff time off. The only other occupants were half a dozen very elderly men who were not ill, but had been admitted for two weeks to give their families, with whom they lived, a break. They were good company and we spent time chatting and playing card games, which they thoroughly enjoyed.

Letty came in to visit and brought me a slab of my favourite toffee, together with my toffee hammer! After she had left, we settled down for a card session, I produced the toffee, cracked it into pieces and, as a gesture, I offered it around. I say 'as a gesture' because they did not have one tooth of their own between the six of them, and I was certain they would refuse. It was not so – their eyes gleamed, the toffee disappeared in one round, and long after I had finished my piece they were still happily sucking away!

The result of the tests was that I saw a surgeon on the Friday before the Monday on which students were back for a new academic year. He told me that my gall-bladder needed removing, and could I come in on the Monday for surgery!

'Term starts on Monday. Could I come in on Monday week?' I asked.

Slightly surprised, he consulted his diary and said, 'Yes, that will be all right. We'll see you on Monday week.'

Surgery was carried out without any problems, and after a couple of weeks' convalescence I was back at school.

Following my next meeting with the consultant, he ordered an extra blood test to check my cholesterol level and as this was high, he told me to see the hospital dietician. To my pleasant surprise, she was one of our ex-dietetic diploma students, and we spent the first ten minutes pleasantly chatting about the course and her career since leaving college.

'Right, now we must get down to business,' she said. 'Tell me every single thing that you eat and drink during an average week.'

I rattled off a typical weekly food intake, following which she ordered me onto a strict fat-free diet. Even my beloved toffee had to go! I looked at her with such a doleful expression when she'd finished telling me the list of things I must not eat that she laughed.

'Come on, now,' I said. 'Do I have to follow this 100 per cent, all the time, or is there a degree of tolerance?'

She smiled and replied, 'Well, let's say 95 per cent of time.'

'Good, that means I can have an occasional treat!'

With that I left, but when I next saw Dr Royds and mentioned the background of the dietician he said, 'In all my years in hospitals [and he was near to retirement], she is the most effective dietician that I have ever worked with.'

I remained on the diet for a year, and this had the effect of reducing the cholesterol to a normal level which has been maintained ever since, assisted by a daily intake of clofybrates which assist in breaking down fat in the blood stream.

The combined effect of all my medical problems led me to adopt my present way of eating. I eat very plainly and in moderation at home, and by doing this I find that I am able, within reason, to indulge myself when we have company or eat out. I still love food and wine, and am blessed with a good digestion. I haven't had an attack of vertigo for a very long time, I now only see the consultant every eighteen months, and have blood tests at eight-week intervals. If I ever have a problem that causes concern I can ring the consultant direct (this has only happened twice in eighteen years). I have never had cause to complain about my treatment and I am a National Health patient.

At college, the school was beginning to miss the strong backing it enjoyed under Dr Pickard. When he believed in something, he gave enthusiastic support, often turning a Nelson eye to the rules in a swash-buckling fashion. As a result, we enjoyed more than our share of senior staff appointments, much to the envy of many other catering schools.

Geoff Tyler, by comparison, was a quiet, relaxed character who acted strictly according to the rules. He could not accept Dr Pickard's thinking on the establishment, and consequently, promotions for any school staff were for a while virtually non-existent. Furthermore, as colleagues holding senior or principal lecturer posts resigned (in most cases following appointment to a high position elsewhere), we were forced to adver-tise for replacements at lower grades. I protested bitterly, but all to no avail and staff morale was noticeably affected.

I was now invited to join the judging panels for two national menu competitions. One, the 'Meal of the Year', was sponsored by the *Caterer and Hotelkeeper*. Entrants planned a five-course menu accompanied with wines of a given country. The panel of judges were Silvino Trompetto – at that time maître chef at the Savoy Hotel – two distinguished wine experts, and two knowledgeable diners. A short list would be agreed from the paper entries and, a day at a time, each pair of competitors prepared, cooked and served their menu to the judges in a private room at the top of the Café Royal. Following the meal, the competitors, chef and waiter joined the judges for coffee and a question and answer session. It was a most interesting and informative exercise, as was the other competition, the established 'Mouton Cadet', which required a menu to be produced suitable for accompaniment by Mouton Cadet red and white wines. The competition formula was similar and equally enjoyable and relaxing.

Since returning from America I'd had little contact with the CTA, and was delighted to receive an invitation to become their first president, which I accepted instantly. I then attempted to attend most council meetings, but after the initial one, which lasted for six hours, I restricted my attendance to two to three hours! Everyone said that I was not expected to be at all meetings, and although I was forced to accept this, it still gave me cause for concern.

All my active life I'd been a severe critic of those on committees who failed to attend regularly or give a fair share of effort. Try as I may, I felt unhappy at giving the CTA council what, in my book, was luke-warm support and after three years regretfully resigned.

One mid-winter morning in 1974 I arose to make the tea and to collect the newspaper and post, which I took back to bed. An official letter had arrived from the Prime Minister asking if I would be prepared to be nominated for an MBE for services to catering education! I was bound to secrecy until after the official announcement in January, but was delighted at the honour, not only for myself, but also on behalf of my colleagues at school.

Letty accompanied me to Buckingham Palace in February 1975, sharing the thrill of driving through the gates in our own car. Entering the palace, along with other award recipients, we walked up the grand staircase flanked by members of the household cavalry, resplendent in their impeccable uniforms with all metal burnished to an eye-dazzling shine. Here we were separated, Letty being conducted to the presentation hall where a regimental orchestra was playing light music, and the recipients to an anteroom, where a member of the royal household gave us instructions on how to proceed for the ceremony. I was privileged and proud to receive the award from Her Majesty the Queen, personally. We came straight back to the college for a celebration lunch with all the staff. It was certainly a day to remember, further enhanced by 128 letters of congratulation received from friends, colleagues and students. Seven days later, we moved house to Jersey Road, Osterley, backing onto a farm section of Osterley Park, where we have lived happily ever since.

Towards the end of June I received a phone call from George Matthews who I had met on the Hotel and Catering Industry Training Board in London. He had left the board, and was in South Africa working with their hotel board. Training in South Africa was carried out in three main centres: Johannesburg, Cape Town and Durban, and some smaller units, one of which was in Soweto. In an effort to improve standards, the board had arranged for a member of a French hotel school to spend six weeks visiting the training centres. He unfortunately had to withdraw, and George was telephoning from South Africa at two weeks' notice to ask if I would take his place. I gathered as much information as possible and asked him to phone again that evening after I had spoken to Letty. The term was almost ended, and Letty and I had booked a holiday which we agreed to cancel as I had insisted she accompany me, so that when George rang back I was able to say we would be on our way.

We flew by British Airways Jumbo, arriving at General Smuts Airport to be met by Leon Malan, Director of the Hotel Board, and Mayron Schoemann, Chief Training Officer, who drove us to a hotel in Pretoria and arranged to collect us later for dinner. The travelling had upset Letty who couldn't face dinner, so I went off with Mr and Mrs Malan and Mr and Mrs Matthews. We went to what Leon described as the best restaurant in South Africa, the Villa Lombardy, owned by Mario, a typical Italian restaurateur. The property included a farm which supplied his kitchen with milk, cream, eggs, butter, vegetables and poultry. We had drinks in a pleasant lounge, and the restaurant consisted of twenty-five seats set in two rooms. Seven black boys served an enjoyable, relaxing dinner which I was sorry that Letty had to miss.

By the following morning, Saturday, Letty was feeling peckish but wanting to eat in our room, so I called for room service. A pleasant native lad with a perpetual smile came to take the order and I requested, very slowly and carefully, two boiled eggs cooked for four minutes and a slice of lemon for my tea (this was in addition to coffee, toast and marmalade), and then repeated the request. The lad returned later with four boiled eggs cooked for two minutes, and a glass of orange juice in place of the lemon!

After breakfast, Mayron and Maryki Schoemann collected us, took us to the bank, back to their house for tea and then on a tour of Pretoria, followed by lunch. The tour of Pretoria continued after lunch, and that evening the four of us dined in the Flamingo Room of the Boulevard Hotel, enjoying a good meal with attentive service.

On Sunday morning we attended mass at the cathedral. Mayron took us out of interest but stayed for the service (he was a member of the Dutch Reform Church). Afterwards we visited the botanical gardens, then lunched at home with the Schoemanns where we met their three children – a nice family and a delightful house. At four o'clock, Leon and his wife drove us to the Sunnyside Park Hotel, Johannesburg, where we were to stay for two weeks. It was a well-appointed and well-run hotel in which we were very comfortable.

Early Monday morning – down to work! I was collected and taken to the Hotel School where I was fairly busily occupied for the next two weeks. Leon Malan had arranged for a member of his staff to look after Letty during the days and she was given an interesting programme to follow.

It was good to meet an ex-Ealing student, Roelf Dapper, teaching at the school, and Letty and I spent a pleasant evening at his home meeting his wife, Margot, and two lively sons. (Roelf is now on the teaching staff at Ealing College.) In the evenings we were invited, or taken to, a number of hotels including the Carlton, President, Tollman Towers (managed by another ex-Ealing student, Robert Vinson), Milpark (where I gave a talk followed by discussion to a group of 100 hoteliers) and the Landdrost, where Harry Murray was in charge. We also saw the original version of *Ipi Tombi* which had opened in March 1974 at the Academy Theatre and was still a sell-out after sixty-seven weeks. Letty and I were taken on the tourist coach trip around Soweto, which we found interesting and extremely thought provoking.

I also spent two days at the Hotel School Ga-Rankuwa for blacks at Arcadia, where I got on well with the staff and students. To our pleasant surprise, the school gave a five-course gala dinner in our honour on the second evening. Following dinner, a Zulu choir entertained with songs which were spine-tingling in both intensity and quality of sound. Letty was presented with a book of colour plates of South African flowers, and I was solemnly handed an authentic Zulu warrior's shield complete with assegai and knobkerrie.

Every evening I recorded my daily experiences and comments about the hotel school at Johannesburg, which was the largest in the country, and Letty would have the notes typed up the following day. Generally speaking, the standards were unimpressive, and I tactfully attempted to offer advice as I went along and at staff meetings.

On 26 July we flew to Cape Town where Letty and I stayed at the Vineyard Hotel. Our room was at the rear and offered a magnificent view of Table Mountain. Leon Malan travelled with us and we were met by our host, Hans Rammesmeyer, who was in charge of training, and Brenda Chance, the South African representative for Edward Arnold, publishers, in Cape Town. In our room was a bowl of Cape flowers and a beautiful display of proteas from Inga Bang, an ex-Ealing student who lived nearby. We enjoyed a pleasant dinner with Hans and his wife, Mirella, who then spent the weekend showing us some of the delightful scenery in and around Cape Town. We went up Table Mountain by cable car, saw the Kirstenbosch gardens, masses of strelitzias, and visited Hut Bay fishing village where we were offered smoked snoek. Tinned snoek was a fish that became available in Britain during, and immediately after, the war when food supplies were scarce, but neither Letty nor I cared for it.

Once again, I spent my days at the training centre, observing and talking to staff and compiling impressions for Letty to type. The training set-up was much smaller than at Johannesburg but the standards were about the same.

We dined at the Mount Nelson Hotel, spent another evening at the home of Mr and Mrs Bang and Inga, and took the wine route to Tulbagh, where Mr and Mrs De Wett Thuron showed us over the plant and we tasted four delicious wines. Lunch was served in the Old Farm House, a public restaurant owned by the KWV, the South African wine organisation. Hans drove us back through the mountains. The scenery was quite magnificent, but some of the roads and bends were hair-raising.

We lunched at the President hotel and, on another day, at the KWV cellars at Paarl following a wine-tasting at Stellenbosch. Our Cape Town visit ended with dinner at Arthur's Seat, followed by a visit to a friend's private house in Constantia which was like a millionaire's dream palace.

On 10 August we flew to Durban where we were met by Gilbert Naidu and taken to his house for tea, followed by a visit to several Indian-owned hotels. In Durban, our hotel was the Cabana Beach, on the shores of the Indian Ocean. On entering the hotel we were greeted by the general manager, an ex-Acton student, who had booked us into a penthouse suite and insisted on us taking dinner with him. The suite was quite opulent, and we thoroughly enjoyed a quiet relaxed dinner for three with plenty to talk about since the Acton days.

The following day Gilbert took me to the school, which was a 100 per cent Indian establishment with a great deal of enthusiasm everywhere, but again, the standards were disappointing. That evening we attended a reception given by the mayor of Durban, a charming person, as was his wife. The British Consul was present, as were all the teachers from the school and members of the local community. Letty and I received an address of welcome to which I briefly replied. The following day, a lunch was held at the school which after a short rest, was followed by a reception and the annual prize-giving. The next day I spoke at a meeting of local hoteliers, which was held at the school, and before leaving Durban Letty and I were able to visit a large cane-sugar plantation and refinery.

On leaving Durban, Leon Malan drove us north-east to the Zululand Safari Lodge, Hluhlwe (pronounced 'Swish-louis'), where we spent two delightful days. On the first day, the Mencke brothers drove us around in a Land-rover, and we observed animals in their natural habitat – just before dusk we got within 20 yards of a white rhino. On the second day, we were taken to a large animal watering-hole. In the centre of the watering-hole was a covered hide with louvered windows so that one could see out without being seen. The hide was approached by a covered way 200 yards from the hole, and we were warned to proceed on tiptoe and keep quiet. Once in the hide, benches were provided for seating in front of the observation windows.

There began one of the most fascinating sights I have ever seen, as families of animals warily approached the hole to drink. As they came into sight in their family groups from the bush, they did not approach in a straight line, but walked from side to side, ever on the alert for predators. The families with young ones were most amusing, particularly the monkeys, who were continually up to mischief and being chastised by their elders. One baby monkey, after cheeking a parent, received a cuff for its pains and scampering away, came perilously close to what we had thought was an old log at the water's edge. As the baby approached, the log stirred, and the jaws of a crocodile opened. Fortunately, the crocodile was too slow, and the monkey scampered back to its mother, leapt into her arms, chattering excitedly, and was fondled and petted to calm it down. The whole cavalcade took one-and-a-half to two hours, was slow and deliberate, and included different kinds of deer and zebras, which were the last animals to arrive. It remains as one of my deepest impressions of Africa. When we regretfully tore ourselves away, I left thinking that after seeing wild animals relaxed in their natural state, I never wanted to visit a zoo again.

Leaving Zululand, we drove across the Transvaal to Pretoria, where we wound up the tour. I completed my report which, on the whole, was scathing, together with a lengthy list of recommendations, and we prepared for the journey back to England.

South Africa is a vast country, and exceedingly beautiful in many parts. Letty and I were disturbed at the ways in which we thought people were labelled in groups – white, coloured, black (Zulu and Bantu) and Asian – and at what appeared to us to be unfair segregation. Attitudes adopted by many people we found unacceptable, and must surely change. It is a country with many problems, which will have to be resolved more fairly than hitherto if a blood-bath is to be avoided. The tragedy is that it is such a vast, wealthy country, that given the goodwill, there should be sufficient for all to share. It is possibly unfair, following a short acquaintance of six weeks, to comment on such a large, complex country, but they were the impressions Letty and I shared. Having said that, we did meet many progressive South Africans who were as concerned about the country's problems as we were.

We returned back home again to find the house and the boys in good shape. The magnificent 200-year-old elm tree outside our front garden had been lopped in our absence because of Dutch Elm disease. John and Michael had volunteered to do the job while we were away, but we considered a tree of that size would be risky for enthusiastic amateurs. We had arranged for a tree surgeon to carry out the job, and the boys removed a thick six-foot high hedge of laurel, elm and bramble from along our garden frontage, together with several yards of fencing, and tidied up in quite a professional manner. Neighbours were so impressed at the hard work and the way John and Michael tackled the job that they wanted to know how much we paid them. When we replied, 'Nothing,' they were surprised, and commented, 'Our sons would want to know how much we were going to pay them before tackling a job of that size!'

School began again in September. We had for some time been having timetable problems fitting all our classes in the Mary King Room, and it seemed the only way out was to hold one or two classes in the evenings. As we wondered how the students would react, we decided to use the classes with older students, and also organised the evenings as a complete management exercise. We encouraged the class to plan the evening according to a theme of their own choosing. This included the food, menus, decoration of the room and anything else, within reason, they considered would contribute to its success. Two classes would be involved, one in the kitchen, one in the restaurant, and each was responsible for the planning, ordering, organisation, supervision and costing. A member of staff was available for advice and assistance, but as far as possible we tried to make the situations the responsibility of the student.

The idea was a winner from the start; the students preferred working in the evenings, and when asked why, replied, 'Everyone is more relaxed. We have no classes to go to afterwards and we can have some fun!'

Almost all the evenings were a success, and were enjoyed by students, staff and customers. Some classes went to endless trouble to achieve the atmosphere they required. Letty and I went in for dinner with two friends on one occasion to find the room jam-packed with tables in order to accommodate a cabaret area! One of the students was friendly with the banqueting manager of the London Hilton and had 'borrowed' the cabaret show of native singers and dancers for the evening. The finale of this excellent and entertaining group's performance was to position two long stout poles on the floor, with a group member at each end. Then, to the slow rhythm of the music, the poles were shuffled inwards and outwards while dancers stepped nimbly in and out. The whole performance was carried out to a chant, with the tempo steadily increasing until everything was happening so quickly, the eye could hardly follow it, and we wondered how many cracked ankle bones resulted.

The performance ended to terrific applause. Then the leader of the group called for volunteers from the audience, and called for Mr Ceserani to join the fun. I was taken in hand for a brief run through by a scantily clad dusky maiden, but once the dance started I had no time to admire her charms – it took total concentration to keep my ankles away from those clacking poles. Victor Delaney hadn't included this dance in his ballroom dancing classes! I managed fairly well at the slower tempo, but once the speed built up it seemed like endless torture. I stumbled off the floor exhausted after what to me had seemed a full five minutes but which in fact, I was assured, was no longer than a minute.

In 1978, Miles Quest, then editor of the *Catering Times*, was asked by the Jersey Tourism Office to recruit a team to carry out restaurant assessments on the island. Annually, in May, a gastronomic festival was held, and a voluntary assessment of restaurants took place by a group of English and French specialists. I was able to join for a week and subsequently assisted for eight years in all. Once I had retired, I was a member of the team for two weeks at a time, of which Letty would join me for the second.

Categories were of gold, silver and bronze according to type, and within the gold and silver, the number of toques would vary according to standard, with the restaurateurs themselves choosing the category for which they wished to be judged. One judge would visit a bronze entry, one or two judges a silver, and two, three or four, a gold. Table bookings were made under an assumed name, and a fully comprehensive detailed mark sheet would be completed on return to the hotel.

One evening, I was out with Ian Tyers, then executive manager of the AA hotels and information services, dining at a restaurant that for many years had enjoyed the reputation of being one of the top six on the island. We knew of the proprietor (an ex-Savoy restaurant manager), but he was not in evidence that evening. We had a disappointing meal with indifferent service, and after independently completing our assessment forms later, we exchanged opinions to find that we could not possibly recommend a gold award. On bringing the matter to the attention of Miles Quest we said that, on the basis of one visit, it would surely be unfair to downgrade the restaurant from gold to silver. He agreed and said he would arrange for a second visit by different judges (this was standard procedure). We also said that we would welcome the opportunity to talk to the restaurateur regarding our experience. 'Why not?' he replied. 'Go ahead.' This we did, by inviting him to come to our hotel where we gave him a full account of our experience. He was most grateful, and following that, counselling was always offered to all entrants and invariably taken up.

During Letty's visit one year we went to a restaurant at Gorey, on the east coast. Our hotel was at Portelet in the west of the island. I had visited the establishment, a silver category entry, on two previous occasions and found it to be of average standard. On arrival, we sat in the reception/bar area, I ordered drinks, the menu came, and I disappeared into the toilet. During my absence, a lady appeared and asked Letty if we had booked.

'Yes. My husband telephoned to reserve a table,' Letty replied.

'In what name, madam?'

'Oh! I don't know,' stammered Letty, in confusion.

I had forgotten to tell her what name I was using that year, and when I returned from the toilet, she was blushing furiously. The lady who had enquired about the name came to take our order, and was obviously doing her best to keep a knowing smile from her face. I thought it was a joke but Letty wasn't so amused. We enjoyed a good meal, however, with attentive service and after paying the bill I introduced myself as a judge, asked to see the proprietor (he was also the chef, and his wife had taken our order), complimented them on the meal and said they would receive a favourable assessment and it would be pointless coming for counselling the following day. We then enjoyed a good laugh about the start to our visit and left.

Lew and Ruth Minor issued an invitation for Letty and I to join them on a trip to Canada that summer, and Bob McIntosh suggested that afterwards we spent some time with them at the summer cottage in Portage and then went back to Lansing. This sounded attractive, and on 30 June we flew to Montreal to be met by Lew and Ruth, and drove to our first night stop. This was Hotel La Sapinière, situated in a year-round resort in the Laurentian mountains, fifty miles north of Montreal. We were introduced to the head chef who was the captain of the Canadian Culinary Olympics team, and spent an interesting afternoon at his home talking shop. We stayed for two nights, and were impressed with the high standard of accommodation, catering and leisure pursuits provided.

Our next port of call was Quebec, where we experienced the reluctance of many of the natives to speak anything other than French. Again we stayed two nights at the Château Frontenac, a seventeen-storey hotel, with an average of seventeen rooms on each floor, which was opened in 1893. It had obviously been a grand hotel in its day, but was by now faded, worn, and well past its best. In the past it had been visited by many distinguished guests including King George V, King George VI and Queen Elizabeth (now the Queen Mother), Queen Elizabeth and Prince Philip, Winston Churchill, Stanley Baldwin and many more, including a long list of stage and screen personalities.

From Quebec we set out north along the St Lawrence river into New Brunswick, following the coastline around the Gaspé peninsula. It was a fascinating trip, passing through many small fishing villages. On the roadside, outside small dwellings, housewives built clay wood-fired ovens in which they baked bread and offered it for sale piping hot. As this coast is famous for lobsters, it was possible to buy a loaf or two, some lobsters at cheap prices and then call into a small supermarket for butter and mayonnaise and a bottle to wash it all down. Picnic tables abound in North America, so there was no problem finding somewhere to eat.

Passing through Shediac, which is known as the lobster capital of the world because of the vast quantities of lobsters caught in the surrounding waters, we decided to stay for lunch. The restaurant we selected was the Fisherman's Paradise, a seafood and steak restaurant where, from a menu with lobster cooked in almost every conceivable way, we were able to select a fresh cold lobster plate at a cost of $9.95. (We were getting $2.38 to the pound.)

After completing the Gaspé peninsula, we flew to Halifax, Nova Scotia, where we stayed one night at the Hotel Nova Scotian and one night at Keltic Lodge, which was as pleasant as the hotel was dull. Lew drove around the 184-mile Cabot Trail, which took us through Cape Breton Highlands National Park with its 377 square miles of breathtaking scenery. We saw the spot now marked by a monument where John Cabot landed in 1497, unfurled the royal banner, and took possession in the name of King Henry VII. The Scottish tradition is strong on Nova Scotia, and a fine museum was constructed in 1954 to house the story of the life and work of Alexander Graham Bell.

Our last visit was to the College of Celtic Folk Arts which was founded in 1939 as a living memorial to the highland Scottish pioneers who left their homeland to endure the rigours and hardships of pioneer life in Canada. The college exists as a summer school where students up to eighteen years of age are given intensive instruction in piping, drumming and dancing along with lessons in the Gaelic language, songs and customs.

It was now time to say goodbye to our hosts, and we flew off to Lansing to be met by Bob and Ruth McIntosh. We stayed a week at their home, ten minutes walk from the university campus, and thoroughly enjoyed seven days of trips and retracing our steps back to Cherry Lane and the many other places and people we had met in 1968–69.

Bob and Ruth then closed the house and prepared to drive to the cottage on the shores of Portage Lake, where they would be staying for six weeks. On the way we called at the National Music Center, Interlochen, where an outstanding music camp for high school students is situated. Seven orchestras at the camp provide orchestral training and routines. Choral music, classical guitar, chamber music, composition, jazz, art, dance and theatre arts are also taught. We had time to attend one concert and were impressed by the high standard of musicianship.

Bob arranged for us to go cherry picking, which was a real eye-opener. The orchard was huge, with trees groaning under the weight of large, black, ripe cherries. We each took a bucket and filled them in no time at all. What was interesting was the cherry picking machinery. A large pair of clamps were fixed firmly around a tree trunk. The clamps were an extension of a pair of arms secured to a powerful machine, which vibrated rapidly backwards and forwards shaking the trees violently, causing the ripe cherries to fall in a black cascade. On either side of the tree was a twenty foot long, four foot wide, endless belt of canvas, affixed to a machine which revolved the belt continuously while cherries were falling, catching them neatly and transporting them to one end of the belt where fruit packers waited to put the fruit into boxes.

The remainder of our time passed all too quickly, and after expressing our grateful thanks to our hosts and good friends for all their kind hospitality, we flew home at the end of July.

At college we had experienced a further change of principal, Geoff Tyler having left to be replaced by Neil Merritt, who rapidly established his aggressive style of leadership, steering the college towards that hoped-for Mecca of so many technical colleges – polytechnic status and degree courses unlimited.

Money was beginning to be in tight supply, and for the first time in many years we began to feel the pinch. Attitudes in the college were changing. New influences on many committees somehow seemed to be taking the emphasis of our thinking away from the students, and directing it towards the staff. The power and influence of the students union was increasing rapidly which was fine when a good set of officers were in post, but if the reverse was the case, then friction appeared to breed. The old style of working based on teamwork and dedication amongst staff that I had grown up with, and grown to believe in, was disappearing.

For the first time since I had entered teaching, I began to lose my appetite for the job. Normally I arose each morning looking forward to the challenge of a new day. I would be in college early, eager to tackle any problems that presented themselves. I no longer felt the urge to do this. I began to dread certain college committees and to dislike certain individuals and their attitudes, and as the year 1979 progressed and I began to contemplate reaching the age of sixty in October, I started to consider retirement. Other deciding factors were that I began to tire quickly, was frequently arriving home tired and irritable, and my sense of hearing was declining. I had taken advice on my ears, and after tests I was told that the hearing in one ear was well below par, but the other was above normal for my age. On enquiring about an aid, I was informed that they did not consider it would be of any use but that I could be fitted and try one out if I wished. This I did but it did not help. I tried three aids in all, at different times and without success, but with one good ear I managed reasonably well except in certain rooms where acoustics gave a problem, and sometimes on the bench in court, when particularly quiet speakers or those with high-pitched tones were talking.

Letty and I discussed the situation and she reminded me that many years ago when I came out of the Army she had been of the opinion that all men should retire at the age of sixty! I had pooh-poohed this at the time.

My decision was finally sealed when I next saw the consultant who, after examining me and checking on my age, gave the opinion that I should retire. I said that I couldn't agree with him more. With that, on my return to college I told Neil Merritt I would be retiring in December and called a meeting to inform the staff.

With the decision made, I felt as though a huge load had been taken off my mind. Later in the year, after doing calculations regarding pension and lump sum payable on retirement, I wrote to the pensions branch of NATFE (the further education sector of the NUT). The helpful advice I received clearly indicated that it would be to my financial advantage to delay retirement until the end of the spring term. I had fully reconciled myself to retiring at Christmas, but as the spring term was a short one and the financial difference was marked, I deferred retirement until Easter 1980.

Neil Merritt was always striving to recruit overseas students, and had made personal connections in America and Canada to assist. He had planned to visit a large institution of further education in Montreal in February, taking his wife and two children on holiday in North America when business was concluded. He particularly wanted to explore possibilities of student exchange between the language and catering schools, and arranged for the two respective heads of schools to accompany him. So, rather unexpectedly, I found myself on an interesting and informative trip.

The well-equipped catering school in Montreal was housed in a large building, part of which was designed as a well-appointed hotel with a substantial amount of accommodation. The Ealing party stayed in the hotel and was fed in the dining-room. The majority of the teaching, textbooks and handouts were in French, and many of the lecturers were partisan French-speaking Canadians. I got on reasonably well with the teaching staff, but detected in a number of them a veiled suspicion, combined with a gentle hostility, which was puzzling as I was only there for a week!

I returned to Ealing with only weeks to go, and I really began to look forward to the last day of term. As I returned from each college committee for the last time and put the minutes of the meeting in their file, it was with a feeling of relief.

On my last day I had planned to go around the college making personal visits to the numerous sections of the college support services to thank them for their help and co-operation, and to say goodbye. The previous evening I wrote out a list of calls to ensure that I left no one out, and on the last day, breezed into college feeling on top of the world.

After making the first call on the list, my mood suddenly changed. I felt miserable, and, realising that I would not be able to make any more calls, I became thoroughly depressed. To say that I was surprised would be putting it mildly. I just could not understand what had happened, particularly as the mood remained with me for the rest of the day and I couldn't wait to get away home to peace and quiet!

What a strange way to complete almost thirty years (all but one term!) in a job that, for the most part, I had thoroughly enjoyed and which had given me so much fulfilment and satisfaction!

CHAPTER 11

1980 Onwards

Retirement

At home during the Easter holiday I initially felt much the same as in previous years, but as the first day of the summer term approached, and the realisation that it was no concern of mine sank in, I slowly relaxed. I arose, made tea, collected the paper and indulged in the luxury of reading the daily news and sipping tea at leisure in bed. Jersey Road lies between the M4 and the A4. Consequently it has a trickle of commuters' cars between 7.45 and 8.45 a.m., and I would sit up in bed smugly satisfied in knowing that the days of joining them were over!

I now appreciated the closeness of Osterley Park and formed the habit of walking around it twice a day whenever possible. It is a pleasant spot, cared for by the royal parks staff, with an ornamental lake containing a varied collection of water-fowl including large families of Canadian wild geese which often fly over the garden giving variations of living Peter Scott paintings. The house is a National Trust property, administered by the Victoria and Albert Museum. The grand neo-classical villa and its landscaped park were created during the second half of the eighteenth century and contain many examples of the work of Robert Adam. The house was presented to the National Trust in 1949 by the ninth Earl of Jersey.

In later years, during the summer months, varied evening concerts and entertainments have been featured. One summer evening, the grounds around the house swarmed with guests in all manner of Edwardian and Victorian costume, both civilian and military. Refreshment marquees were busy and numerous parties brought picnic hampers. At the side of the house in between the cedar trees a large, square stage had been erected, and as I approached the strains of a lively Russian dance came over the loudspeakers and a troupe of dancers leapt onto the stage. An entertaining twenty minutes' programme of traditional folk music and dance followed, warmly applauded by an appreciative audience. That provided an unexpected bonus to my evening exercise! The interior of the house is frequently used as a setting for film work and a collection of vans, equipment and a caterers' wagon can be seen parked outside on these occasions.

The farmer lives in a house half-way up the drive from Jersey Road to Osterley House, and has established a small but popular farm shop for the sale of produce. His wife has a collection of about a dozen horses of various types including Shetland ponies, which are employed in giving riding lessons to young people.

Our branch library is ten minutes' walk away. Alongside is Osterley bowling green, and Andrew Durkan, a county-level bowler, said that I should take up the game when I retired, have a set of woods as a retirement gift, and that he would give me some instruction. At the end of Jersey Road is Wyke Green Golf Club, so I was well situated for a retirement full of interesting pursuits if I wished.

People often talk to me about retirement, discussing how to cope, the merits of making plans and expressing many points of view. I consider that one's way of life after finishing full-time employment is a personal matter which everyone should endeavour to work out to suit themselves.

In my case, I had made it clear that although leaving Ealing, I was not yet prepared to sit back. As a result, sufficient requests for my services in various ways have come along over the years enabling me to be selective. I have refused anything that would involve stress or too demanding a commitment, and have endeavoured to slow down and operate at a more reduced pace than hitherto.

Time passes quickly and life is full of interest. I am in close and continuing contact with many varied sections of industry and its education and training activities. Judging competitions occupies a good proportion of time, and book revision and updating is an ongoing pursuit which now benefits from the more relaxed time available.

A further bonus in retirement is the convenience of travel from home. Osterley station, on the Piccadilly line, is five minutes' walk; Piccadilly Circus can be reached within forty minutes; Heathrow is twenty minutes away; and the M4, M3 and M25 are within a few miles.

Many people suggest that I now work harder than when I was at college, but this is quite untrue. I enjoy what is, for me, a perfect retirement, being involved in a sensible number of projects all of which give me enjoyment, satisfaction and keep the brain active, working within an environment that has been my life for half a century.

In April 1980, I attended a Catering Teachers Association Conference at Thomas Danby College, Leeds, at the conclusion of which I was delighted to be presented with a gift that has been used every day since. A hand-beaten, engraved, silver serviette ring, fashioned out of a piece of antique silver.

Letty and I had spent a happy farewell evening in the Mary King Room at Ealing College with old staff colleagues, and on a later occasion, the director and heads of schools arranged a pleasant surprise by organising a farewell dinner in the Robert Adam Room of Boodles Club. This was made possible by the courtesy of Richard Edmunds, club manager, and Cecil Bill, my old number two at Boodles, who was then almost on the point of retirement and who cooked the meal. It was a most delightful evening. After receiving a kind invitation from the Royal Air Force Catering Officers Association to be an honorary member, I was really beginning to enjoy retirement!

Letty and I spent a weekend in Folkestone where I was attending a CTA branch meeting one Saturday. We stayed with Stan Regnaud and his wife, Lilo. Stan had retired from Westminster two years earlier, and had bought a handsome bungalow with a good-sized garden. The house and garden, which was almost completely given over to vegetables, were precision and orderliness personified – such organisation was typical of Stan Regnaud. Lilo worked part-time for a fine-arts dealer, and Stan did all the shopping and cooked a three-course lunch and dinner daily. He had switched over strongly to healthy eating, but still enjoyed fish and chips once a week and an occasional egg and bacon meal. He baked cakes with little or no fat and was thoroughly enjoying his way of life. After dinner on the first evening we stayed chatting for so long that both Letty and Lilo gave up saying 'What on earth do you two find to keep talking about?' and retired to bed. Stan and I had so many things in common that we kept going until the early hours. It was a thoroughly entertaining weekend that passed quickly. As we left on Monday morning and said goodbye, little did we realise that this was the last time we would see Stan as sadly he passed away later in the year as a result of a brain tumour.

One of the most worthwhile competitions that I am involved in judging is the 'Student Taste of Britain', open to teams of four full-time, part-time or sandwich-course students under the age of twenty-one. Teams are asked to devise a three-course, sit-down waiter or waitress served menu for twenty covers around the theme 'A Taste of Britain'. The meal has to be suitable for serving at a college luncheon to be held in April, and cost price for food, drink and coffee should not exceed £10 per head. A local or national theme may be developed, but no restriction is placed on the nationality of accompanying drinks. Teams are required to submit the menu, accompanying drinks, costs per head, recipes, detailed methods of preparation and service, and a full schedule of estimated costs for food and drink.

The initial paper entries are divided into four regions, and copies (known only by numbers) are sent to each judge two weeks before a meeting at which the final four teams (one from each region) are selected. Each regional winning team is subsequently asked to prepare, cook and serve their menu for twenty covers in the college training restaurant, with one table of six reserved for the judges. The teams are not allowed any assistance in the kitchen by their lecturer and they commence work at 9 a.m., with lunch to be served at 1 p.m. A team of waiters or waitresses are provided to serve the meal.

The competition offers a stimulating challenge to the students, an opportunity to develop teamwork, research the regional foods of their part of the country and to do their own thing. Over the years we have had many memorable meals and been continually impressed by the quality of work and effort put in by the better hard-working teams. The four final menus in 1987 were:

1 *Aperitif: Hope and Glory*
   (Plymouth gin, Drambuie, Somerset cider)

Scallops in saffron and dill sauce	*Lamberhurst Priory Müller Thurgau 1985*
Grilled breast of duck with spinach, black pudding, apple, juniper and lime sauce	*Châteauneuf-du-Pape Château St André 1984*
A proliferation of roots, Byron potatoes	
Boozy bread and butter pudding	*Lemon refresher Lindisfarne Mead*
Coffee and Grasmere ginger-bread	

2   Medallions of Dee salmon and   Lamberhurst Schonenberger
      Dover sole with a sauce of   1985, Tunbridge Wells
      cream, mustard and poppy
      seed

      Thin slices of locally reared   Pinot Noir Réserve
      veal, pan fried, with spring   Personeue 1983
      onions and a sauce of wine,   Huguel Riquewihr Alsace
      redcurrants and yoghurt

      Buttered baby carrots, spinach
      envelopes with creamed
      wild mushrooms

      Grated potato bound in a light
      batter and shallow-fried

      Sweetpaste tartlets filled with   Brown Brothers Orange
      farmhouse Cheshire   Muscat late harvest 1983,
      cheese, apple purée and   Milawa Vineyards, Victoria,
      walnuts, served with a fresh   Australia
      egg-custard sauce lightly
      flavoured with walnut

      Coffee served with Scotch
      whisky or Drambuie

3   Fresh crab broth with rice   Madeira
      purée finished with egg
      yolks and double cream

      Braised saddle of venison   Châteauneuf-du-Pape
      garnished with glazed   Sparkling Malvern Water
      chestnuts, apple halves
      filled with rowan jelly, cider
      and juniper sauce

      Spinach soufflé, Ashbourne
      carrots

      Sliced, steamed potatoes in
      natural yoghurt, double
      cream, topped with mature
      English Cheddar   ·

      Piped potato nests filled with
      finely chopped onions,
      garnished with Hampshire
      truffles

      Cream cheese mousse   Veuve Cliquot
      dressed with bilberries   Ponsardin demi-sec
      steeped in Can-y-Delyn,
      served with Welsh
      shortbread

      Coffee with Irish Mist

4	*Pike and tarragon charlotte (a pike and tarragon cream served in a wholemeal shell)*	*Pinot d'Alsace AOC Cave de Kientzheim 1985*
	Prime Scotch rump filled with produce from the forests and glens	*Château Lamathe Cissac 1982 AC Haute-Médoc Cru Bourgeois*
	Cauliflower soufflé layered with peas	
	Braised Golden Maris Pipers served in a basket of chips, garnished with glazed carrots	
	Potatoes cooked in milk and butter, garnished with mint leaves	
	Fresh butter and oatmeal shortbread filled with local curds and local fruits	*Kallstadter Steinacker Auslese 1983*

The remainder of 1980 passed pleasantly. I spent two weeks on restaurant assessment in Jersey, Letty joining me for the second week, and I appreciated, on return, being able to relax and not having to chase into college. Volunteers were being requested at a magistrates meeting for service on the domestic courts panel, and as the number of hands showing was below the required number, I decided to assist.

An interesting consultancy project was occupying me on average three to four days a month, and although I was thoroughly enjoying my newly found freedom, I still had mild feelings of guilt if I spent too much time without some form of paperwork to deal with. The habit of years was hard to shake off!

In 1981, at the college degree presentation ceremony held at the Queen Elizabeth Hall, I was privileged to receive an Honorary Fellowship, and this was followed in the next few months by honorary memberships of the Association Culinaire Française, and of the City and Guilds of London Institute. Rather than keeping the certificates in a drawer I framed and hung them on the wall of my study where they are now, in the company of many other certificates and photographs of friends, colleagues and events in my life that I now frequently glance at and recall with pleasure.

A new competition was launched during this year – '*The Observer/*

Mouton Cadet Dinner Party Menu', open to readers of *The Observer*. Each competitor had to submit a menu with three courses suitable to be accompanied by the Mouton Cadet white and red wines. Recipes are required for the first two courses, but not for the third which may be either sweet or savoury.

There is a panel of three judges: Paul Levy, Jane Grigson and myself. At our initial meeting we agree a short-list of six who are invited to the cellars of Hedges and Butler at hourly intervals on one day to cook and serve one course. We look for food that is interesting, light, not too demanding for a busy person to prepare and fun to eat. Above all, it must complement the wines.

After all dishes have been presented and the judges have deliberated, the competitors join us over a glass of champagne for a discussion, following which three competitors are selected to proceed to the second stage. This takes place a week later, when at two-hourly intervals, each competitor cooks and serves both courses. The winner and guest go to La Varenne school in Paris for a week's course on contemporary French cuisine. All three finalists and their companions, accompanied by the judges, win a three-day trip to Bordeaux during which they visit Château Mouton-Rothschild, and all six finalists receive cases of wine.

It is an interesting competition that has retained its popularity and attracts a wide variety of entries. Six cookery books have been published by past winners, and the 1983 winner, Frances Bissell, and the 1984 winner, Richard Cawley, have written on food for press and magazines.

In 1986, because of the high standard of entries, we arranged for a second set of six 'cook-offs', which we shall continue in the future, and in 1988 we again changed the rules to allow four competitors a day, on three successive days, to each cook two courses. This seems to have strengthened what was already a successful, esteemed competition.

The Higher National Diploma in Hotel and Catering Operations was being phased out, with three or four years left at most, and I was asked to take over as external assessor for the gastronomy option for six colleges. It was an interesting exercise which gave me an insight into current teaching and student thinking on this vast fascinating subject.

I also became more heavily involved in that excellent competition, 'Student Catermind', as question-master for all the regional heats, and assistant to Magnus Magnusson in the grand final. During this period I set all the questions, and with the amount of travelling involved at the worst time of the year, it was an arduous although enjoyable commitment.

One year, the Scottish heat was being held at the University of Stirling in a large, modern lecture theatre. The temperature had been below zero for several days, and the central heating had broken down twenty-four hours previously. I entered the theatre in my warmest clothes and a muffler, cap and gloves but was so cold that I kept them on all evening, with the exception of the gloves which I was forced to remove to be able to turn the cards over. To make things worse, on returning to the hotel before nine o'clock and requesting some hot food all they could supply was coffee and biscuits.

'Student Catermind' must go down as one of the most popular competitions of all time, and reflects considerable credit on the time, thought and energy devoted to it by Sheila Mitchell and Harry Andrews, two leading personalities and stalwarts of the Industrial Caterers Association. Year after year, with unflagging effort, they beaver away unselfishly, devoting a tremendous amount of their time. After three years of full involvement I was more than ready to hand over.

A competition which started in 1979 and has continued is the 'Quality Food Awards', sponsored by *Super Marketing*, a grocery trade publication, and it has given me a completely new type of work involvement. Any food product for human consumption (not including drinks) introduced for sale through the retail grocery trade during the last fifteen months may be entered.

As the competition has gained popularity, so the number of entries and variety of products has increased. All entries are now categorised and judging takes place over two days at the South Glamorgan Institute of Higher Education, where the entries are prepared for judging by students under supervision. On day one, well over a hundred products are tasted and whittled down to about sixty for the final day. The highly esteemed awards are presented by category, usually at a luncheon in a West End London hotel.

In 1982, it was decided that a new edition of *The Theory of Catering* should be prepared for 1984. After agreeing on a division of the work required with Ron Kinton, I found it a relaxing pleasure to be able to write without the pressure of a full-time job. Normally an early riser, I would sit in my room overlooking the park and contentedly scribble away for an hour or two and call that sufficient for the day.

Albert and Michel Roux were writing their first book at this time, in French, which was then translated and typed. They asked if I would check it over for them and this I was more than pleased to do. Michel Roux would call in on his way from the West End to the Waterside Inn at Bray, and leave about twelve recipes. These were checked by the time he returned about a week later when we would discuss my comments and he would leave a fresh batch. It was an interesting task, particularly as it gave me a preview of what has been a well-received and successful publication.

During the year I also judged in the Army cookery competition at Aldershot, and at the Torquay Gastronomic Festival. Whilst on Jersey I was invited over to judge the Guernsey Food Festival and Letty flew to Guernsey with me in an Islander plane a few feet above the sea.

The Mouton Cadet menu competition for professional chefs which required competitors to cook and serve a menu suitable for serving with the two Mouton Cadet wines, white and red, had been offered annually since 1968. I was invited to join the panel of judges in 1973 but by 1983, David Russell (the originator of the competition) and his fellow judges considered it needed a fresh challenge as it appeared to have gone stale. The decision was made to allow competitors a wider choice of Mouton-Rothschild wines, and the competition was renamed the 'Mouton Menu Competition'. The effect was remarkable. The list of competitors entering began to include entries (a chef and waiter) from the very best of restaurants and hotels, and the quality of the menus improved considerably. Judging became more difficult, and whereas in the past we had selected three, or occasionally four, menus for cook-offs, in the 1986/87 entry, because of the exceptionally high standard, we had to settle for five, and that only after a difficult paper judging session.

All judges receive copies of each entry approximately two weeks before meeting, produce short-lists, and by discussion and argument whittle the lists down to those selected to cook and serve their menu. Cook-offs take place one a day in the cellars of Hedges and Butler, wine merchants, Regent Street. Starting at 8.30 a.m., the chef is allowed to bring in a young assistant, who is intended to fetch and carry and assist with elementary tasks only. The waiter, who is usually a head waiter or restaurant manager, is also allowed a young assistant.

The menu is prepared for eight – five judges and three guests – is served at one o'clock sharp, and usually ends at about three-thirty. The two competitors are then invited to sit with the judges, offered coffee and brandy, and a relaxed discussion ensues for about thirty minutes. This enables the judges to explore the thinking behind the menu, and to assess the quality of the competitors further.

The menus for the 1986–87 competition were:

1 *Gratin de Coquilles St Jacques aux Poires de Terre*

Raw, sliced scallops overlapped in the centre of a plate. Thinly sliced cooked Jerusalem artichokes arranged round the outside, sprinkled with cooked spinach and julienne of carrot and leek. Coated with an hollandaise sauce containing mussel or scallop juice, truffle juice and cream, and quickly gratinated under the grill.

Wine . . . . Mouton Cadet Blanc Sec 1985

Poulet en Cocotte Fermier aux Lentilles, Carottes, Petits oignons, Champignons de Paris

Wine . . . . *Château Mouton Baron Philippe 1979*

Beaufort and Camembert à l'Ancienne

Wine . . . . *Château Mouton-Rothschild 1970*

Feuilleté de Poires Caramelisées au Sabayon de Vanille

Rectangles of puff pastry, halved, spread with pastry and almond cream and a few slices of caramelised pears. Remaining half of pastry added, covered with sliced pears and lightly coated with golden caramel. Served with kirsch-flavoured sabayon sauce.

Wine . . . . *Château Coutet 1981*

2   *Bavarois de Homard Moscovite*

Lobster and caviar mousse with a sauce of shallots, chervil, fish stock, Sauternes, cream and butter.

Wine . . . . *Mouton Cadet Blanc Sec*

Canon d'Agneau en Trellis, Sauce Marc de Bourgogne

Squares of boned loin of lamb wrapped in pig's caul, spread with onions and carrot purée, covered with a trellis of puff pastry. Served with courgettes, kohlrabi and savoyade and a red-wine sauce finished with Marc de Bourgogne.

Wine . . . . *Château Mouton Baron Philippe 1979*

Assiette de Brie aux Morilles et Truffes

Brie halved and sandwiched with a mixture of cream cheese, cooked shallots, chives, truffle and morels, served with a little dressed salad.

Wine . . . . *Château Mouton-Rothschild 1970*

Parfait de Miel en Coulis de Vanille

Honey-flavoured parfait piped with meringue to form a beehive shape, decorated with chocolate twigs and bees, served with an egg-custard sauce, garnished with raspberries.

Wine . . . . *Château Coutet 1980*

3   *Turban de Ceteaux à l'Orientale et Fondue de Pétoncles et Homard*

Threads of Chinese vegetables, wrapped in fillets of baby sole, nestling on a pool of ginger butter. The centre filled with a fondue of lobster and scallop medallions bound in their own sauce.

Wine . . . . Mouton Cadet Blanc 1985

Côtelette de Pigeonneau de Lait Poêlée Lié de Vin Nems de Sous Bois à l'Ecorce de Chou

Cutlets of milk-fed squab with a farce made from the thighs and offal of the bird and a slice of foie gras. Encased in thin crêpinette, cooked in butter, served with a sauce made from the bird's carcass, vegetables, red wine and juniper and finished with old port lees.

Wine . . . . Château Mouton Baron Philippe 1975

Fourme de Montbrison (Auvergne)
Tomme de Savoie (Haute-Savoie)
Mothe St Heray (Poitou)

Selection of three French cheeses served with a small salad dressed in vinaigrette with grilled caraway seeds.

Wine . . . . Château Mouton-Rothschild 1971

Fraîcheur Glacée aux Agrumes à l'Arome Gentiane, sa Compôte son Sirop, Tuile aux Noix Ecrasées

Iced parfait of citrus fruits with a hint of Eau de Vie Gentiane, garnished with a small compôte of fruits, served with a crisp nut biscuit.

Wine . . . . Château Coutet 1978

4 *Oreiller de Turbotin et St Jacques au Fumet des Moules et Vermouth Cressonière*

A ramequin of turbot, scallop and turbot mousse lined with blanched green of leek served with a cream, vermouth, mussel and watercress sauce and decorated with a slice of truffle.

Wine . . . . Mouton Cadet Blanc Sec 1985

Eventail de Canard Sauvage Rosé, Piqué au Gingembre et Cassis

Duck breast studded with ginger, fried, sliced and served with a garnish of duck forcemeat and oyster mushrooms, vegetables and a caramelised blackcurrant sauce.

Wine . . . . Mouton Cadet Rouge 1982

Fourme d'Ambert
Pont l'Evèque

Wine . . . . Château Mouton-Rothschild 1976

Roule au Crème au Beurre de Cannelle, Sauce Citron au Miel et aux Pistils de Safran

Sponge roll brushed with sherry filled with a buttercream made with Italian meringue, cinnamon and diced apricots. Served with an egg-custard sauce flavoured with lemon, honey and saffron.

Wine . . . . Château Coutet 1979

5   *Le Soufflé d'Oursins au Parfum d'Ecosse*

A soufflé of sea urchins garnished with dice of lobster served in the sea urchin shells.

Wine . . . . Mouton Cadet Blanc 1983

Médaillons de Cailles aux Diamants Noirs Périgordins

Roast breasts of quail garnished with artichoke bottoms, quail egg and potatoes and a truffle sauce. Garnished with julienne of truffles and chervil. Served with a salad of frisée endive, asparagus heads and lollo leaves.

Wine . . . . Château Clerc Milon 1970

Stilton
Vacherin

Wine . . . . Château Mouton-Rothschild 1971

Pommade de Glace Vanille en Tasse, Panachée de Baies Rouges

Vanilla ice-cream piped into a coffee cup made from biscuit mixture, the handle piped with choux paste, stood in a saucer made from puff pastry with red berries around the cup, decorated with mint leaves.

Wine . . . . Château Coutet 1975

I include all finalist menus because the trade press never seems to be able to find space to do so. This is an aspect of quality competitions that annoys me – there are excellent examples of menu thinking, frequently with original ideas from which others can learn, but the information is restricted to the judges and a handful of people.

The Mouton Menu Competition is a demanding test for a chef, as he is required to work in partnership with his manager or waiting colleague in the planning of the menu and its accompanying wines. The meal has to be prepared, cooked and served in a strange kitchen to a highly critical panel of judges. Each course must be perfectly balanced in terms of presentation, temperature and seasoning, and form a suitable partner with the accompanying wine. There must be no obvious repetition of ingredients in succeeding courses, and the cheese should be carefully selected and only served in prime condition. Unlike most other competitions, in the Mouton, the chef has to understand how to eat, what wines complement his food and how to select and serve cheese at its very best. It makes excellent experience for someone who has the ambition to own his own restaurant.

1983 was, on the whole, a year in which I continued with ongoing work, undertaking occasional consultations, judging competitions and revising books. By now, any remaining feelings of guilt at sitting back for long periods and doing nothing other than walking, gardening, reading or watching television had long since disappeared. Letty and I were happy, relaxed and thoroughly enjoying our chosen form of retirement.

The one new project that year was to act as technical adviser to a twenty-minute film being produced for a major food manufacturing company. A highly professional film crew was employed and the shooting took place in a college over a weekend, with two chef-lecturers assisted by two students demonstrating the products. The most interesting part followed when, over two days, the twenty hours of film were edited down to twenty minutes. I sat with the sponsor in the back of a studio watching the editor operating a highly complex control panel at which he sat for over twelve hours on each day with hardly a break. Food and drinks were brought in and he continued working whilst eating and drinking. It was a new and fascinating experience.

In 1984 things hotted-up. The Roux brothers offered their first annual scholarship and I was invited on the judging panel. Young chefs could

Judging the Diners Club/Roux brothers' scholarship practical test results at the Inn on the Park Hotel, London, 1985
From the left: Edouard Hari (Head Chef, Inn on the Park Hotel), Peter Kromberg (Head Chef, Inter-Continental Hotel), Nick Gill (Chef/Proprietor, Restaurant Nick Gill, London), Bill Vine (Réunion des Gastronomes), Albert Roux (Chef/Director, Le Gavroche, London), Michel Roux (Chef/Director, Waterside Inn, Bray), Victor Ceserani

apply for the first of three stages; initially a paper entry, using a specific commodity, they were required to make a main course proposal. Six selected entries were then asked to cook-off in one of three regional centres. Two were chosen from each heat for a final cook-off at the Inn on the Park, London. Here they had to prepare a classic dish at thirty minutes' notice, followed by a sweet, for which they were given a mystery box of ingredients, all of which were required to be used. Arrangements are made for the winner to be employed for a period in a three star Michelin restaurant in France, the type of experience any ambitious young chef welcomes.

I became involved in three more competitions: the 'Chef of the Year' at Hotelympia, in January, which I also judged in 1986; an essay competition on champagne offered by the Champagne Bureau which was a relatively modest affair; and the 'Pub Caterer of the Year Competition' launched by the newly published *Pub Caterer* magazine, for which we worked out the following criteria:

1 Variety of choice – interesting and original
2 Presentation – attractive, appetising, not garish
3 Ease of service – comfort of seating
4 Quality of food – size of portion – value for money
5 Hygiene – food – service – server – environment, including toilets
6 Overall feeling of ease, and attitude of staff

As with most competitions this has taken several years of adjustment and learning from experience resulting in its current format. Initial paper entries (for which menus total around 400) are divided into six regions of Britain. A group of pubs in each region are visited anonymously by a panel of judges singly or in groups. The selected pub in each group is the regional winner and a finalist. All six finalists are visited by the main judging panel anonymously and again singly or in groups. After lunch the bill is paid, we introduce ourselves and invite the landlord and his wife to have a drink and a chat with us. We finally have a look around the kitchen and meet the chef or cook.

One requirement for a finalist is to offer food seven days a week, but even so we can occasionally be unlucky. I travelled to Preston one year with the editor of *Pub Caterer* on a bitterly cold day. There was no heating on the train and we then had half an hour's journey from the station to the pub. On arrival, it seemed exceptionally quiet. We called up for a drink at the bar and then wandered along to the food counter, to be greeted by a notice. 'We apologise for the inconvenience, but are unable to serve food today and tomorrow as the kitchen is closed for alterations'! Fortunately, there was heat in the train for the journey home! Before making the return journey two weeks later, the editor's secretary rang the pub in an assumed northern accent to make sure they were open and food would be available.

Some of the interesting dishes noticed on our travels include Turkish lamb; mushrooms filled with pâté, fried in batter, served with garlic mayonnaise; flake smoked mackerel in a tangy cheese sauce, topped with fresh breadcrumbs, served with granary bread; pork and chicken liver coarse pâté served with salad, fruit and hot granary bread; and duck in black cherry sauce.

We also look for a reasonable choice of vegetarian dishes, and in many cases found that the better pubs seemed to be ahead of restaurants with the selection of dishes on offer.

Pub Caterer magazine has proved to be a lively, interesting, helpful publication, and speedily followed the success of 'Pub Caterer of the Year' with three other competitions: 'Steak and Kidney Pie of the Year', with a first prize of £500; the 'Kitchen Master Challenge', with a first prize of £1 000; and the 'Pub Meal of the Year', with a first prize £1 000. For this last entrants are invited to suggest a three-course meal from their existing menu. Six finalists are selected and invited to a suitable venue to prepare, cook and serve their meal. The winning menu for the last competition was:

Mushroom kibbeh and salad

Moroccan-style roast lamb with pilau rice served with four dips . . .
Tzatziki   (yoghurt, cucumber and mint)
Hummus   (chick-pea salad)
Tahini   (sesame seed salad)
Tabbouleh (crushed wheat salad)

Mandalina (a chilled orange-flavoured sponge)

The 'Kitchen Master Challenge' invites publicans to create a three-course meal costing not more than £2.50 to produce. Six chosen finalists cook-off at the annual Pub Caterer Show held at the Birmingham Exhibition Centre. The 1987 menus included those shown on the next page.

Melon, ham and pimento

Haddock casserole with garlic sauce and pitta or French bread

Peach caramels

* * *

Chilled tomato soufflé

Kidneys in orange sauce

Mon ami (cream, cottage cheese, honey, saffron, peaches)

* * *

Stuffed tomato bonne femme

*Medallions of pork with pineapple, onion, brandy and Indian spices,
served with turmeric rice*

Neapolitan crêpe surprise

* * *

Orange and tomato soup

Beef with pine nuts and prunes

Peach brulée

* * *

Grilled grapefruit with rum and brown sugar

Chicken and yellow bean stir-fry with soft noodles and fresh herbs

Kiwi and raspberry pavlova

* * *

Cod and tomato brioche

Lamb chops, angel style

Hawaiian cream

* * *

Another project helpful to pub caterers was a skill school, held two hours a week for ten weeks for licensees looking to develop their food expertise. A pilot course was offered at Birmingham College of Food where I attended the last session, and I was gratified to witness the enthusiasm of the two lecturers and the course members, which clearly indicated the success of the course. Subsequently the course time was increased to three hours a week and it is planned to be offered at catering colleges in different parts of the country.

In May, Letty and I decided to renew our previously brief acquaintance with Venice by taking a week's holiday. We were thoroughly enchanted with the city, walking for hours along the canals and piazzas, absorbing the unique atmosphere. When our legs grew weary we would take a water-bus, and never tired of travelling up and down the Grand Canal and its subsidiaries where there is always something of interest to observe. On arriving home we agreed that we wanted to repeat the trip in two years' time, and we did.

Our second trip that year was to explore the east coast, ending at Norwich, where we planned to stay at the Hotel Nelson, one of a small group of hotels owned by a property company founded by Mary King's brother. Leaving home we motored due east and spent two splendid days enjoying the kind hospitality of Gerald Milsom at Maison Talbooth. We visited both of his establishments at Dedham, and in between explored the Constable country. We then headed north, called in at Gerald's excellent fish restaurant at Harwich for lunch and then following the coast, stopping at places of interest, made our way to Norwich where we spent two interesting days.

In June, *Caterer and Hotelkeeper* launched the first of its 'Catey' awards at a large, glittering gathering in the Great Room, Grosvenor House, Park Lane. It was a splendid evening with so many industry personalities present that it was impossible to say even a few words to many old friends and acquaintances. After dinner had been served, we all sat back in anticipation of the climax of the evening, which appeared to be taking the form of an Oscar presentation. I had thoroughly enjoyed dinner, the wine and the company at our table, and sat back completely relaxed, sipping a glass of port, applauding with interest as the various recipients were called, particularly when three good friends in Michel Bourdin, Michel Roux and Richard Shepherd were called to the stage.

By that time, with one award remaining, I was considering whether I could indulge in a second glass of port when Richard called over, 'Vic! It's you!' Initially, when my name was called to receive 'Personality of the Year', I felt so embarrassed that I wanted to sink under the table, but that quickly faded and I proceeded with a surge of pleasure to receive the statuette from Judith Chalmers and Sir Charles (now Lord) Forte.

Towards the end of summer, Prestige Hotels and *Caterer and Hotelkeeper* arranged to play a Sunday cricket match, for which I volunteered to act as an umpire. Weather prospects looked good – it was a pleasant, warm, sunny day and the match was to be played at the Maori sports club ground, Worcester Park. It was a day of fun, good humour and light-hearted, but seriously played, cricket. Among the *Caterer's* team were the editor, Joe Hyam, his brother (an accomplished player), Richard Shepherd and Roy Ackerman who kept wicket. Included in the opposition were an ex-Ealing student, Geoffrey Tucker, and Terry Holmes, then manager of the Stafford Hotel.

Sir (now Lord) Charles Forte presenting the Caterer and Hotelkeeper
'Personality of the Year' award, 1984

Prestige won the toss, elected to bat, and knocked up a respectable
total. Following tea the *Caterer* team batted steadily but looked to be
heading for defeat when, with two wickets remaining, the skies opened
up with a typical summer rainfall. I was wearing a white cotton sunhat,
and as the brim became rain-sodden it drooped on all sides. I felt certain
that the captains would call the match a draw and chase off for the
pavilion, but not a bit of it! Play continued until the inevitable defeat
was handed out by Prestige, and we left the field like a pack of drowned
rats. Once in the club house and changed this was soon forgotten, and
the pleasant social evening that followed was thoroughly enjoyed by all.

At the Ealing degree presentation, Mary King and Rocco Forte were
made Fellows of the college. Mary was escorted by Michael, one of her
twin nephews, who drove them to the Queen Elizabeth Hall for the
ceremony.

I had now completed over fifty years in the industry and a small group
of good friends and colleagues had arranged to take Letty and me to

dinner that same evening at the Ritz. Realising that there would be insufficient time following the degree presentation to come home, change and travel back to town, I rang the manager of the Ritz, who kindly offered us the use of a room for two hours.

Michael King drove us to the front door of the hotel, and as Letty and I walked up the steps I glanced twenty yards to my left at the staff entrance where I used to clock in and out fifty years ago! We had a comfortable room where we were able to bathe and change, and Letty put her feet up. I then rang Michael Quinn, the head chef, to say hello, and twenty minutes later there came a knock on the door. It was Michael, with a bottle of champagne, come to wish us a pleasant evening. He stayed chatting for a few minutes and had no sooner left than a second knock on the door revealed Ken Ellerton, the projects manager of the *Caterer and Hotelkeeper* magazine, who was in the party, together with Joe Hyam, Colin Lazaro and Colin Morrison, all also from the magazine. After they had helped us finish the champagne, we proceeded downstairs to the bar to meet up with the rest of the party. Michael Duffel, the manager, then appeared to wish us well and presented me with an inscribed copy of *The London Ritz* as a memento of what had been a truly memorable evening.

A few days later at Westminster College, Battersea Park Road, the Catering Teachers Association held their Silver Jubilee Conference with the theme 'How might catering education best serve society?' A well-chosen panel of speakers spoke frankly without pulling punches, and it was a proud day for the many teachers who over the years have worked so hard to maintain a worthwhile association and to implement its motto, 'He who dares to teach must never cease to learn'.

In November I was honoured to receive a letter from the Académie Culinaire de France Filiale de Grande-Bretagne informing me that I had been proposed and unanimously accepted as a Méritant member. This news came as a great delight because the Académie is undoubtedly the most serious and respected body of chefs in the country, with a limited membership which is carefully vetted and exclusive.

The Académie was formed to promote the art and science of cookery; to maintain the highest standards of the classic and contemporary cuisines of France, Britain and other countries; and to discover and recognise the best apprentices and commis chefs, to assess their abilities, and to assist in their future development. The Académie organises competitions for chefs in order to develop keenness, innovation and higher standards.

At present, a small sub-committee of which I am a member is exploring the possibility of establishing an Academy of Culinary Arts to offer courses at postgraduate level. It is a tremendous challenge, fraught with many difficulties, but we are steadily persevering and hopeful of achieving ultimate success. To see the culinary arts recognised as a discipline equal to other disciplines for which degrees are awarded, and recognised as such, has been a dream of mine for the last twenty-five years. It is an uphill battle against the élitist world of the academics who too often regard those who 'think with their hands' as being lesser mortals.

In 1985, a body established by the London borough, called Lambeth Accord, asked for help. The purpose of the organisation is to assist the disabled by setting up a 'worklink' as a resource to offer the opportunity to:

1 discuss what the applicant wants to do about work
2 improve job-seeking skills and interview techniques
3 obtain information on local employment, training and educational options
4 explore what the applicant could do in a multi-skills workshop related to local opportunities
5 come for a few weeks to try out a variety of skills
6 train and gain work experience for up to one year in office administration and catering and related service industries, including on the job work experience with employers.

Advice and assistance was needed to establish a catering workshop and recruit a trainer. The worklink was already established in several skills, and catering was to be the next addition to the list. Initially I was sceptical, and did my utmost to discourage it as I did not believe that anybody other than fit people can cope with the hard work and hurly-burly of the great majority of jobs in the catering industry. The organisers, however, were so sincere and persuasive that I finally reluctantly agreed to assist.

A large disused office block had been allocated by the council for the project, and there was the skeleton of the old staff kitchen and restaurant to use as a base. Plans were evolved for equipment and alterations, and a job description produced for a trainer. When asked what I thought the response would be to the advertisement for a trainer, I said that as the salary was equivalent to a junior lecturer we would be lucky to receive a handful. To my surprise, and the organisers' delight, thirty applications were received, from which we were able to produce an interesting short-list of eight candidates. Fortune continued, for following the interviews we had three candidates who were all highly suitable. When we then made our final choice and offered the post the response of the successful candidate was most gratifying. Roger Robinson has since gone on to do a sterling job, which I was able to see when invited to lunch several months ago.

I still retain my initial reservations, but am prepared to be convinced by results to change my opinion. Roger has now been three years in the post, and continues to retain the enthusiasm and dedication which were apparent when being interviewed for the post.

Presumably as a result of the Catey award, I received an invitation to join the panel of judges for the annual Glenfiddich Book Awards. During the following week a total of fifty books on food, cookery and wine arrived covering a wide range of subjects, and made useful, interesting reading.

I received an invitation to speak at an Essex branch conference of the Hospital Caterers Association, and was pleased to learn that the chairman was to be Philip Sessions, an ex-Ealing student. He was very kind, collecting me from home and returning me safely at the end of the day.

Letty and I received an invitation to the preview of the Mouton label collection which was on show at the Victoria and Albert Museum. In 1945 Baron Philippe de Rothschild commissioned a noted artist to design the label for the Mouton Baron Philippe of that year. He continued the practice, changing the artist each year, most of whom enjoyed international recognition. When the artists submitted their work for the Baron's approval, many included their preliminary sketches and these were tucked away in a cupboard. In the early 1980s the Baron's daughter discovered the sketches and decided to mount them, along with a complete set of labels since 1945, to form a collection. The collection had been on display in several countries, and now was to be seen for the first time in Britain.

The final pleasant memory of that year occurred in November at the Athenæum Hotel, one of the Rank group. Stuart May, Managing Director of Rank Hotels, upon realising that twenty-five years had passed since he left Ealing, decided that a celebration was called for and arranged a reunion dinner for his class who were nicknamed 'The Glorious Fourth'. Only two of the class were unable to be traced, one last heard of in Tanzania, and the other in South Africa. Two flew over from the United States and one from Canada. Those who attended included Blain Jefferson, now a private hotel owner in Yorkshire; John Jennison, tenant of The Kings Arms, Old Amersham; Andrew Kettley, restaurateur in Newport Beach, California, USA: Kevin Rayner, a manager with the Sheraton Organisation; Ann Wallis, Director of School Meals, North Wembley; Peter Yarker, proprietor of the Dukes Hotel, Bath; Nicholas Brown, an accountant within the industry; Roger Brown, proprietor of The Bell Hotel, Tewkesbury; John Brunhold, General Manager at the Holiday Inn, Annaheim, Los Angeles, USA: Malcolm Hill, Outside Catering Executive, Cornwall; David Tyrrell, Director of Outside Catering, Ewell, Surrey; and Ingrid Beaton (widow of Ian Beaton) restaurateur, north Devon.

In the first two years of their course they had been in two groups, and as with all Ealing potential management students in those days, spent a good part of their time in practical kitchen and food service situations. Because Ron Kinton and I were their first-year tutors we were invited along with our wives. Most of the group were also accompanied by wives, and together we enjoyed a splendid evening with so many tales and reminiscences passing around that the time swiftly flew by. The menu Stuart planned for us was:

Terrine de Pigeon et Basilic	*Chablis Montains 1983*
Suprême de Barbue aux Poivres	
Contrefilet de Boeuf Dauphinoise *Légumes du Marché*	*Château Giscours 1980*
Torte aux Truffes	
Friandises	*Cognac* *Liqueurs*

Early in 1986 I received a phone call from Mr G. B. Chiandetti, a director of Trusthouse Forte, asking if I would be prepared to act as the external assessor for a graduate chef training scheme that had recently been launched. I replied saying that I really had enough to occupy me at present, but was prepared to hear more about the details, and made an appointment to call and see him.

The concept appealed to me at once. The idea was to take selected promising young chefs or cooks, male or female, in or outside of the company, and put them through a strenuous three-year development programme. The more I heard about the scheme, the more I realised that it was too tempting for me to refuse, and I finally agreed to assist on a limited number of days a year. It is a decision I have not regretted. Even at the end of the first year, the way the graduates had developed and gained confidence was most rewarding.

In May, Letty and I returned to Venice for another thoroughly pleasant and relaxing week, which was all the more enjoyable as we had by now begun to know our way around the city. We have formed the habit of taking two or three shorter breaks during the year, and we select parts of Britain unfamiliar to us to visit. These have included Scotland, north and mid-Wales, the Lake District, the Peak district of Derbyshire, Exmoor, Dorset and Yorkshire. On the continent, we took the car to Britanny, and made separate trips by coach to Switzerland and Italy. Holland, in May, and Yugoslavia, in September, were on the itinerary for 1987, and possibly a long weekend when the rhododendrons and azaleas would be at their best at the Mendip Park Lodge, Frome, Somerset.

One of the most magnificent displays of rhododendrons and azaleas in the country is a short distance away from our home, in the Isabella Plantation in the centre of Richmond Park, to which we always endeavour to make an annual pilgrimage. As members, we attend most of the Royal Horticultural Society shows in Vincent Square hall alongside Westminster College, and usually take the opportunity to lunch in the training restaurant afterwards. This makes for a very pleasant day, as we invariably have an enjoyable meal, and it is always pleasant to have a brief chat to the students who are serving at table.

The first time I went to a show in the new hall, just off Vincent Square, I was reminded of the time in the 1930s when the badminton club from school spent a day there at the All-England championships. It was quite a thrill seeing the game played at top level for the first time, and when, at the end of the day, our master managed to acquire twelve dozen used shuttles for us to take away, our joy was complete. Shuttles were expensive. The age of plastic birds had not yet arrived, and we usually played with tatty old shuttles, the feathers from which had almost completely been lost. Consequently the flight, instead of being true, was of a constantly changing pattern which, on reflection, I suppose made for the sharpening of our reflexes, for without quick reflexes there was little chance of hitting the bird. Not only was the quality of the used shuttles from the championships something we had never seen, but in addition, their idea of a used bird was, to us, almost perfect. Consequently we enjoyed several weeks of playing with respectable shuttle-cocks before the supply was exhausted.

My sense of hearing was deteriorating, and with considerable regret I felt obliged to apply for transfer from the active bench to the supplemental bench of justices. The application was approved which meant that I could continue carrying out the duties of a magistrate, with the exception of sitting on the bench. I had been experiencing similar difficulties in large committees, and tendered resignations from the Council of Management of Hotelympia and the City and Guilds advanced cookery, larder and pastry moderating committees. I often find in conversation, particularly when in groups or noisy rooms, that I may hear only one word in six. This makes active conversation difficult, especially with softly voiced speakers, but I am philosophical about it, and consider that to go through life with all parts of the body working A1 all the time is probably expecting too much.

During 1986 I judged a hospital cooks competition at Walthamstow Technical College, and Prue Leith invited me to present the awards at her school's first graduation day. I was pleased to receive the invitation as it gave me the opportunity to see over her new school. It was a very hot summer's day, and strolling along from the station at about one o'clock, a few doors away from the school was a pub. From the outside of the pub to the front door of the school was a solid mass of young people, clutching glasses of all shapes and sizes, chatting, laughing and joking, and thoroughly enjoying the sunshine.

On entering the school, I met an ex-Ealing student who was a member of the teaching staff, and then Prue and the remainder of the staff. After a brief chat we adjourned to the main demonstration theatre where about 100 cheerful faces (the same group that had been outside) were awaiting.

Prue opened the proceedings in her typical informal, friendly style and she has obviously developed a tremendous rapport with all her students. I said a few words, then made the presentations, and thoroughly enjoyed what was a quite hilarious afternoon.

I found myself reflecting on that afternoon at Walthamstow with a quiet chuckle when, at the Ealing graduation ceremony in the autumn at the Queen Elizabeth Hall with all the assembled company standing and the organ playing, as a member of the platform party, dressed in cap and gown, I solemnly proceeded in procession from doors half-way down the hall and onto the stage. They were two completely different ceremonies, both for the same purpose, and each perfectly suited to the occasion.

Soon afterwards, Ron Kinton and I were talking to Edward Arnold, our publishers, when they made the suggestion that we consider taking on a younger colleague as an associate with a view to the future. This sounded a prudent suggestion, so Ron and I decided to go our separate ways to think out potential suitable names. On meeting a week later, we were pleased to find that we had both come up with the same name – David Foskett. I had recruited David onto the teaching staff at Ealing several years ago, and he had proven to be a keen, first rate, conscientious chef-lecturer. His background was ideal. He was trained at Westminster Technical College, had experience in the West End and industry and had spent a period in the research kitchens of a large food manufacturing company, during which time he studied for, and gained, food technology qualifications. Some time after he had joined us at Ealing I advised him to invest five years on part-time study, initially to gain membership of the industry's professional body, the HCIMA, and then to gain a degree in education. After successfully completing his HCIMA examinations, he enrolled at Garnett College for the part-time degree course where his tutor was Ron Kinton. Ron had left Ealing several years earlier to take a post in teacher training. Here again David was successful in gaining his degree with honours.

Ron and I had assessed him independently, but arrived at the same conclusion. David was delighted to be offered the opportunity to join us and obviously he will bring a further dimension into our work. The first task undertaken by the three of us was the preparation of a follow-up textbook to *Practical Cookery* entitled *Contemporary Cookery*, which

Ronald Kinton (on left), co-author of the student textbooks, with Victor Ceserani, assessing the induction stove at Brown's Hotel, London, 1985

was published in June 1988. Following this, we started work on the sixth edition of *The Theory of Catering*, and so we had plenty of book work to keep us occupied for some time.

Letty and I had been considering spending a long weekend at Charles Wurz's Hotel, Mendip Lodge, in Frome, but on the spur of the moment we did an about-turn and flew off to Amsterdam for our first look at the Dutch capital. Our hotel was in the centre of the city, and apart from a day's visit to the delightful garden display of bulbs at Kirkenhopf and a canal boat cruise, we walked ourselves leg-weary each day. We found the Kirkenhopf gardens most interesting and learned that they were opened after the war as a showcase for the Dutch bulb industry. As the Dutch are the largest suppliers of bulbs in the world, and the gardens are only open for two months of the year while the bulbs are in bloom, it is not surprising that they have become world famous and during the eight weeks are visited by large numbers of people from all corners of the globe.

We enjoyed the overall atmosphere of Amsterdam, found it dirty, scruffy and untidy in many parts as, indeed, is London and many other cities, but the friendly, easy-going attitude of the Dutch was infectious. Places to eat, whether for a meal, snack or just a drink, were plentiful, and Letty was delighted to find an establishment close to our hotel where we could have a satisfactory meal with a bottle of wine at a reasonable price and be offered her favourite sweet, Zabaglione, as a single portion. To the best of my knowledge this is almost unknown in England. Most establishments that feature it on the menu stipulate for two portions only, although I am informed that the Romeo and Juliet restaurant, Sutton Row (not a well-known establishment) offers single portions of this delicious sweet.

Having heard so much about the red-light district, we set out one evening to explore, but had difficulty finding the main street. A young, smartly dressed Dutch lady in her mid-twenties was passing, and slightly tentatively I asked her the way. She smiled, and for the next two to three minutes in flawless English gave a vivid commentary on the various streets that make up the district, told us a little of its history, warned us to be very wary of pickpockets, wished us a pleasant visit and proceeded on her way. We only had to walk a hundred yards, turn a corner and there we were, with large numbers of sightseers, many tourist coaches and a few customers. It was amazing to see how some people used the visit as a family outing, with young children of tender age accompanying many parent groups. Passing by house after house with ladies of all shapes, sizes and race in view through uncurtained illuminated windows, gave me the impression of looking in a butcher's shopwindow to select the Sunday joint. It was a thought-provoking visit showing a down-to-earth practical approach to man's oldest need. It was seemingly sordid and distasteful, and yet one could not help but wonder what the figures in Holland were for rape compared to ours.

A few weeks later we suddenly decided to make a three-day nostalgia trip to the Isle of Wight. We stayed at the Albion Hotel, Freshwater Bay, near where Alfred Lord Tennyson had lived, and had planned to take our favourite walk above the bay on Tennyson Down, which stretches for two to three miles to the Needles, a famous landmark of three large rocks in the sea. The walk was severely curtailed, however, for by the time we had climbed the steep slope up to the down (with two stops on the way) and had walked a further mile, we were leg weary and had to return.

The time passed swiftly and happily as we visited all our old favourite haunts which included Sandown and Brown's pitch-and-putt course; The Crab Inn, Shanklin; Bembridge; Foreland; Lane End; Seaview; Ventnor; and Cowes, where during Cowes week we would walk along the length of the promenade as the yachts were turning for home on their final leg, hoisting their multi-coloured spinnakers. The vast number of yachts involved made a memorable, colourful sight as the wind stretched sails to the full and the crews strove to reach the finishing line. There would be the royal yacht *Britannia* at anchor and warships of visiting nations, all gaily displaying lines of coloured pennants. The Albion provided a satisfying dinner nightly, with a good selection of wines which sent us to bed happy and contented each evening.

In July at Osterley Park a number of Chinese evenings were held, organised in conjunction with the Victoria and Albert Museum and the Chinese Office in London. It was a great success, all four evenings being completely sold out with many people in costume arriving with picnic baskets and wine coolers. Several stalls were erected alongside the lake selling Chinese items of all kinds, the largest stall manned by a selection of Chinese restaurateurs, dispensing hot and cold food. They sold huge quantities of take-away food from large steamer containers, and the queues of people waiting to be served seemed almost endless. Entertainment included dancing and martial arts. A floating pavilion donated by a Chinese official and anchored to the bottom of the lake is the sole reminder of a series of splendid evenings. Reaction by the local residents who regularly walk in the park to the pavilion is, however, very mixed. They either consider it a decorative addition or an impertinent, unwelcome intrusion, completely out of keeping with the overall ambience.

August of 1987 (normally a quiet month for me), turned out to be busy and interesting. At fairly short notice I was asked to assess the six finalists in a 'Clean Kitchen Award'. This involved visits to eight kitchens (without prior notice), two each of hotels, restaurants, hospitals and industrial caterers. A trip to the north-east took me to the Nissan motor plant where, in addition to viewing the kitchen, I learned a great deal about the Nissan company and the effect its management style and working practices were having on the area. In Blackpool I visited a small hospital with a kitchen and surrounding area in pristine condition, then went into the town to see behind the scenes of a fast-food operation. Outside

Exeter was a British Telecom staff canteen; there was a restaurant in East Molesey, Surrey; a very large hospital at Northwick Park and two large hotels in London. I was delighted to see such high standards of hygiene organisation in daily practice. The exercise left me thinking – if only we could legislate for all kitchens to be maintained at this standard, we would undoubtedly see a sharp reduction in the annual number of food poisoning cases. Good food starts with clean food, and this should only be prepared, cooked and served in a clean kitchen.

Once again, on the spur of the moment, we flew to Paris for a long weekend, even though August is the hottest month of the year. We arrived at our hotel early on Friday evening and took a leisurely dinner at a brasserie across the square. I enjoyed a delicious dish of rabbit with prunes and armagnac sauce, and was served by a smart young waiter who had worked in London. On the Saturday morning we visited Claude Monet's house (which was most interesting), the garden, which he planted mainly for his painting, and his studio. In the afternoon we strolled, window shopped and sat outside various bars sipping tea or mineral water. We had booked for the *Folies Bergère* that evening, but as it was so warm, we decided to take the metro to Montmartre and stroll. We dined in the garden of Mère Catherine which soon filled up, and we enjoyed a good dinner in lively surroundings.

On Sunday morning we visited the recently opened Arts Museum in a large converted railway station, which proved to be an interesting way to pass the morning. I had reserved seats that evening for dinner on a bateau mouche, and in the afternoon we decided to stroll and located the landing stage. This we found without any bother and I checked my reservation at the same time. I was informed that jacket and tie were mandatory, and as I had brought neither on the trip, offered to cancel the reservation. 'Non, non,' replied the manager, 'we will lend you a jacket and tie.' In the event, I borrowed a tie from our hotel reception, which looked reasonably well on one of my sports shirts, and wore my half-tailored leisure jacket.

In my own mind I had thought that the evening would be a tourist 'rip off', but was pleasantly surprised with the events that followed. Embarking, we were escorted to reception for an aperitif, then to a sensibly positioned table for two with a bottle of champagne and a pianist playing light classical music. Just before sailing, a jazz trio circled the decks to see us off. An attractive menu with a reasonable choice was offered, plus a bottle of wine, and we enjoyed a good meal. The boat was large and about 95 per cent full, mainly with French nationals. We cruised slowly along the Seine with the various places of interest being flashed on numerous indicators above eye-level around the deck. It was an unexpectedly delightful evening that was dictated by the leisurely pace of the boat and the food, wine and attentive service. It was quite dark when we returned to the strains of Handel's music and a giant catherine wheel on the landing stage flashing sparks as it revolved to welcome us back. It was a fitting finale to our visit to Paris which we had last visited on our silver wedding over twenty years previously.

In September, I was offered the opportunity, which I accepted with alacrity, to make the 'chef's pilgrimage' to visit Paul Bocuse with the senior executive chef, Jean Bellavita, from Trusthouse Forte. We flew to Lyons, then motored to Collonges-au-Mont-d'Or to meet Paul Bocuse and take lunch in his ground-floor restaurant. After lunch we were shown over his banqueting hall a short distance away, where he has installed a massive fair-ground type mechanical organ. A flexible card of music was switched on and while the organ thundered out its cheery music, we strolled around the hall reading the many plaques on which are printed the names of the most famous chefs in history including Albert Roux, Anton Mosimann and Michel Bourdin.

My colleague had some business to transact, but later that evening we returned, this time for dinner in the upstairs room. Before dinner we stood at the entrance to the kitchen watching the operation of a busy service for ten to fifteen minutes. Everything in the kitchen was spotless, the top of the stove, the floor, the chefs – a most impressive and unusual sight, and a model for anyone who cares to see what a busy commercial kitchen should look like. Both meals were superbly cooked, presented and served, and I consider that the standard of room service was among the most elegant and efficient that I have experienced. The visit made clear to me why the French chefs have unanimously styled Bocuse 'The Emperor'.

The following morning we proceeded to the Moulin de Mougins where we met Roger Vergé and took lunch in the garden restaurant. Whilst reading his book some time ago, I had formed the impression that he was a warm, kindly man, and on making his acquaintance was delighted to find that impression confirmed. We then flew to Nice where we were to have met Louis Outhier, and dined at his restaurant, L'Oasis, at La Napoule, but as the booking had gone astray we had to defer this until lunch the following day. Dinner in the hotel (the manager was Michael Cipolla, son of Louis, the chef who opened the Carlton-Tower Hotel) was a slight anticlimax after the previous day.

Louis Outhier, a beaming extrovert, greeted us warmly the following day, put on his apron, and said that he was going to cook our lunch. We sat in the garden restaurant and thoroughly enjoyed the last meal of our trip. Louis is planning to close his restaurant shortly and re-open it as a school. I was intrigued to learn how many applications were received by all three chefs from all over the world from people wishing to work in their kitchens for periods of time, and the charges they were prepared to pay.

For our Autumn break we had booked a week's holiday in Dubrovnik at a hotel ten minutes' walk from the old town. The hotel was comfortable, the food adequate but not memorable, the weather perfect, with the sun shining daily from dawn to sunset, and the temperature never fell below 70 °F. We found the old walled town delightful, strolling around the market every morning where vendors would cut up green and black figs to press into our hands along with grapes as tasters before buying. After a mineral water under a shaded café umbrella and a leisurely walk around the ancient streets, we would head for our favourite bar overlooking the harbour, where we would sit for an hour or so watching the world go by. Several short boat trips took us to neighbouring islands and resorts which were full of interest and history. The Yugoslavs were friendly and helpful, and we left having thoroughly enjoyed a memorable trip.

My next involvement was as a judge in the *Caterer and Hotelkeeper* 'best lunch for under £10 competition' which took myself and fellow judges, among other places, to the Colonial Restaurant, Glasgow, where chef/proprietor Peter Jackson's culinary skills were in evidence; The Tudor Rose, Whalley, north of Blackburn, where Rosemary Newman served a delicious lunch for under £5; La Giralda, a most popular restaurant, and rightly so, at Pinner Green, Middlesex, where David Brown, the chef/proprietor, offers such good food and value for money that he serves over 250 meals a day; and finally, the eventual winner, The Old Manor House, Romsey, Hampshire (close to Broadlands, Lord Mountbatten's home which is open to the public) where Mauro Bregoli, the chef/patron, offers excellent fare and presents a splendid wine list in an impressive Tudor house. The judges' visits to all restaurants were unannounced, and tables were booked ahead under an assumed name.

1987 proved to be my busiest year since retirement. In the autumn, with Letty as my travelling companion, we assessed some sixteen restaurants as one of four sets of assessors, submitting reports for an in-company incentive scheme for Thistle Hotels. For Trusthouse Forte, accompanied by two company executives, I visited fifteen restaurants from which we selected six to assess the quality of the food being produced. The six head chefs at a later stage were required to prepare, cook and serve a three-course meal for four covers in the kitchen of a catering college which was judged by Paul Bocuse, Roger Vergé, Gilbert Ponée and yours truly. An interesting set of menus was produced, the winner's menu being:

Filo pastry purses filled with breast of quail, served with a truffle sauce

A composition of delicate fish served on rosemary sauce

*A plate of three desserts: one English pudding of berries, one raspberry
mousse, and a tulip of brandy snap filled with seasonal berries
on a raspberry coulis*

I was delighted to learn that Trusthouse Forte plan to start a graduate
waiter scheme and a 'Waiter of the Year' award to run on alternate years
with the 'Chef of the Year'. There is a lot to be done to improve the status
and respect of service staff, and encouragement and incentive by
schemes of this type can help.

My last 'working' visit of the year was to Ecole Lenôtre, Plaisir, 25 km
from Paris alongside the main factory of Gaston Lenôtre. Here they
produce a wide selection of high quality foods sold in the Lenôtre shops
in Paris and used in the numerous outdoor catering functions run by the
company. Gilbert Ponée, a master pastry-cook and confectioner, is the
school manager, and courses are taught in hot kitchen, cold kitchen,
pastry and confectionery, and bakery. It is a highly successful school
dedicated to the French culinary arts, which has earned a worldwide
reputation, evidenced by the number of students applying to take
courses.

A question I am frequently asked is, how do I manage to keep my
weight down when I seem to do so much eating out? My brief reply is, '10
per cent knowledge, 10 per cent common sense, and 80 per cent discipline!' I find that I can now control my weight and keep it within a
pound or so of 140 lb by stepping on the scales each morning to look for
the 140 lb mark.

At home, with Letty, I eat simply and drink alcohol in moderation, no
more than half a bottle of wine a day, and that not every day. When we
have company and when eating out I completely relax, forget the weight
and enjoy a good meal with a glass or two of wine and if the following
morning the scales are over 140 lb then I cut back until 140 lb is again
achieved.

I could never resigned myself to a 'cranks' diet, as one of the two
greatest pleasures of my life has been, and is, good food. I count my
blessings that, in spite of being without a gall-bladder, my appetite is
sound and I thoroughly enjoy a good well-prepared or cooked meal.
When I speak of good food, many people think I am referring to *haute
cuisine* exclusively, but this is not so. A piece of freshly baked crusty
granary or wholemeal bread, with a portion of correctly matured
cheese – farmhouse Cheddar, Stilton, dolcelatte, Brie or fourme
d'ambert – accompanied by a tankard of bitter or a glass of red wine is
just as enjoyable, as can be a plate of fish and chips in our favourite fish
restaurant in Richmond; properly cooked, slightly crisp vegetables;

Letty's lamb hot-pot; Michael Sullivan's crab soup at the Heathrow Penta; Richard Shepherd's spinach soufflé with anchovy sauce at Langan's; and Michel Bourdin's coulibiac at the Connaught. I could go on to fill another book with examples, which is probably why I always join in with the song from Oliver by Lionel Bart – 'Food, glorious food'!

I would never have considered the writing of my autobiography as being worthy of the time it has taken, but several years ago Bryan Bennett, my publisher and good friend, made the suggestion. I rejected the idea out of hand because of the time it would take. He then suggested that I write a small number of pages daily or weekly, which I thought might be a possibility, but I never managed to get down to it. Then, in September 1986, Lee Brown, publisher of the magazine *Pub Caterer*, drove us to Kidderminster for a competition and back the following day. As we said goodbye she remarked, 'You should write an autobiography Victor.' That second comment sparked me off, and I commenced writing a day or two later. Being an early riser helped as I usually put in my daily stint of an hour or two before eight o'clock; the task was nearly completed in June 1988.

The interest and excitement generated by the industry still motivates me and makes me want to continue to be involved, particularly when a project concerns young people, or endeavours to improve standards. I enjoy visiting catering colleges, and seeing and hearing how the almost continually changing pattern of courses are operated. Standards vary considerably, and in some cases I have been concerned at the poor levels of work and teaching. Some colleges use lack of equipment or accommodation as an excuse, but I believe that given the right teaching staff with a positive attitude, an effective job can be done in almost any situation. Shortage of cash is frequently a problem but the answer to this is to look at colleges like Birmingham College of Food where Eddie McIntyre, the Principal (who trained as a chef), personally orchestrates an aggressive teaching programme, geared in many ways to producing revenue. Hustle and bustle is the order of the day in industry, so what is wrong with having that scenario in practical sessions in college? It calls for more time and effort on the part of the teachers. That, I suspect, is often the problem.

If students have been carefully selected for the industry, are motivated by their tutors, and then given a busy time in training kitchens and restaurants, they will usually react well and gradually acquire a work tempo that stands them in good stead when they enter industry. Obviously, there must be time for explanation and discussion, but the bulk of this can be dealt with in the class-room.

It is good to see a college where the students are smartly dressed, proud of their uniform (irrespective of whether they are on a craft or degree course) and moving briskly with purpose. This must also impress visitors from industry and encourage their confidence in that particular department.

Sound, regular contact with industry by all teachers of catering and related subjects is essential if students are to be prepared to enter that industry in the right frame of mind. I believe college and industry should work as a partnership to help equip the students to form a sound foundation for their careers. An advisory panel of local industrialists to meet with school staff once a term to discuss teaching plans and problems and industry's plans and problems can be a great help. Industrialists should be encouraged to visit colleges frequently, sit in, or observe classes, be able to question why certain topics are being taught, or why they are being taught in a particular way. The teacher should be able to justify what he is teaching; if he cannot, changes should be made.

College responsibility should be to equip students to fit into industry as it is today. (I consider it a failing on the part of the college when they declare, as I have heard on more than one occasion, that a sizeable number of their students leave the industry within a short space of time after leaving college.) Frequently, the industry and its conditions are blamed, overlooking the fact that a measure of blame may lie with the college and its staff. Effective teachers will keep themselves up to date by visiting industry whenever possible, talking to colleagues in industry, and working for an occasional short period if the opportunity arises. Armed with the invaluable information that can be gained in this way, plus their own industrial background, teachers will increase their confidence and effectiveness. A more purposeful and rewarding catering education should follow.

The more all concerned strive to improve and strengthen catering education, the better equipped should the students be. This, in turn, should have the effect of making improvements in industry.

Our industry is, in many cases, an integral part of tourism. An increasing tourist industry will make an ever-increasing contribution to the national economy and this is surely a worthwhile goal to aim at for all concerned.

In retirement I eat out and have the opportunity to see over a wide variety of establishments from five star restaurants to pubs. Too many use pretentious flowery language that builds up customer expectation, which, when the dish is presented and eaten, is frequently disappointed. The use of incorrectly styled French, often wrongly spelt, is another source of irritation. Only if a thorough understanding of French culinary language is present within the establishment and the chef or cook has the knowledge to prepare and cook French recipes in a correct manner, should any such dishes feature on a menu. I consider it dishonest practice to do otherwise. This is particularly so when many establishments use excellent examples of attractively styled dishes, written completely in English. Most of the new wave of English chefs who have successfully emerged over the past two decades use this style.

Even when dishes are written in French, a simple description in English should follow, sufficient to give customers an understanding of what they are ordering. Basically, a menu is a means of communication between the caterer and customer, and, ideally, the customer should be able to read and feel confident that he is ordering dishes that he likes and wants. This is particularly important for customers who may have a food allergy.

The same principle applies to wine lists. Most people are ignorant about wines, although they know what they like when drinking it (myself included). It is helpful to be able to understand more about the wine by means of a carefully worded sentence or two.

Dishes from many parts of the world are becoming increasingly popular and it is sound policy to offer a small selection, but only if the chef can produce them to a reasonable standard. The menu written daily by Richard Shepherd at Langan's Brasserie, London, is a hotch potch by academic standards of menu compilation. Some dishes are written in French, some in English. Items such as sausages and mash, white onion sauce, black pudding, bubble and squeak and rice pudding are interposed between many more traditional English dishes, classical French dishes and an occasional ethnic speciality. It is interesting to note, however, that Langan's is and has been for over a decade, one of London's most popular restaurants. It serves an average of 600 customers daily, six days a week – a success story that defies pedantic rules. The choice on the menu is large and varied, the quality is good and the amount of repeat business indicates clearly that customers are satisfied and getting value for money.

Eating out in good company is for me an interesting and a continuing source of pleasure, whether it be in a modestly priced establishment or a Michelin starred restaurant. I am critical of the way food is cooked and presented and of the way it is served with its accompanying wines, but I do not voice this criticism unless the food is so badly cooked that it cannot be eaten or if, as happens occasionally, I am asked to give a critique. When I criticise I endeavour to be constructive and helpful. I deplore the unfair practice of speaking sharply to a member of the waiting staff with a complaint. Usually the fault does not lie with them. If the waiter or waitress appears sufficiently competent to deal with the complaint, I lodge it with them. Otherwise, I ask to see the restaurant manager.

There are all too frequent faults in food preparation and presentation including: soups of poor quality, lacking in flavour, consistency and temperature; overcooked poached fish; fried fish garnished with mounds of salad or served with slices of lemon from which you cannot squeeze the juice instead of segments; plates overcrowded and overgarnished with unsuitable items such as slices of orange, rings of pepper or raw onion, mustard and cress or limp lettuce leaves; vegetables lacking in flavour and colour cooked almost to a mush; and large, clumsy and overdecorated sweets with whipped cream. Food presentation is important and can stimulate the appetite; clumsily presented food can have the reverse effect.

With regard to the service of food, I often think that many of the traditional practices of fifty years ago continue to be taught and practised whether or not they are suitable for contemporary use. All traditional ideas of service should be questioned. They should only be used if justified in the light of modern requirements.

Why, when presented with a menu either at table or in a lounge, is a wine list not offered at the same time? Why is butter cut up, curled or shaped in small pieces and put on all tables in the room just before service, irrespective of the room temperature, so that it becomes so soft that you can hardly pick it up with a knife? Why, when a plate of food is served, does a waiter loom over you with an oversized peppermill before you have even tasted the food to decide whether it requires pepper or not? Why, if you politely point this out to him, does he not leave the mill on the table or return when you have tasted? Why are accompanying sauces not left on the table so that they are to hand if you would like a little more? Why is bread cleared from the table without asking if you have finished with it? Why is salad served on unsuitable crescent shaped dishes, so that it is impossible to turn the salad, to coat it with the dressing, without spilling it on the table cloth? Why do waiters and waitresses not wear uniforms that can be laundered daily? One of the most unpleasant odours is under-arm perspiration and to receive that when food is being served is unforgivable. Why, when an order for a small party is being taken, can a simple code not be used by the waiter to indicate which items have been ordered by which customers, so that when the commis lays the cutlery and serves the food, the table conversation is not interrupted by, 'Who's the fish?', 'Who's the soup?', and so on?

The fact that so many of these faults in food preparation and service occur so frequently can rightly be attributed to the departmental heads – the chef and restaurant manager. However, I consider that it is also a reflection on the quality of senior management. Presuming that they eat daily, they should be aware of what is going on and take the necessary remedial action.

A weakness in knowledge of the food and beverage operation is often apparent in younger managers emerging from colleges which have poor quality food and beverage courses within their curriculum. The tradition on which the reputation of Ealing College was based was for all potential management courses to include a strong food and beverage element with a sound practical content both in college and industry.

It would be interesting to hear the views of some of the ex-Ealing students of the 1950–1970 era on this point. People like Chris Pollard, who, assisted by his wife Vivienne (also an ex-student), built up the Hamard Catering Group in South Wales; Stuart May, now Managing Director, Rank Hotels; James Brown, now General Manager, Royal Garden Hotel; J. Stirling Gallagher, Managing Director, Sutcliffe Catering Group Ltd.; and many others.

In a final reflection on life I count my blessings for having enjoyed my self-chosen first job. I chose to become a chef because that is what I wanted to be and it is a decision I have never had occasion to regret, even though in the early years many people would look down their noses when they heard what I did. I was proud to be a chef and proud to work at the Ritz Hotel, and the attitude of those who found this calling to be less than respectable was, to me, annoying.

Over the past decade or so as the image of the chef has changed so dramatically – thanks in no small measure to many talented chefs from the continent working in Britain, and the bright, keen bunch of innovative young British chefs who are rapidly carving out reputations for serving good food – the calling has achieved respectability.

If any young boy or girl asks for my advice on becoming a chef, I ask them four questions to which I expect unequivocal answers:

1 'Do you like and are you interested in food?'
2 'Are you prepared to undertake a full-time job that involves hard and sometimes heavy work, which may be under pressure, in a hot kitchen?'
3 'Are you prepared to work unsociable hours with, possibly, split duties?'
4 'Have you, or do you intend to gain, some form of part-time work in a trade kitchen before committing yourself to a full-time job?'

If, and only if, they have satisfactorily answered the questions will I help them to get a start.

My very last thought is that I suppose it could be said that a chef has the unique opportunity of being better equipped than most to undertake his or her last journey. With an angel cake and a devilled chicken, a chef would be prepared for a start in either direction!

Résumé

1934	Apprentice chef, Ritz Hotel, London
1937	Commis chef, Orleans Club, London
1940	HM Forces, Royal Fusiliers, and Army Catering Corps
1946	Chef, Boodles Club, London
1950	Teacher training college, London
1951'	Lecturer, Professional Cookery, Acton Technical College
1956–86	Judge, Senior and Junior Salon Committee, Hotelympia
1959–63	First Chairman, and founder member, Catering Teachers Association
1962	*Practical Cookery* first published
1962–72	Chief Examiner, City and Guilds of London Institute
1964	Head of School of Hotelkeeping and Catering, Ealing College of Higher Education
1964	*The Theory of Catering* first published
1966–76	Chairman, Junior Salon Committee, Hotelympia
1968–69	Visiting Professor, and degree of MBA, Michigan State University, USA
1970	*Understanding Cookery* British edition published
1974–79	Member of the Council and Education Committee, Hotel and Catering Institute
1974–81	Judge, Mouton Cadet Menu Competition

1975	Awarded MBE for services to catering education
1976	*Questions on Practical Cookery* first published
1977–81	Judge, Meal of the Year Menu Competition
1978	*Questions on Theory of Catering* first published
1978–81	Judge, Jersey Hotel and Restaurant Exhibition
1978–85	Judge, Jersey Hotel and Restaurant Star Grading Awards
1978–85	Judge, Torquay Gastronomic Festival
1980–	Judge, Quality Food Awards
1980–	Judge, Student Taste of Britain Competition
1981–	Judge, Mouton Cadet/*Observer* Menu Competition
1981–82	Judge, Guernsey Food Festival
1982	Honorary Fellow, Ealing College of Higher Education
1982–	Judge, Mouton Rothschild Menu Competition
1984	*Caterer and Hotelkeeper* Personality of the Year Award
1984–	Consultant, *Caterer and Hotelkeeper* and *Pub Caterer* magazines
1984	Honorary Fellow, City and Guilds of London Institute
1984–	Judge, Pub Caterer of the Year Competition
1984–87	President, Catering Teachers Association
1985	Membre d'Honneur, Association Culinaire Française
1985	Membre Méritant, Académie Culinaire de France
1985–	Judge, Pub Meal of the Year Competition
1985–	Judge, Steak and Kidney Pie of the Year Competition
1986–	Assessor, Trusthouse Forte Graduate Training Scheme
1987–	Assessor, Thistle Hotels Guild Awards for Excellence in Food and Food Service
1987	*Cookery: an Introduction* first published
1987	Organiser and Judge, Trusthouse Forte Chef of the Year Competition
1988	*Contemporary Cookery* first published
1988	Honorary Member, Chefs and Cooks Circle
1988	Grand Cordon Culinaire, Conseil Culinaire Français de Grande-Bretagne

Index